JOURNAL FOR THE STUDY OF THE OLD TESTAMENT
SUPPLEMENT SERIES
76

Editors
David J A Clines
Philip R Davies

JSOT Press
Sheffield

God is King

Understanding an Israelite Metaphor

Marc Zvi Brettler

Journal for the Study of the Old Testament
Supplement Series 76

For Monica

אשה טובה אשרי בעלה

a fine wife—happy is her husband

Ecclesiasticus 26.1

Copyright © 1989 Sheffield Academic Press

Published by JSOT Press
JSOT Press is an imprint of
Sheffield Academic Press Ltd
The University of Sheffield
343 Fulwood Road
Sheffield S10 3BP
England

Printed in Great Britain
by Billing & Sons Ltd
Worcester

British Library Cataloguing in Publication Data available

ISSN 0309-0787
ISBN 1-85075-224-9

CONTENTS

PREFACE

This book has had a long gestation period. My initial interest in God's kingship derives from my study of the book of Judges in 1982, when I struggled to understand Gideon's rather strange claim that divine kingship precludes human kingship. This interest grew into a doctoral dissertation supervised by Professor Nahum Sarna of Brandeis University, which was submitted in August 1986. My doctoral work was partially supported from grants from the Lady Davis Foundation and the Memorial Foundation for Jewish Culture. My gratitude to Professor Sarna, who first introduced me to the critical study of the Bible when I was an undergraduate in 1975, is very deeply felt. I would also like to thank my other dissertation advisors, Professors Tzvi Abusch and Michael Fishbane, who always encouraged me to find an independent approach to the Bible. I am also indebted to my teachers at the Hebrew University of Jerusalem and to my former colleagues at Yale University, who freely shared their knowledge with me and emphasized the importance of inter-disciplinary approaches to biblical study.

The current book is a very substantial revision of my dissertation, following the excellent comments of David Clines, one of the editors of the JSOT Supplement Series. Many of the more technical and polemical aspects of the original have been omitted, and all Hebrew has been translated, in the hope that this work will be accessible to scholars of religion. I would like to thank the Jewish Publication Society for permission to use their Bible translation, *Tanakh*. In revising this work, I was ably assisted by Mr William Schniedewind of Brandeis University, who suggested many ways in which the original manuscript could be improved. Mr Michael Rosenbaum assisted me in many technical matters. Professors Janet Soskice of

Cambridge University and Mark Smith of Yale University were kind enough to share unpublished material with me. Drs Naomi Schmidt and Alex Pringle helped me master the world of computing. The Brandeis libraries, especially the Judaica department and the Interlibrary Loan Office helped me find many obscure works. Without all of this help, the current work could not have been completed.

My debts to my family are felt so deeply, they are difficult to articulate. My mother was my first Hebrew teacher; my father set an invaluable example of the importance of studying Judaica. My daughter Talya has brought me much concrete joy as I have struggled to understand the meaning of the abstract 'God is king'. My young son Ezra also gave me much joy during the final tedious stages of preparing this volume. My wife Monica has patiently endured being first a dissertation widow, and then a book widow, but has still shown great support for my scholarly endeavors. It is with much love and admiration that I dedicate this book to her.

ABBREVIATIONS

AB	Anchor Bible
AfO	*Archiv für Orientalforschung*
AnBib	Analecta Biblica
ANEP	J.B. Pritchard (ed.), *Ancient Near East in Pictures*
ANET	J.B. Pritchard (ed.), *Ancient Near Eastern Texts*
AnOr	Analecta Orientalia
AOAT	Alter Orient und Altes Testament
AS	*Assyriological Studies*
ASTI	*Annual of the Swedish Theological Institute*
BASOR	*Bulletin of the American Schools of Oriental Research*
BDB	F. Brown, S.R. Driver and C.A. Briggs, *Hebrew and English Lexicon of the Old Testament*
BHS	*Biblia Hebraica Stuttgartensia*
BiOr	*Bibliotheca Orientalis*
BKAT	Biblischer Kommentar: Altes Testament
BWANT	Beiträge zur Wissenschaft von Alten und Neuen Testament
BZAW	Beiheft zur *ZAW*
CAD	*The Assyrian Dictionary of the Oriental Institute of the University of Chicago*
CBC	Cambridge Bible Commentary
CBQ	*Catholic Biblical Quarterly*
CBOT	Coniectanea Biblica, Old Testament
CIS	*Corpus Inscriptionum Semiticarum*
CTA	A. Herdner, *Corpus des Tablettes en Cunéiforme Alphabétique*
DBSup	*Dictionnaire de la Bible, Supplément*

DJD	Discoveries in the Judaean Desert
EI	*Eretz Israel*
EM	*Encyclopedia Miqrait*
EncJud	*Encyclopedia Judaica*
FOTL	Forms of Old Testament Literature
FRLANT	Forschungen zur Religion und Literatur des Alten und Neuen Testaments
HAT	Handbuch zum Alten Testament
HSM	Harvard Semitic Monographs
HSS	Harvard Semitic Studies
HTR	*Harvard Theological Review*
HUCA	*Hebrew Union College Annual*
ICC	International Critical Commentary
IEJ	*Israel Exploration Journal*
IES	Israel Exploration Society
JAOS	*Journal of the American Oriental Society*
JBL	*Journal of Biblical Literature*
JCS	*Journal of Cuneiform Studies*
JJS	*Journal of Jewish Studies*
JNES	*Journal of Near Eastern Studies*
JQR	*Jewish Quarterly Review*
JSOT	*Journal for the Study of the Old Testament*
JSOTSup	Journal for the Study of the Old Testament, Supplement Series
JSS	*Journal of Semitic Studies*
JTS	*Journal of Theological Studies*
KAI	H. Donner and W. Röllig, *Kanaanäische und Aramäische Inschriften*
KAT	Kommentar zum A. T.
LXX	Septuagint, Rahlfs edition
MRS	Mission Ras Shamra
MT	Massoretic Text
NCBC	New Cambridge Bible Commentary
NJPS	New Jewish Publication Society Translation
OTL	Old Testament Library
OTS	*Oudtestamentische Studiën*
PAAJR	*Proceedings of the American Academy of Jewish Research*
PBI	Pontifical Biblical Institute
PEQ	*Palestine Exploration Quarterly*

pTJ	Targum pseudo-Jonathan (Ginsburger edition)
RB	*Revue biblique*
RGG	*Religion in Geschichte und Gegenwart*
RSV	Revised Standard Version
SBL	Society of Biblical Literature
SBLDS	SBL Dissertation Series
SBLMS	SBL Monograph Series
SBT	Studies in Biblical Theology
SEÅ	*Svensk Exegetisk Årsbok*
TDOT	G.J. Botterweck and H. Ringgren (eds.), *Theological Dictionary of the Old Testament*
THAT	E. Jenni and C. Westermann (eds.), *Theologisches Handwörterbuch zum A. T.*
TJ	*Targum Jonathan* (Sperber Edition)
TO	*Targum Onqelos* (Sperber Edition)
TLZ	*Theologische Literaturzeitung*
TZ	*Theologische Zeitschrift*
UT	C.H. Gordon, *Ugaritic Textbook*
VT	*Vetus Testamentum*
VTSup	*VT* Supplements
WMANT	Wissenschaftliche Monographien zum Alten und Neuen Testament
ZAW	*Zeitschrift für die alttestamentliche Wissenschaft*

INTRODUCTION

The image of God as king is no longer evocative to most readers of the Bible. Monarchy is no longer the powerful and predominant political system that it once was in the ancient world. 'The kingship of God' has been overused in religious rhetoric; it has lost the vivid associations that it might have carried in ancient Israel. It is this set of associations that the current work sets out to recover.

The kingship of God is among the most overworked topics in biblical research; studies abound that explore the formula יהוה מלך, 'the LORD is/has become king', that attempt to determine when the conception of God's kingship entered into Israelite religion, that place the conception within its ancient Near Eastern context or that focus on the evolution of the kingship of God from its incipient form in the 'Old Testament' through its 'maturation' in the New. However, what the Israelites meant by calling their God a king or the extent to which kingship imagery was projected onto him has not been previously explored in detail. This is what I shall attempt here.

This project is fraught with difficulties. First, it must be decided what conceptual tools may be most fruitfully applied to unlock the full significations of God as king. In Chapter 1, I briefly explore the modern study of metaphor and show how certain methods used in studying metaphors may be applied to the study of God as king. My approach implies that any attempt to understand 'God is king' must involve a complete depiction of human kingship in ancient Israel, the metaphor's vehicle, just as the metaphor 'my love is a rose' may only be understood by someone who knows what a rose is. Since Israelite kingship encompasses a complex and very incompletely understood set of institutions, a re-examination of Israelite kingship is a necessary part of this study. The seemingly extraneous, lengthy expositions on human kingship, the vehicle of the metaphor, are however an essential prerequisite for understanding the image of God as king.

Two central problems immediately emerge in studying 'God is king' as a metaphor, where God's kingship in Israel is patterned after human kingship. We must consider the possibility that some references to God as king predate the Israelite monarchy, in which case the Israelite monarchy could not have been the vehicle of the metaphor. Second, we must allow for the possibility that the image of God as king might have shaped human kingship rather than vice versa.

Neither of these problems can be resolved with complete certainty. The dating of biblical texts is notoriously problematic; only the schematic periodization of texts as archaic, classical and post-exilic can be made with some assurance.[1] This represents a division of literary texts spanning about one thousand years into only three periods! Nevertheless the song in Exodus 15 which is traditionally dated to the late second millennium (Robertson, 1972:155) and is thus pre-monarchic, ends 'The LORD will reign for ever and ever!'[2] (v. 18). If this early date for the entire poem is accepted,[3] the conception that God is king predates the establishment of the monarchy.[4] This is certainly possible—the conception that gods were kings is well-documented in the literature of Israel's neighbors,[5] and could have been borrowed lock, stock and barrel from them. However, the vast majority of biblical texts, including those depicting God as king, are traditionally dated from after the establishment of the monarchy. Furthermore, this study notes many cases where God's depiction as king specifically mirrors depictions of the Israelite king rather than the reverse.

Certain biblical and extra-biblical (Tigay, 1986:77) names with the element *mlk* (often translated 'king') have also been used to date the emergence of the metaphor 'God is king'. These names might be especially significant since various people in the premonarchic period (e.g. Abimelek in Judg. 8:31 or Malkiel in Gen. 46:17) have these names, possibly suggesting that 'God is king' was a pervasive pre-monarchical theological conception. However, it is uncertain whether these names actually belonged to these pre-monarchic figures or are anachronistic, backward projections from the period of the monarchy. Furthermore, it is uncertain whether these names should be vocalized *melek*, 'king', or *mōlek*, the divinity Molech (Heider, 1985:229-232), in which case they have no bearing on God's kingship. For these reasons, these *mlk* names are not discussed here.

Concerning the second problem—names although 'God is king' did become a popular image in ancient Israel, there is no evidence that *in Israel* the human king was generally patterned after God.[6] The work of Frankfort (1978) and others has seriously undermined the position popular earlier in this century (e.g. Hooke, 1933:8) that divine kingship was a prevalent notion in the ancient Near East. The observation of Jacobsen (1970:164) about Mesopotamian religion equally applies to Israel: 'In almost every particular the world of the gods is therefore a projection of terrestrial conditions.' The earthly reality preceded and served as the basis for speculation about the divine. Thus, in cases where common imagery is shared by God and the king, I assume that human imagery has been projected upon God rather than vice versa.

Much of this study ignores the comparative evidence adduced by others to explicate God's kingship. I do not mean to question the validity or importance of this type of study. The study of biblical religious institutions must take both diachronic and synchronic forms. The diachronic study would certainly include an investigation of how certain notions entered into Israelite religion from other religions. This is a valid venture, although it is difficult to isolate the formative period of ancient Israelite religion, let alone to reconstruct the intellectual and religious interrelationship between Israel and its neighbors for that period. My study is largely synchronic, paralleling the methods of structural linguistics. It takes as a given that the metaphor 'God is king' did exist in ancient Israel: instead of exploring *where* it *originated outside* of Israelite society it explores *how* it *functioned within* Israelite society. To illustrate by analogy: a person examining the biblical word *hêkāl*, 'palace, temple', may either study its etymology, tracing Sumerian *É.GAL* through Akkadian *ekallu(m)* into Northwest Semitic, noting the attendant phonetic and lexical shifts. Alternately, someone may examine every case of *hêkāl* in the Hebrew Bible within its context and in relation to other words in the same semantic field. Each type of study will raise different questions and will yield certain types of solutions; each is legitimate for particular purposes. In general, etymological studies are particularly valuable when the root in question is poorly attested to in the Bible. If we based our understanding of common biblical words on their meanings in cognate languages, the results would be disastrous.[7] If we may follow this analogy, the image of God as king is a prevalent theologoumenon, so contextual study of the image's meaning within the Bible is more productive than the attempt to define its meaning through a search for its putative origin.

A largely contextual study of the kingship imagery used of God in Israel does not invalidate the effort to uncover its external underpinnings. It does, however, represent a change in the direction of research and supplements the cross-cultural methods traditionally used to study this image and much of biblical religion. For example, a recent collection of essays entitled *Ancient Israelite Religion* (Miller et al., 1987) devotes almost half of its pages to 'Sources and Contexts'. Finally, a proper comparative approach to the metaphor god is king in Israel and the surrounding cultures should first study how the metaphor functions within each society, and only then should compare the societies to each other.[8] Religious notions must be understood within specific systems, and rites or institutions 'shared' by different religions might actually have very different meanings or functions (Geertz, 1973:87-125). Therefore, a person studying the metaphor 'god is king' in various societies must first study how the metaphor functions within each society, and only then should compare the various societies to each other. Thus, this contextual study of the metaphor God is king in Israel may be used as a preliminary to a cross-cultural, comparative study of the meaning of the metaphor in various societies.

Fully exploring the extent of the metaphor can become tedious. Just imagine explaining the metaphor 'my love is a rose' to someone who has neither seen nor smelled a rose! Inevitably, 'unpacking' a metaphor turns 'energic speech into boring paraphrase' (Hall, 1985:6). Furthermore, by its very nature, 'No metaphor is reducible to a literal equivalent without consequent loss of content...' (Soskice, 1985:94-95). However, by examining in detail the institution of Israelite kingship in relation to the attributes of God as king, a new type of window is opened toward understanding the biblical God. A detailed study of the overused, 'dead' metaphor revives the image of 'God is king', and brings us closer to understanding the ancient Israelite conception of God.

Chapter 1

THEORETICAL CONSIDERATIONS ON METAPHOR

Since the time of Athenagoras at least, the good theologian and insightful faithful have recognized the language of both popular devotion and formal theology to be highly metaphorical and not found that to be particularly problematic (Soskice, 1987:105).

But if we would speak of things as they are, we must allow that all the art of rhetoric. . . [is] for nothing else but to insinuate wrong ideas. . . and so [figures of speech such as metaphor] indeed are perfect cheats. . . (Locke, *Essay Concerning Human Understanding*, quoted in Soskice, 1985:13).

Metaphor is one of our most important tools for trying to comprehend partially what we cannot comprehend totally: our feelings, aesthetic experiences, moral practices, and spiritual awareness (Lakoff and Johnson, 1980:193).

Thou shalt not commit metaphor (Black, 1962:25, paraphrasing a predominant attitude).

We are in the midst of metaphormania (Johnson, 1981:ix).

The role of metaphor in religious studies has been debated for centuries. Some scholars have derided metaphorical language as imprecise, obscuring the possibility of proper apprehension of the divine, while others have insisted that metaphorical language is intrinsic to all God-talk. Those in the first camp have sometimes contrasted 'precise' scientific language with metaphorical, 'fuzzy' religious language, belittling the latter. However, recently scholars have begun to question whether this distinction between scientific and religious language can be so rigidly drawn (MacCormic, 1976; Soskice, 1985 and 1987). Linguists and philosophers have recently emphasized that metaphorical language is a basic part of all types of human communication (Lakoff and Johnson, 1980). This newer intellectual climate recognizes that understanding the role of metaphor in religious language is no longer a luxury (Tracy, 1979; Johnson, 1981; Soskice, 1988:131).

The classic Renaissance work on biblical rhetoric, Judah Messer Leon's *The Book of the Honeycomb's Flow* (ספר נופת צופים), recognizes the centrality of metaphor to biblical rhetoric (Rabinowitz, 1983:510-513). However, the examples he cites do not involve the use of metaphors about God. Among modern works on biblical rhetoric, Caird's *The Language and Imagery of the Bible* (1980) contains a section on metaphor. He acknowledges that 'All, or almost all, of the language used by the Bible to refer to God is metaphor' (p. 18) and delineates the main metaphors used of God, including 'God is king' (pp. 177ff.). However, his study is little more than a sketch which points to the necessity of a large-scale study of an important biblical metaphor. In a critique of the myth and ritual school, Johnson (1958:233) noted the 'purely figurative language' used in reference to God's kingship, but he does not develop this insight. In the prologue to his work on the monarchy, Halpern explicitly recognizes the importance of metaphor (1981:xxv-xxvi), but he does not intensively follow up his observations in the body of his study. Porter, in his *Metaphors and Monsters* (1983) fruitfully applies metaphor scholarship to a short but difficult unit, Daniel 7–8. Newsom (1984) explores the use of metaphors by Ezekiel in his oracles against Tyre. Fretheim (1984), in a study of God's suffering, appreciates the metaphorical nature of most biblical language. His study comes closest in scale and method to mine. Camp (1987) offers a detailed description of the different functions of the metaphor 'Wisdom is a woman' in Proverbs. These studies have begun to exploit the new studies on metaphor and suggest the importance of an in-depth study of 'God is king', which was a 'strong' (Soskice, 1985:62) metaphor in ancient Israel. Several works have studied how particular metaphors used of God in the Bible relate to current theological or liturgical problems. The studies of Sallie McFague are typical of this genre. In her earlier work (1982), she develops the metaphor 'God is a friend', which is not a common biblical metaphor, and shows how it may be constructively used in modern Christian theology. Her newer study (1987) more powerfully emphasizes the centrality of metaphor to theology, and examines the metaphors of God as mother, lover and friend. These works are mostly prescriptive rather than descriptive—they want to determine how we should speak of God and not how the ancient Israelites perceived God through metaphors. Ramsey (1971b) is similar; although it contains a stimulating classification of biblical metaphors, its central concern is how various metaphors which function as 'models' may be combined with his conception of 'cosmic disclosure' to create a meaningful contemporary religious language.

'Metaphor' is notoriously difficult to define. Max Black (1962:28-29) notes, '"Metaphor" is a loose word, at best, and we must be aware of attributing to it stricter rules of usage than are actually found in practice'. Ricoeur (1977:18) claims that we can only define metaphor metaphorically, creating an unavoidable paradox. Nevertheless, the current definitions must be discussed to the extent that they determine whether 'God is king' may be studied as a metaphor. Once this is done, the insights of modern studies on metaphor may be used to explicate the kingship of God in the Bible.[1]

Theorists of metaphor may be divided into three camps: those who posit that metaphor is determined by semantics, the study of words; those who define metaphor through pragmatics, the study of utterances; and those who take an intermediate position, that metaphor belongs to both disciplines. A scholarly consensus is slowly being reached that the third, compromise position is correct.

L. Jonathan Cohen, 'The Semantics of Metaphor' (Ortony, 1979a:64-77) is representative of the first view. Cohen subscribes to the linguistic theory that a word's meaning is a sum of its constituent components. According to this system, 'man' would be analyzed in this system as male-adult-human (Lyons, 1977:317-35). Cohen claims (p. 74), 'An expression has a metaphorical occurrence in a sentence sequence if and only if the extent of cancellation is so great as to exclude it from identifying a topic independently of some special circumstance'. Thus, his sample sentence, 'Their legislative program is a rocket to the moon' (p. 68) is metaphorical because 'legislative program' and 'rocket to the moon' in most normal circumstances have little or nothing in common with each other. In his more technical terminology, many semantic components of 'legislative program' and 'rocket to the moon' must to be cancelled before their common core may be uncovered.

The opposite position, that metaphor is a matter of pragmatics, is taken by John Searle, who claims, 'Metaphorical meaning is always speaker's utterance meaning' (Ortony, 1979a:94; see also Loewenberg, 1974). Thus, the first stage of decoding a metaphor is knowing if it is metaphorical (Searle, 1979:114), and metaphor can only be understood because of 'shared strategies' between speaker and hearer (p. 120). Searle has overstated his case; intentionality may in some circumstances be important in decoding metaphor, but it does not play an exclusive role in determining if an utterance is metaphorical. For example, no 'shared strategy' can make 'a desk is a piece of furniture' into a metaphor or can remove 'man is a wolf' from its metaphorical status. It is only because of certain semantic clashes that certain utterances in particular situations may be used as metaphors.[2]

I agree with Black, Ricoeur and others, that metaphor must be studied within both semantics and pragmatics (Black, 1962:29-30; Ricoeur, 1977:89-90; Gardner and Winner, 1979:129-30; Porter, 1983:5). It is the situation in which 'Bob is a wolf' is uttered that will determine whether it is metaphorical. If it is uttered about a person (an issue of pragmatics), it would be a metaphor, since in typical speech 'wolf' and 'person' have little in common. In other words, they must go through extensive cancellation (a semantic process) before being identified. However, when the same statement 'Bob is a wolf' is uttered by the owner of a wolf farm of one of his animals, it would not be metaphorical. Thus, in many cases, both pragmatics and semantics play a role in determining whether a statement is metaphorical.

Whether or not pragmatics plays a role in determining metaphors is determined by the metaphor. For example, 'Bob is a fox' or even 'Something's rotten in the state of Denmark' (see Booth, 1979a:49) will not be metaphorical in some circumstances (e.g. if Bob is not human, and if the 'something' is an egg), and will be metaphorical in others (e.g. if Bob is human and the 'something' refers to a plot). There are certain instances, however, where the semantic conflict between the two elements in the metaphor is so great that pragmatics plays no role in determining whether a statement is metaphorical. This is the case with 'God is king' since no utterance context can subvert the semantic clash between God and king because the ancient Israelite would have been aware that certain elements intrinsic to kingship could not be projected onto God. For example, Israelite kings were typically human and part of a dynasty, qualities that were inappropriate to the Israelite God. Because of the conflict between these intrinsic features of Israelite kingship and the intrinsic features of God, the statement 'God is king' should be considered metaphorical. A similar position is articulated by Soskice (1985:77) about other metaphors: 'It is difficult to believe that the prophets, although perhaps lacking a developed set of grammatical distinctions which enabled them to designate metaphors as metaphors, were unaware that in speaking of God as a herdsman or planter were using language not strictly appropriate to him'.

It is possible that 'God is king' has not been studied as a metaphor since it is considered by scholars to be a 'dead' or 'faded' metaphor (Wellek and Warren, 1973:301 n. 26), much like the 'leg' of a chair. However, this is not true of the metaphor in the biblical period. Dead metaphors do not have associated submetaphors (Soskice, 1985:73). For example, usually when we say 'don't kick the "leg" of the chair', leg is 'lexicalized' or 'dead'. However, when someone says: 'Don't kick the chair's leg or step on its toe', by using the word 'toe' which is a submetaphor of 'leg', the metaphor has been revived. (See Ricoeur, 1977:290-91.) Similarly, since the metaphor 'God is king' produced many submetaphors or entailments throughout the biblical period such as 'God is enthroned' or 'God's majesty is celebrated with great noise', it cannot be a dead metaphor. In fact, the metaphor was a vital enough throughout the biblical period to prevent certain expected kingship terms and images from being used with Israelite kings.[3] The metaphor remained live throughout the biblical period, as indicated by its innovative use in the book of Daniel (see below, pp. 105-106) and beyond, in other apocalyptic uses (Gray, 1979:225-73) and in the New Testament (Gray, 317-373; cf. Bright, 1953).

Modern theorists of metaphor would consider the biblical statement 'God is a king' to be metaphorical; we must now see how these theorists would interpret such metaphors. There is no consensus on this matter; the approach of individual scholars depends on how they perceive metaphors as functioning. The 'interactive' or 'tensive' view of metaphor promulgated by Black (1962:38-43) on the basis of I.A. Richards (1936:89-138), has been accepted by most scholars, though with some modifications and reservations.[4] This theory suggests that the metaphorical statement makes the vehicle (in this case 'king') look more like the tenor (in this case 'God', cf. Black, 1962:43)[5] by focussing on a 'system of associated commonplaces' (p. 40). In order to understand how a metaphor functions according to this view, we must uncover the 'associated commonplaces' or 'associated implications' (Black, 1979:27) between the tenor and the vehicle. For example, when we hear the metaphor 'my love is a rose', we must search for the shared implications between the 'love' and 'rose' which make the metaphor meaningful in a particular context. These elements might include

beautiful, scented and flushed. These shared elements are netaphor-
ically) called the 'grounds' of the metaphor (Paivio, 1979:151; Miller,
1979:220).

'Unpacking' the metaphor (Cohen, 1979:7), i.e. reaching its
grounds, is a complex operation. Scholars generally agree that most
metaphors cannot be adequately paraphrased, with the possible
exception of dead metaphors (Henle, 1967:193-95). This is because
paraphrases never denote and connote the same as the original
metaphor (Lakoff and Johnson, 1980:128-38), and any paraphrase
would cause the metaphor to lose its power, which is largely
generated through its compactness (Henle, p. 194). A radical
statement of this sentiment is found in de Man (1983:235):

> In the manner of a vibration spreading in infinitude from its center,
> metaphor is endowed with the capacity to situate the experience at
> the heart of a universe that it generates. It provides the ground
> rather than the frame, a limitless anteriority that permits the
> limiting of a specific entity. Experience sheds its uniqueness and
> leads instead to dizziness of the mind. Far from referring back to an
> object that would be its cause, the poetic sign sets in motion an
> imaging activity that refers to no object in particular. The
> 'meaning' of the metaphor is that it does not 'mean' in any definite
> manner.

Despite these problems, unpacking the metaphor by exploring its
'associated commonplaces' is a worthwhile venture. It can serve the
same function as most literary criticism—it makes the original more
transparent and conveys to the uneducated reader how the work
affected the critic (Davidson, 1979:45).

Unpacking the metaphor involves a further difficulty. It is
uncertain whether these 'associated commonplaces' are only shared
constituent components of the vehicle and the tenor, or if they
include shared emotions conveyed by the vehicle and the tenor or
even extend to images shared between them. Psychological studies of
metaphor suggest that there is a dual decoding of verbal and
imagistic elements in deciphering metaphors (Paivio, 1979:163-69;
Miller, 1979:203-09). Ricoeur (1977:98, 213) too has emphasized
both elements, noting that 'metaphor is a semantic event that takes
place where several semantic fields intersect' and that in deciphering
a metaphor 'What must be construed is the common element B, the
Gestalt namely the point of view in which A (the tenor) and C (the
vehicle) are similar'. Henle (1958:191) speaks of a metaphor covering
the 'similarity of feeling' between vehicle and tenor. Soskice

(1985:95; cf. 1988:134) describes this large set of common features as 'a community of relations'. Once we speak of shared images and feelings, the similarities between the vehicle and tenor become extensive; according to some theorists of metaphor, they are infinite (Davidson, 1979:44; Booth, 1979b:174). This study can just begin to explore them.

I have suggested that 'God is king' is a live biblical metaphor which is best explicated by examining the common elements shared by the biblical conceptions of God and king. This may be accomplished in at least two different ways. The first involves collecting all contexts in which God is explicitly called מלך, 'king', or the root מלכ, 'to reign', is used of him. The elements of royalty that are projected onto him are then catalogued and studied to see what elements of human kingship are contextually explicit. This method was used, for example, in Eissfeldt's influential study of God's kingship (Eissfeldt, [1928] 1962b). However, this overlooks the fact that 'God is king' has many associated submetaphors which may be invoked without the explicit use of the root מלכ, 'to reign'. A comparison to a different metaphor may illustrate the problem of the methodology of Eissfeldt and his followers. Lakoff and Johnson (1980:4 and passim) have suggested that an important conceptual metaphor in our society is 'argument is war'. Their suggestion cannot be examined by counting the number of times that this expression explicitly appears in literary or spoken sources, but by seeing the prevalence of such phrases as 'Your claims are *indefensible*', or 'If you use that *strategy*, he'll *wipe you out*' or 'He *shot down* all of my arguments'. Similarly, in investigating the metaphor 'God is king', we must study phrases such as 'God sits on a throne' or 'the members of the court surround God' or 'the members of the heavenly court are called בני אלים (sons of God)'. This suggests a second method for studying the metaphor God is king: outlining the characteristics and terminology associated with human kingship and seeing the extent to which they are applied to God. This would be parallel to investigating the metaphor 'argument is war' by outlining the features of 'war' and comparing them to the terms we use in talking about 'arguments'. This method has been used to some extent by Mettinger (1986-87) and is adopted here.

This method could incorrectly suggest that there is a unified, complete image of God as king which is invoked every time kingship imagery is used of him. However, I have stated earlier that the meaning of a metaphor in a particular context is a function of pragmatics, the utterance situation. Therefore, the image conveyed by 'God is king' will differ in varying contexts. To illustrate by analogy: 'My love—you are a rose' will convey a different image if uttered by a person (1) who cherishes roses for their beauty; (2) who is red-green color-blind; (3) who loves roses' scent; (4) who 'appreciates' roses only for their thorns. Thus, the way in which a metaphor is unpacked must be sensitive to its context (Morgan, 1979:143; Fraser, 1979:181-82; Klein, 1981). This issue is especially significant in unpacking the metaphor 'God is king' since the attitudes in ancient Israel toward the institution of monarchy were varied, as they were informed by complex sets of social, geographical, religious and chronological factors. For example, it would certainly be interesting to know how the image of God as king within the Yahweh-only group[6] differed, e.g. in the period of Josiah, a reformer king, and Jehoram, an apostate king. However, it is difficult if not impossible to either date texts exactly within the biblical period or to determine what ideological group produced a particular text.[7] Therefore, in this study I will only distinguish between pre-exilic and post-exilic texts.[8]

It is possible that in some groups in ancient Israel, 'God is king' was not understood as a 'mere' metaphor. Judg. 8:22-23, 1 Sam. 8:4-9 and 10:19 imply that for some people in ancient Israel, God's kingship precluded the possibility of Israelite, human kingship. The argument of these texts is fallacious, since 'God is king' as a metaphorical statement does not preclude the truth of literal statements such as 'Solomon or Jeroboam is king'. Thus, in Mesopotamia, the denotation of several deities as 'king' was not seen as interfering with the institution of human kingship (Roberts, 1987:380-84). In Israel, however, there was a tendency to reify certain metaphors. For example, the metaphor 'Israel is God's servant' is taken quite literally in Lev. 25:55, where it becomes the basis for precluding Israelite servitude. This reification of divine metaphor requires further study; in this context, it is sufficient to note that for most people in ancient Israel 'God is king' was not reified, and was understood as a fully metaphorical statement, and therefore did not impinge on human kingship.

The method suggested for studying metaphors forces us to fully describe human kingship (the vehicle) before we can understand the metaphor 'God is king'. For ancient Israel, this is a complex task, since many different types of sources describe kingship, and it is difficult to put them in chronological order and to evaluate their historical veracity (see Mettinger, 1976). However, for understanding the metaphor 'God is king', popular perceptions of kingship are more important than the historical realities. This may be illustrated by analogy—to understand the metaphor 'man is a wolf' we must study popular perceptions of wolves rather than their 'real', biological behavior. Similarly, in understanding the metaphor 'God is king', we need not know exactly what transpired in the royal palace, information that might become accessible through archival material, but how various groups of the ancient Israelite population perceived or understood kingship. Thus, genres such as the prophetic story (see Rofé, 1970), which might play a minor role in reconstructing actual Israelite kingship, are important since they provide a wealth of evidence on how kingship was perceived.

Determining the identity of the 'I' in Psalms is very important for the reconstruction of ancient Israelite royal practices. The 'I' of the psalms of the individual is usually anonymous and has been identified with people ranging from personified Israel to impoverished individuals (see Eaton, 1976:1-11, Feininger, 1981:93-94 and Croft, 1987). The identification of the 'I' as the king has recently gained popularity (Eaton and Croft). If the 'I' is the king, some fifty psalms could be used to reconstruct royal norms and rituals (Eaton, 27-86). Most arguments that these psalms are royal are not convincing; they confuse possibility and probability[9] and presume rather than prove that the king was prominent within the cultus (e.g. Croft, 75-76).[10] It is therefore appropriate the return to the position of Gunkel and Begrich (1933:140-71) that approximately ten psalms are royal.

Since the biblical depiction of human kingship is incomplete, many scholars have used ancient Near Eastern material to supplement the biblical account. However, although various court groups had contacts with foreign powers and it is clear that certain biblical words and motifs are borrowings from nearby cultures (see Machinist, 1983 and references there), it would be incorrect to assume that most Israelites invoking the metaphor knew the detailed workings of extra-Israelite political institutions. Thus, to the extent that Israel's understanding of non-Israelite kingship shaped the metaphor 'God is king', we should pay attention to the biblical descriptions of these institutions, particularly as they appear in the Joseph story, Kings, Esther, Ezra-Nehemiah and Daniel.

These accounts of non-Israelite kingship are often more detailed than the biblical descriptions of Israelite kingship. Some cases, such as the Joseph story, are probably a projection of Israelite institutions onto foreigners (Redford, 1970:187-243). However, Esther and Ezra-Nehemiah are generally thought to reflect the foreign institutions that they describe (Berg, 1979:20, n. 13; Bickerman, 1967; Porten, 1978). Ideally, in periods when Israel was the vassal of foreign kings, we should try to see if the metaphor 'God is king' was patterned after Israelite kingship or after the foreign overlord.

There is no single way of organizing all of the concepts and terms that are connected with human kingship; any categorization is somewhat arbitrary and will include some ambiguous categories and overlapping subheadings. The following division has not avoided these pitfalls; nevertheless, it offers a convenient grid through which both human and divine kingship may be explored:

1. Royal Appellations (e.g. רעה, מלך, 'king, shepherd').
2. Royal Qualities (e.g. wise, wealthy).
3. Royal Trappings (e.g. scepter, throne).
4. The King and Domestic Affairs (e.g. builder, the royal court).
5. Becoming King (including a reinvestigation of the 'Enthronement Psalms').

Each of these topics will form a chapter. Each chapter is divided into subtopics, where specific terms or ideas are discussed extensively, first in relation to human kings, and then to see the extent to which God shares the same properties. Conspicuously absent is a section on the king and foreign affairs, which would examine the extent to which God's kingship is patterned after an overlord with Israel as a vassal. A responsible study of God as suzerain would involve a complete re-examination of covenant forms and terminology, a task that far exceeds the compass of this work.

It is striking that the metaphor 'God is king' has not been previously studied using the methods proposed here. Three factors may have contributed to this: (1) biblicists have shared philosophers' distrust of metaphors; (2) biblical scholars have lost interest in the kingship metaphor because of its patriarchal bias; (3) biblicists are uncomfortable with anthropomorphisms.

Over twenty-five years ago, Max Black (1962:25) characterized the predominant attitude among philosophers as 'Thou shalt not commit metaphor'. This attitude was particularly strong among the logical positivists, who denied the meaningfulness of any non-tautological statement about God. More recently, the influential perspective of the logical positivists has begun to wane, and many philosophers now claim that metaphor is central to both science and religion (MacCormic, 1976, Soskice 1985:97-117). Lakoff and Johnson (1980) have powerfully argued that metaphors are inextricably involved in the way we structure the world. Philosophy has come full-circle; the old view of Aristotle that 'it is from metaphor that we best get hold of something fresh' (Ricoeur 1977:33-34) has gained popularity again. Given this trend, the central metaphor 'God is king' deserves serious study.

Most biblical texts describe God in male terms. This has made the biblical God less accessible to many modern worshippers, and has forced a search by such scholars as Trible (1978) for alternative models that might exist within the text itself. This has sometimes forced the abandonment of patriarchal models, including a loss of interest in the metaphor 'God is King' (McFague, 1982 & 1987). However, another alternative within feminist biblical theory exists. In the 1987 Society of Biblical Literature Presidential Address, Elisabeth Schüssler Fiorenza argued that we must continue to examine ancient texts contextually, but must add an '*ethics of accountability*', that evaluates 'the ethical consequences and political functions of biblical texts in their historical as well as in their contemporary sociopolitical contexts' (1988:15). According to this model, an accurate and representative representation of all models used of God in the Bible remains important, although this 'history of religion' venture should be supplemented by an evaluative component.

Discomfort with the anthropomorphism involved in religious metaphors such as 'God is king' may be partially responsible for the absence of serious studies of biblical divine metaphors within biblical theology.[11] One might expect the two major biblical theologies to seriously treat the means through which God is described in the Bible by investigating divine metaphor and anthropomorphism. The opposite is true. Eichrodt (1961:145) sidesteps the whole issue by declaring 'according to the ideas of Jahwism, it cannot be said that Israel regarded God anthropomorphically, but the reverse, that she considered man theophoric'. Von Rad (1962:212; see also Vischer, 1949:9) has a different solution; he discusses anthropomorphism under 'God as spiritual'(!) and notes that the biblical anthropomorphisms used are second best to 'Christian faith [which] has been able to accommodate the recognition of God's spiritual nature without prejudice to his immediacy in religion, because it has its focus in the person of Jesus. . . '. This position is developed in greater detail by Mauser (1970). If any of these attitudes is typical, it is easy to understand why serious study of the anthropocentric metaphor 'God is king' in the Hebrew Bible has been avoided.[12]

Chapter 2

ROYAL APPELLATIONS

Introduction

This chapter examines which of the appellations that the ancient Israelites used of their kings were also applied to God. I have intentionally avoided the terms 'title' or 'epithet' which are generally used in such contexts. These terms are at home in the scholarship concerning Mesopotamian royal titles (Hallo, 1957 and Seux, 1967), but cannot be comfortably transported from Assyriology to biblical studies, since the Bible lacks the long 'royal titularies' which characterize Mesopotamian inscriptions. I have therefore chosen 'appellation' as a neutral term for the nouns or noun phrases that denote kings.

This chapter studies appellations which were, to the best of our knowledge, not specific to one king or one situation.[1] These are: מלך, 'king', נגיד, 'divine designee', משיח, 'anointed one', בחיר יהוה, 'the chosen of the LORD', רעה, 'shepherd', נשיא, 'exalted one', ראש, 'head', אלהים, 'God', אדון, 'master', שפט, 'judge', נר, 'lamp', רוח אפינו, 'our life-spirit', מגן, 'shield', צמח, 'branch' and משל, 'ruler'. The meaning of these terms is often difficult to determine. In this study, I will follow Barr (1961), and use contextual-semantic and not etymological factors to determine their meaning. This methodology has been further developed by Sawyer (1972), who is heavily influenced by structural semantics. It is especially important to consider contextual-semantic features since previous scholars such as Buber (1967) have come to incorrect conclusions after giving primary consideration to the etymologies of royal appellations.

The discussion of each term will first focus on the use of each appellation with the Israelite king, investigating which aspect(s) of kingship each term conveyed, and seeing how widely each appellation was applied to kings of different types (real–ideal; Northern–Southern;

Israelite–foreign) at various periods. By its nature, this type of study is often very technical and complex, but it is necessary, since it is impossible fully to appreciate the meaning of the image God (the tenor) the king without first understanding human kingship (the vehicle) in all of its aspects. After completing the study of each appellation, I will examine the extent to which it is used of God. At the conclusion to the chapter, I will describe the patterns which may be discerned concerning the royal appellations which are projected onto God and those that are avoided. These patterns can later be compared to patterns from other chapters, to help define the extent of the metaphor 'God is king' in ancient Israel.

I distinguish between words which primarily denote 'king' (e.g. מלך, 'king') and appellations of kings which are primarily not used of kings (e.g. רעה, 'shepherd'). Words in the first category are 'primary royal appellations'; the others are 'secondary royal appellations'. מלך, 'king' and נגיד, 'divine designee' are the only two primary royal appellations in the Bible and will be studied first.

מלך, *'King'*

מלך, 'king' is the 'general word' (Sawyer, 1972:50-51) for the monarch in biblical Hebrew. It is used to denote human rulers in most books in the Bible, from archaic poetry (Judg. 5:3) through Late Biblical Hebrew (e.g. Chronicles and Daniel, passim, and in the Aramaic of Daniel), and into post-biblical Hebrew (Ben-Yehuda, 1959:3045). As a general term, it denotes the king in his various roles, including military (1 Kgs 12:23-24) judicial (1 Kgs 3:16-28) and religious (2 Kgs 23). Sometimes the Israelite king is called more specifically מלך ישראל, 'king of Israel' (1 Sam. 26:20; 2 Sam. 6:20 and frequently of the Northern kings). It is possible to speak metaphorically of Leviathan (Job 41:26) and of the master of the underworld (Job 18:14) as kings, and to call locusts kingless (Prov. 30:27). The superlatives מלך מלכים, 'king of kings' (Hebrew) and the Aramaic equivalent מלכא (מלך) מלכיא are never found with Israelite kings. They are used of the Babylonian king Nebuchadnezzer (Ezek. 26:7; Dan. 2:37) and of the Persian king Artaxerxes (Ezra 7:12). These terms are probably calques from the Akkadian *šar šarrāni* (von Soden, 1981:1189b; Seux, 1967:318-319). Similarly, המלך הגדול, 'the great king', used in 2 Kgs 18:19, 28 (=Isa. 36:4, 13) of Sennacherib king of Assyria is an Akkadian calque derived from *šarrû rabû* (von

Soden, 1972:937b; Seux, 1967:298-300). Though גדול, 'great' without
a definite article is used to describe non-Mesopotamian kings (Ps.
136:17; Qoh. 9:14), המלך הגדול, 'the great king' was never applied to
Israelite kings, since like 'king of kings' it was inappropriate for any
king who reigned during or after the Israelites might have borrowed
the term from the Assyrians.

The substantive מלך, 'king' is used of God forty-seven times in the
Bible.[2] To the extent that these contexts may be dated, the term first
appears in early Hebrew poetry (Num. 23:21; Deut. 33:5; Robertson,
1972, shows that these passages are later than generally suggested),
runs through Classical Biblical Hebrew into Late Biblical Hebrew
(Mal. 1:14; Zech. 14:9, 16, 17) and is used once in Biblical Aramaic
(Dan. 4:34). מלך, 'king' is used of God mostly in poetic passages of the
Bible; only in 1 Sam. 12:12 and Dan. 4:34 is it used in prose. This is
not surprising, since one of the predominant characteristics of
biblical poetry is heightened style, including the extensive use of
figurative language (Kugel, 1981:59-95). It is therefore expected that
calling God a king, that is invoking a metaphor, is predominantly
found in passages that are recognized as poetic. Some major works
like Ezekiel and Proverbs never explicitly call God 'king'. Context
determines where God is called 'king'; the term is used to emphasize
some royal aspect of God. Usually, the aspect of God as warrior is
emphasized (e.g. Psalm 24, Zechariah 14), often as the leader of the
so-called 'holy war', but once as a victor in a mythological battle (Ps.
74:12). In Jer. 8:19 God as king is expected to protect his capital city.
Less frequently, God's aspect as judge is emphasized through the
appellation 'king' (Isa. 41:21; Ps. 5:3; 10:16). Three times God is
called 'king' where these two attributes intersect (Isa. 33:22; Ps. 98:6;
Ps. 99:4). God's praiseworthiness is emphasized through his appellation
'king' (esp. Ps. 145:1, cf. 47:7; 84:4; 95:3). Other passages call God a
'king' where he is depicted as a shepherd (Mic. 2:13), as beautiful (Isa.
33:17), as enthroned as deserving of proper honor or 'royal treatment'
or when an oath is taken in his name (Zeph. 1:5; cf. the phrase
חי . . . המלך, 'by the life of the king'). These are all qualities which God
as king shares with mortal kings.

Although God as king and human kings share these attributes,
sometimes God possesses them in a more powerful or extreme form.
For example, Jer. 10:7, 9, a description of God's overwhelming power
as a warrior (cf. v. 6 גבורה, 'power') says ובכל מלכותם מאין כמוך 'and
among all their royalty there is none like you'. Furthermore, God is

called 'king' in certain contexts where the shared aspects of kingship between people and God are different not only in extent, but in essence. Thus, in Isa. 43:15 and Ps. 149:2 God as king is the ברא, 'the creator' or the עשה, 'maker' of Israel. The designation of God as 'king in (or 'over') Jeshurun' in Deut. 33:5 is similar. These attributes adhere to God as king by analogy to human kings, who unify and lead their nations. However, Israelite kings are never called the 'creators' or 'makers' of Israel. God's attributes as king extend beyond those of Israelite kings. Given the tensive model of metaphor developed in the previous chapter this is not surprising: a metaphor provides a basic frame of comparison, but does not confine the tenor (God) to the vehicle (human kingship).

Phrases calling God a king are often in the syntactic form מלך 'king of' (construct) + substantive, or מלך 'king' + adjective or מלך + prepositional phrase. In Isa. 44:6 and Zeph. 3:15, texts which are anti-Davidic, God is called מלך ישראל, 'king of Israel', thus usurping the (human) throne of kingship. Similarly, he is called מלך יעקב, 'king of Jacob' in Isa. 41:21.[3] In many cases the *nomen rectum* used with God as king expresses God's superior kingship. Since biblical Hebrew lacks a true grammatical superlative (Thomas, 1953), these phrases function as superlatives—God the king is מלך הגוים, 'king of the nations' (Jer. 10:7), מלך עולם (וער), 'everlasting king' (Jer. 10:10; Ps. 10:16), מלך כל הארץ, 'king over all the earth'[4] (Ps. 47:8; cf. Zech. 14:9) and מלך שמיא, 'king of heaven' (Dan. 4:34). Adjectives in the semantic field of strength or greatness modify God as king; he is גדול, or רב, 'great' (Mal. 1:14; Ps. 48:3), גדול על כל אלהים (Ps. 95:3), 'the great king of all divine beings' and עז, 'ruthless' (Isa. 19:4). The adjective רב, 'great' in the phrase מלך רב, 'a great king' is unusual. רב is usually used quantitatively (as 'many'), while גדול is usually used qualitatively (as 'great') rather than quantitatively ('many'). This suggests that the phrase מלך רב, 'great king' used of God in Ps. 48:3 is a calque from the Akkadian *šarrû rabû*, though probably mediated through a Northwest Semitic language.[5] The phrase was probably borrowed from a (human) overlord, but it was applied to God as king.

In comparing the use of 'king' with God to its usual use with human kings, certain patterns emerge. Many of God's titles as king exactly parallel the use of 'king' with Israelite monarchs. Thus, God is מלך ישראל, 'king of Israel' and is called 'the king Yahweh' just as David is called 'the king David'. God as king serves many of the same functions as the human kings. However, the metaphor is also used as a tool to show how God's attributes extend beyond those of human kings. For example, God in his role as warrior-king never loses in battle. He not only heads his peolple, but also created them. Finally, he is no mere king: he is the greatest king. Though the royal titles reflecting Mesopotamian origin מלך מלכים, 'king of kings' and המלך הגדול 'the great king' are not applied to God in the Bible, God is called מלך רב, 'great king' as well as other superlatives such as 'everlasting king', 'king over all the divine beings' and 'king over all the earth', terms never applied to Israelite kings, historical or ideal. These and other superlative expressions use the metaphor 'God is king' to turn God into the overlord *par excellence*, whose kingship surpasses that of any human monarch.

נגיד, *'Divine Designee'*

נגיד, *nāgîd*, which is usually misleadingly rendered 'prince',[6] is used in pre-exilic texts of kings only; I therefore categorize it as a 'primary royal appellation'.[7] For reasons adduced below, I translate this term 'divine designee'. In pre-exilic texts, it is used of the early (until the ninth century) kings Saul, David, Solomon, Jeroboam (I) and Jehu, most of whom began or sought to begin a dynasty. The use of נגיד, 'divine designee' with Hezekiah (2 Kgs 20:5) is textually uncertain, since the term is missing in the parallel Isa. 38:5. If נגיד, 'divine designee' is original there, it may reflect the projection of a term from the reign of David onto Hezekiah, rather than an indication that נגיד, 'divine designee' was actually used of kings in the late eighth century (Tadmor-Cogan, 1982:198). It is unclear why it is used in Ezek. 28:2 of the king of Tyre. In post-exilic sources, the use of נגיד is extended; it refers to various types of royal officials (1 Chr. 9:10, 11, 20; 1 Chr. 12:28; 2 Chr. 31:13; 35:8 and Neh. 11:11 of priestly נגידים and in 1 Chr. 9:20 and 2 Chr. 32:21 of military נגידים). This usage continues into post-exilic Hebrew (see Ben-Yehuda, 1959:3510-3511). In its pre-exilic use with kings, it is usually (e.g. 1 Sam. 10:1; 13:14; 2 Sam. 6:21; 7:8; 1 Kgs 14:7; 16:2; etc.) God who 'designates' (usually צוה, 'appoint' or משח, 'anoint') someone לנגיד 'as a divine designee'. The biblical evidence has suggested to most scholars that: (1) נגיד, 'divine designee' is an early term, possibly taken over from pre-monarchic leaders, and (2) it is a sacral term, connected to God's endowment of 'charismatic leadership' to an individual.[8] However, the term נגיד, 'divine designee' is never applied to pre-monarchic leaders; this suggests that the term originated with the monarchy and is not a carry-over from the so-called 'charismatic leaders' of an earlier period.

Recently, both Mettinger (1976:158-162) and Lipiński (1974) have independently suggested that the term נגיד originally meant 'crown prince'.[9] They base this on (1) 1 Kgs 1:35, where David says to Solomon ואתו צויתי להיות נגיד על־ישראל ועל־יהודה, 'him I designate to be *nāgîd* of Israel and Judah'. (2) 2 Chr. 11:22 ויעמד לראש רחבעם את־אביה בן־מעכה לנגיד באחיו כי להמליכו, 'Rehoboam designated Abijah son of Maacah as chief and *nāgîd* among his brothers, for he intended him to be his successor'. (3) The etymology of נגיד from the root נגד in the sense 'to designate', as seen in 1 Kgs 1:20, 'and so the eyes of all Israel are upon you, O lord king, to tell (from the root נגד) them who shall succeed my lord the king on the throne'. However, each of these proofs is weak. (1) This text is *sui generis* among pre-exilic texts as having a human subject designating the *nāgîd*, and there is no reason to give this text priority for interpreting נגיד. (2) In 2 Chronicles, *nāgîd* may not have its technical pre-exilic meaning of 'king'; instead, it may have its typical post-exilic meaning of 'high official'. (3) If the substantive *nāgîd* were related to the verb להגיד, 'to designate', we would expect the substantive to reflect the *Hiphil* form of that root. Furthermore, Mettinger's etymological argument is fanciful; it is similar to someone explaining why a prophet is called a נביא on the basis of 1 Sam. 9:7, where a person worried about what gifts to bring a prophet says, 'What can we bring (נביא) the man?' Mettinger has mistaken a typical biblical word-play for an etymology (Shaviv, 1984).

The evaluation of Fritz (1976:351) 'Die ursprüngliche Bedeutung von נגיד ist kaum zu ermitteln' is realistic. Though its original sense will remains obscure, certain important aspects of the usage of נגיד may be noted:[10] (1) When used of kings, it is largely confined to the first kings, namely Saul, David and Solomon; (2) while a king may be anointed (משח) to kingship by either God (1 Sam. 15:17) or a person (2 Sam. 2:4), pre-exilic verbal expressions with *nāgîd* (with only one exception) have God as their subject (Alt, 1967a:254, esp. n. 54). (3) Although *nāgîd* appears eleven times in the narratives in Samuel–Kings, it is relatively infrequent in the poetic books.

The previous section concluded that the term נגיד emphasized the relationship between God and the king. This usage made the term inappropriate as a royal appellation of God, and therefore it is never used of him in the Bible.[11] This is typical of a metaphorical statement; God as king need not share all of the appellations that typified the Israelite king.

משיח, *'Anointed, Messiah'*

Although the root משח, 'to anoint' is usually discussed in connection with kings, the substantive משיח, 'anointed one' is not a primary royal term. Morphologically, it is a *qāṭîl* form of משח, 'to anoint' (Bauer-Leander, 1965:470), and can refer to anyone anointed. The high priest is called הכהן המשיח, 'the anointed priest' (Lev. 4:3, 5, 16; 6:15), and the patriarchs are called משיחי, 'my anointed ones' (Ps. 105:15 = 1 Chr. 16:22), probably to characterize them as important people.[12] Thirty-one of the 39 instances of משיח, 'anointed one' refer to the king, but in contrast to its Jewish and Christian post-biblical usage, משיח, 'Messiah' never to the future, ideal king (see Baumgartner, 1974, 610 s.v. משיח 5). The biblical narrative records anointing of kings by the people (e.g. 2 Sam. 2:4; 5:3), suggesting that originally anointing was a secular rite (Mettinger, 1976:185-203 and Pardee, 1977:14-18), 'perhaps a purificatory rite which was used to prepare for the change in status' (Pardee, 17). However, it is not generally noted that when the substantive משיח, 'anointed one' is used of kings, it is never in the unbound form; it is always in a construct with either יהוה, 'Yahweh' or אלהי יעקב, 'the God of Jacob' or it appears with an attached personal pronoun which refers to God, as when Cyrus is called משיחו, 'his anointed one' (Isa. 45:1). Thus, although anointing may have its historical origins as a secular ceremony, the use of the substantive משיח, 'anointed one', always stresses the bond between the human king and God, at whose bequest the king is ruling. Therefore, משיח, 'anointed one' like נגיד, 'divine designee' is never used of God, since without exception in the pre-exilic corpus, משיח, 'anointed one' always appears either in a construct with God or with a pronominal suffix referring to him. This usage makes it inappropriate to God.

בחיר יהוה, *'The Chosen of the LORD'*

בחיר יהוה, 'the chosen of the LORD' like the previous two terms studied, stresses the relationship between God and the king, while emphasizing the king's subordinate role. It is used of Saul in (the appendix) 2 Sam. 21:6[13] and of a Davidic king in Ps. 89:3. It is not, however, exclusively used of kings; Israel (e.g. Isa. 43:20; Ps. 105:6), Moses (Ps. 106:23) and the Servant of God (Isa. 42:1) are called God's chosen. The term בחיר יהוה, 'the chosen of the LORD' is semantically inappropriate to God, and is never used of him.

רעה, *'Shepherd'*

Shepherd is one of the oldest appellations for kings in the ancient Near East, used already in ancient Sumer (Hallo, 1957:141, 147-149; Seux, 1967:244-250; Levenson, 1976:105 n. 55). It frequently refers to kings, particularly in Jeremiah, where the Targum usually renders it as מלך, 'king' (e.g. Jer. 2:8; 10:21; 12:10). The full significations of this title are elaborated in Ezek. 34:4-6: a good shepherd cares for his flock's sick and weak and keeps his flock whole, being sure that no sheep stray away (cf. Jer. 50:6). A king has similar responsibilities, caring for his sheep's (namely the nation's) well-being, keeping them whole and protected. In Jeremiah, the term רעה, 'shepherd' is sometimes used ironically, to emphasize the king's failure to discharge specific responsibilities (e.g. Jer. 2:8; 10:21). 'Shepherd' designates both foreign (e.g. Jer. 6:3; 12:10) and domestic kings, and is used of reigning kings (e.g. Jer. 50:6) and of the future ideal Davidic king (Jer. 3:15; 23:4; Ezek. 34:23-31; 37:24). It is likely that the metaphorical use of 'shepherd' of Israelite kings contributed to the literary depiction of David (and possibly Moses) as actual shepherds.[14]

Although the image of God as a shepherd is frequent in the Bible, and he is compared to a shepherd (Jer. 31:10), or the verb רעה, 'to shepherd' is used of him (e.g. Ezek. 34:1-16), he is only called a רעה twice, in Psalms 23 and 80.[15] Psalms 23 unpacks the metaphor in some detail; an individual envisions God as his shepherd (v. 1) because God feeds him and provides him with water (v. 2), guides him properly (v. 3) and comforts him with the shepherd's crook (v. 4b). This final image is highly innovative; the shepherd's crook is typically used to control the sheep, and represents the shepherd's authority. For example, the crook is a symbol of royalty in Mesopotamian art and literature, and is found on the relief on the top of Codex Hammurabi (cf. CAD Ḫ s.v. ḫaṭṭu, 1948:90-91 and Olivier, 1979:45-47). The creative psalmist has reversed this image; for God the shepherd the staff symbolizes the benevolent guidance which the shepherd has provided.[16] In Ps. 80:2, a northern psalm (Ginsberg,

1982:31), God is appealed to as רעה ישראל 'O shepherd of Israel' and נהג כצאן יוסף, 'who leads Joseph like a flock'. Here the title is used in the vocative to encourage God to shepherd his people, namely to come to save them (vv. 3-4, 15-20). Thus, the two contexts where the appellation 'shepherd' is used of God emphasize the care and concern which God shows for Israel. This contrasts with the way human kings treat their flock Israel (Jer. 23:1-2). God is like the ideal future king, who is depicted as a proper shepherd (Jer. 23:4; Ezek. 34:23). To summarize: in the metaphorical application of 'shepherd' to God the king, God surpasses the typical Israelite royal shepherd. He is the ideal king, who can even reverse certain of the typical entailments of the shepherd submetaphor, using his shepherd's crook to comfort rather than chastise his 'flock'.

נשיא, *'Exalted One'*

נשיא, 'exalted one' is a notoriously difficult term; its etymology and function have been hotly debated (Baumgartner, 1983:686-687). The term has many referents, but 1 Kgs 11:34, which says of Solomon כי נשיא אשתנו, 'but I will keep him as an exalted one', and Ezek. 34:24 and 37:25, where the future Davidic descendant is called נשיא, 'exalted one', suggest that the term can be used to designate a king. Etymology and usage suggest that a translation 'one lifted up' or 'exalted' (BDB s.v. נשיא; cf. Bauer-Leander, 1965:470 n. α) is appropriate.

The distribution of the term is problematic. It is frequently used in P texts of the pre-monarchic tribal leaders, the heads of the clans or tribes, who in different contexts can number from twelve (e.g. Num. 7) to two hundred and fifty (Num. 16:2). The other large cluster of use is in Ezekiel, where it is used over thirty times in reference to a single individual (Driver, 1972:298, #21).

If we accept a pre-exilic date for P (Hurvitz, 1983:83-94), its נשיא, 'exalted one' probably reflects some element of the ancient tradition. It is unlikely that the נשיאים, 'exalted ones' are a post-exilic anachronism retroverted into earlier periods since נשיאים, 'exalted ones' are not active in the leadership of the exilic or post-exilic community. If P is largely exilic or post-exilic and modeled its portrayal of the desert leadership structure after contemporaneous institutions, it would have named the desert leaders זקנים, 'elders' or חרים, 'prefects' (cf. Jer. 27:20; 29:1; Ezek. 20:3; Ezra 3:12; Neh. 2:16).

נשׂיא, 'exalted one' is rarely used of the pre-exilic king outside of Ezekiel. 1 Kgs 11:34 calls Solomon's descendent a נשׂיא, 'an exalted one' but the Septuagint indicates that the MT's reading is uncertain (J. Gray, 1976:291 n. g). It is expected that the king would not be called a נשׂיא, 'exalted one' since the pre-monarchical נשׂיאים 'exalted ones' were not exclusive wielders of power, and may have even been elected officials (Speiser, 1963). Thus, despite its positive etymology, the usage of נשׂיא, 'exalted one' suggested incomplete power. If a non-royal official named נשׂיא continued to function during the monarchical period, as suggested by 1 Chr. 4:38; 5:6 and 2 Chr. 1:2,[17] the term נשׂיא, 'exalted one' would be especially inappropriate to kings. The diminutive use of נשׂיא, 'exalted one' might explain why the term is used in the MT of 1 Kgs 11:34, which refers to the diminished power of the Davidic dynasty as a result of Solomon's sins (Levenson, 1976:64).

The use of נשׂיא, 'exalted one' in Ezekiel 1–39 is complex. Sometimes it unambiguously refers to the king, whether Davidic (Ezek. 37:24, where מלך, 'king' = נשׂיא, 'exalted one' of v. 25;[18] Ezek. 19:1) or of foreign powers (e.g. 26:16; 30:13; 38:2). Twice נשׂיא, 'exalted one' in Ezekiel probably refers to royal officials, a usage we saw in Chronicles (7:27; 32:29). The referent of נשׂיא, 'exalted one' in chs. 40–48 is hotly debated (Levenson, 1976:57-62); some claim that he is a Davidic king, while others see him as a non-Davidic figurehead. The usage of נשׂיא 'exalted one' elsewhere in the Bible and the general ideology of Ezekiel support the proposal of Levenson (pp. 66-69; cf. 75-107) that the נשׂיא, 'exalted one' was a Davidic king who was intentionally not referred to as מלך, 'king' to indicate his lack of full royal power.

Although much remains uncertain about the use of the term נשׂיא, 'exalted one', it is likely that this appellation invoked the comparison of the king to a non-royal official who did not wield great power. Therefore, a king would only be called a נשׂיא, 'exalted one' in special circumstances, where his royal authority and power were being called into question. It is therefore not surprising that this term, despite its 'exalted' etymology, is never used of God.

ראשׁ, *'Head'*

ראשׁ, 'head', has a very wide semantic range and is often used non-anatomically to indicate 'first' or 'finest'. In the field of officialdom,

ראש, 'head' described a high official, who often seems to be equivalent to the נשיא, 'exalted one'.[19] He functioned through the post-exilic period (Ezra 8:17; Neh. 10:15). In many contexts, it is difficult to tell if ראש, 'head' refers to a specific type of official or is a general term for leader. It is an appellation for the king in Hosea 2:2 and in Isa. 7:8-9. Isaiah's use of ראש, 'head' for the kings of Damascus and Samaria is determined by poetic needs; he needs a word that may refer both to kings and to cities. Thus, this text does not indicate that ראש, 'head' was a generally used royal appellation. Its use in Hosea 2:2 is more significant; it is probable that Hosea, who might have had a negative attitude toward the monarchy (Gelston, 1974) is intentionally avoiding the term 'king'. This may be similar to the use of נשיא, 'exalted one' in Ezekiel to diminish the king's royal status. It is therefore not surprising that the appellation ראש is never applied to God since it is an ambiguous term which can convey the lack of full royal power.

אלהים, *'God'*

One of the most obvious cases of a shared title between God and the king seems to be Ps. 45:7, a royal wedding psalm: כסאך אלהים עולם ועד, which could be rendered, 'your throne, O God is everlasting'. The king seems to be addressed in the vocative אלהים, 'O God'. However, this is unlikely for two reasons: (1.) In v. 8 אלהים *'elōhîm* is used in a context that unambiguously refers to God. If the same *'elōhîm* referred to the king in the previous verse, too much semantic confusion would be caused by the shift in referent. It is therefore likely that *'elōhîm* in v. 7 has the same referent as in v. 8, namely God.[20] (2.) Although kings are compared to a מלאך אלהים, 'messenger of God' or even compared to אלהים, God in respect to strength (Zech. 12:8), good judgments (2 Sam. 14:17), cleverness (2 Sam. 14:20) or power (2 Sam. 19:28), kings are never elsewhere called God. They are portrayed as firmly entrenched in the earthly rather than the heavenly realm. Possibly this passage should be understood as *sui generis*, a remnant of the ancient Near Eastern ideology of divine kingship. However this ideology is not omnipresent in the ancient Near East (Frankfort, 1978) and was probably unknown in Israel (North, 1932: 36-38), contrary to claims such as David 'must himself have been regarded as a potent extension of divine Personality' (Johnson, 1967:16).

Most likely, Ps. 45:7 should be translated as 'your throne is like

God's throne, everlasting' though some other explanations, many involving clever emendations, are possible.[21] According to Emerton (1968) this is the sense of MT; others claim that we need to emend it to כסאך כאלהים, 'your throne is like the divine', where כאלהים is understood as ככסא אלהים, 'like the divine throne', following common biblical usage (Emerton). The כ fell out by haplography, possibly influenced by אלהים in the following verse.[22] Thus, אלהים, *'elōhîm* is not an appellation shared between God and the king.

אדון, *'Master'*

אדון, 'master', is typically used by subordinates in relation to superiors. It refers to slaves in relation to their masters (Exod. 21:5ff; Prov. 30:10), Joseph as vizier (Gen. 44:5ff.), Jacob to the stronger Esau (Gen. 33:8ff.), angels explaining visions to mortals (Dan. 10:16ff.), a war commander (2 Sam. 11:11), a prophet, especially of Elisha (2 Kgs 2:19, 4:16, 28 etc.), a priest (1 Sam. 1:15, 26) and Moses (Exod. 32:22; Num. 32:25, 27 etc.). Superior officers were addressed אדון, 'master' by subordinates in the Hebrew epistles found at Lachish and Yabneh Yam (Donner-Röllig, 1979, nos. 192-197, 200). However, the predominant human use of אדון, 'master' is with the king who is the master *par excellence*. אדון, 'master' is a full-fledged royal title—it is not used in books such as Hosea and Micah which use royal appellations that undercut the king's royal status. Its use spans the range of biblical kingship: Saul is called 'master' (e.g. 1 Sam. 22:12) and post-exilic (foreign) kings are called 'masters' (Dan. 1:10 and the Aramaic מר in Dan. 4:16, 21[23]). The intimate association between the appellation אדון, 'master' and the king is shown in the lament over dead kings in Jer. 22:18 and 34:5, where the king is lamented: הוי אדון, 'Ah, master'. אדון is used with kings more often than with all other types of individuals together and the phrase אדני המלך, 'my master, the king' appears over sixty times in the Bible. It is particularly favored as a polite form when addressing the king in the vocative (e.g. 2 Sam. 19:27; 1 Kgs 1:24). Another phrase using אדון, 'master' is בי אדני, 'if you please, my master'. It is used to entreat someone who wields power, e.g. a vizier (Gen. 43:20; 44:18), an 'angel' who has just given an oracle of reassurance (Judg. 6:13), a priest (1 Sam. 1:26), and of course, a king (1 Kgs 3:17, 26).

אדון, 'master' is frequently used as an appellation for God. Many questions have been associated with this divine appellation. I will survey the following four issues: 1. the use of אדון, 'master' of God;

2. *'ădōnāy* (with a final *qāmeṣ*) used of God alone; 3. the combination אדני יהוה, 'the master, Yahweh'; and 4. אדני, 'master' read as a surrogate for the tetragrammaton יהוה.

אדון, 'master' in the unbound form appears only five times in the Bible; only in Ps. 114:7 is it used of God, emphasizing his power or dominion over nature. Seven of the eight times האדון, 'the master' is used, it refers to God. It usually emphasizes his power (note esp. Isa. 1:24; cf. Isa. 3:1; 10:16; 19:4),[24] and twice appears in the pilgrimage formula.[25] אדון, 'master' in the singular construct is only used of God, only in the phrase אדון כל הארץ, 'master of all the earth'. Its use in the phrase ארון (הברית) יהוה אדון כל־הארץ (Josh. 3:11, 13), 'the ark (of the covenant) of Yahweh, master of all the earth' suggests that this name is connected to the ark, perhaps in God's role as warrior, whose manifestation (the ark) was carried forth during certain battles (cf. 1 Sam. 4). Elsewhere, God is called אדונים, 'masters', a plural of majesty (Gesenius, 1974 §124 g, h). This appellation is found in Isa. 19:4 and Mal. 1:6, and אדני האדנים, 'master of masters' is used in Deut. 10:17[26] and Ps. 136:3, אדנינו, 'our master' is found six times and אדניך, 'your master' once.[27] Dan. 2:47 calls God מרא מלכין, 'master of kings' possibly based on Deut. 10:17, and in Dan. 5:23 he is מרא שמיא, 'master of the heaven'. These contexts usually emphasize God's strength, though several times his role as creator is subsumed under this appellation.[28] However, in Neh. 8:10, a late text, אדנינו, 'our master(s)' is used in a context that does not emphasize God's strength. The uses of אדנינו 'our master' with God is syntactically differentiated from its use with humans; with God, the syntax is יהוה אדנינו, 'Yahweh our master' (Ps. 8:2, 10; Neh. 10:30), while with kings אדנינו precedes, as in 1 Kgs 1:11, 'our master, David'. To summarize: God is called אדון, 'master', often in contexts that emphasize his power. He shares this title with human kings, though to a large extent God as אדון, 'master' is distinguished from humans syntactically and morphologically. I will now turn to the issue of morphological differentiation.

The morphology of *'ădōnāy* is problematic. If the ending *āy* is the possessive singular suffix following a plural noun, the presence of a קמץ (i.e. *āy*), rather than a פתח (i.e. *ay*), is anomalous. Eissfeldt (1970:24-26 and 1974b:68) claims that the ending is 'a nominal afformative, which reinforces the meaning of the basic word'. However, this contention is based on doubtful Ugaritic evidence.[29] Even if the Ugaritic evidence were clear, this feature is not evident

elsewhere in biblical Hebrew, and there is no obvious reason why it
should only be preserved with *'ădōnāy*. Instead, the *-āy* of *'ădōnāy*
should be understood as a frozen form of the first person singular
suffix attached to the plural of majesty, which we saw above is often
used when God is called ארון. Frozen forms have become fossilized
in forms of address in other languages, as in French *Monsieur*, Syriac
מריא, 'my master' and Rabbinic Hebrew רבי, 'my teacher' (Dalman
1889:20-21). The ending is *āy* rather than *ay* since the word froze in
its pausal form (Bauer-Leander, 1965 §29t). This pausal form may be
explained in two ways: (1) The word may have been frequently used
as a vocative to open petitionary prayers, and therefore naturally
appeared frequently in its pausal form; it froze in this frequent form.
This is supported by two cases of suppletion, in Psalms 35 and 51,
where *'ădōnāy* is used in the vocative, opening a colon, while other
divine names are used elsewhere.[30] (2) The form is not a true pausal,
but is an attempt to differentiate the way the term was used with
God (see Gesenius, 1974 §135q). Melammed (1948) has collected
cases where morphological patterning is used to differentiate the
divine from the human.

It is difficult to determine how many of the one hundred and thirty
four[31] texts using אדני, *'ădōnāy* use it in the posited original sense of
'0, my (powerful) master'. This problem is complicated by manuscript
divergences in particular instances, with some texts reading אדני,
'ădōnāy and others the tetragrammaton יהוה.[32] In some cases,
'ădōnāy may be an error for *'ădōnî* or might indicate that there is
some ambiguity whether a person or God is meant.[33] In many cases,
אדני, 'master' is used to denote 'my powerful master'. This is clearly
seen in the exclusive preference of the expression of entreaty בי אדני,
'if you please, my master' rather than בי יהוה, 'if you please Yahweh'
or בי אלהים, 'if you please, God'. However, there are cases where אדני,
'master' is used in contexts which do not emphasize his personal
divine strength (Eissfeldt, 1974b:64-65).

To summarize: God was called ארון, 'master' by analogy to human
kings, and at some point in biblical Israel the form אדני, 'my master'
which probably originated as a vocative petition form, became
fossilized. The original function and connotation of אדני, 'O my
(powerful) master' remain in some contexts (e.g. Ps. 35), but in
others, אדני, *'ădōnāy* could be construed as a proper noun, in the
sense that its function is *identification, and not signifying*'.[34] This
development is discussed in more detail below.

אדני יהוה, 'my master, Yahweh', which appears 280 times (Baumgartner, 1967:13) is always read according to the Masorah as אדני אלהים, 'my master, God'. This phrase is largely confined to cases where people are speaking to God or where a prophet is reporting what God spoke; fewer than one percent of the cases fall outside of these categories. The first type of usage parallels the royal use of אדני, 'my master'; just as a person usually addresses the king אדני המלך, 'my master, the king' so one polite form of addressing God is אדני יהוה, 'my master, Yahweh' (e.g. Gen. 15:2; Jer. 1:6). Prophets, especially Ezekiel,[35] recite their prophecies using אדני יהוה, 'my master, Yahweh' in their reporting formulae to emphasize God's power over his people; in these cases, אדני, 'my master' retains its semantic content, invoking God's power, and should not be construed as a personal name (Greenberg, 1983b:64-65). Throughout the biblical period this phrase was read אדני יהוה, 'my master, Yahweh' and only later, when the tetragrammaton was read as אדני, 'my master' was the expression read אדני אלהים, 'my master, God' probably so אדני, 'my master' would not be read twice in succession creating a strange redundancy. Some of the cases where אדני יהוה, 'my master Yahweh' is used, that are neither addressing God nor reporting formulae, emphasize God's strength (e.g. Isa. 25:8; Zeph. 1:7; Zech. 9:14; Ps. 73:28).[36]

At some point it became taboo to pronounce the tetragrammaton יהוה. In the words of *b. Kiddushin* 71a, 'The holy one, blessed be he said: I am not called by the name by which I am written; I am written *yh* and am called *ad*'. Exactly when this change took place is not known; the tetragrammaton was pronounced from the First Temple[37] into the Second Temple period, though clear tendencies against its pronunciation, even under limited circumstances, had developed by the end of the Second Temple period (Alon, 1949:33-34). The existence of the Elohistic Psalter (Pss. 42-83), which strongly prefers the name *'ĕlōhîm* over the tetragrammaton, might be a pre-exilic reflection of this tendency. Further evidence may be found in Neh. 8:10, where קדוש היום לאדנינו, 'for the day is holy to our master' parallels v. 9 היום קדוש־הוא ליהוה אלהיכם, 'the day is holy to the LORD your God', suggesting that 'master' was seen as interchangable with LORD and God. Evidence from Qumran is mixed. The authors of some scrolls wrote the tetragrammaton, either in 'Aramaic' or paleo-Hebrew script, while others, especially when paraphrasing biblical texts, substituted אל, אלהים, 'God' or אדני, 'my master' (Skehan, 1980). The predominant surrogate is אדני, 'my master' which is used in 1QH in the frequent formula אודכה אדני, 'I thank you, my master', which is based on Isa. 12:1, 'I thank you, O LORD'. 1QIsaᵃ to 3:17a has the tetragrammaton instead of MT's אדני, 'my master'; this suggests that the scribe writing in the late second century BCE (Cross in Trever, 1972:30) heard or subvocalized the tetragrammaton as אדני, 'my master' (Skehan, 40 n. 14; Kutscher, 1959:164). It is unclear why the accepted surrogate for the tetragrammaton became אדני, 'my master' rather than אלהים, 'God', especially given the evidence of the Elohistic psalter. Both surrogates are problematic; אלהים, 'God' may be used of foreign deities and אדני, 'my master' is not an exclusively divine appellation. Perhaps since אדני, 'my master' which emphasized God's power, carried more semantic content than אלהים, 'God' it was seen was seen as a better tool for understanding God.

Much of the evidence concerning the meaning of אדני, 'my master' and its use in different periods converges. God was called אדון, 'master' by royal analogy. The honorific title of important people, but especially of royalty, was given to God in 'speaking phrases', especially in the phrase אדני יהוה, 'my master Yahweh'. אדני, 'my master' in general was used to refer to God, expressing his royal power. This aspect was seen as so significant that אדני, 'my master' became the standard surrogate for the tetragrammaton during the Second Temple period.

שפט, *'Judge'*

שפט, 'judge' is sometimes used in parallelism with or in place of מלך, 'king'. Absalom, who is attempting to assume the throne, says (1 Sam. 15:4) מי־ישמני שפט הארץ, 'if only I were appointed judge in the land'. Foreign rulers may be called judges (Amos 2:3;[38] Ps. 2:10). The future king is called a 'judge' (Isa. 16:5). The late Dan. 9:12 שפטינו אשר שפטונו, 'our judges who judge us' probably refers to the Davidic kings. This appellation is natural, since in both Hebrew and other Semitic languages the root שפט has broad connotations of rulership (Richter, 1965:59-71 and Niehr, 1986), and part of the king's functions included administration of justice (cf. pp. 109-13), thus covering שפט, 'judging' in its narrower sense. This appellation is not used to indicate limited royal power.

שפט, 'judge' is used as a divine appellation ten times in the Bible, ranging over a wide variety of texts, though all occurrences may be

pre-exilic literature.[39] Isa. 33:22 כי יהוה שפטנו יהוה מחקקנו יהוה
מלכנו הוא יושיענו, 'For the LORD shall be our judge, the LORD shall be
our prince, the LORD shall be our king: he shall deliver us' reminds
us that when God is called a שפט, 'judge' he is not a mere local
tribunal, but the King sitting in judgement. Various elements of the
king as judge are transferred to God; for example God, like the king
(Isa. 16:5; Ps. 122:5) is pictured as sitting in judgment (Ps. 9:5).
However, God as judge is portrayed as more righteous and more
powerful than any human judge (see pp. 113-14).

נר, *'Lamp'*

In 2 Sam. 21:17, David's officers call him נר ישראל, 'the lamp of
Israel'. This metaphor is interpreted in at least two ways: McKane
(1977:461) claims that נר, 'the (shining) lamp', is symbolic of joy and
may represent a house full of vitality. However, this is nowhere
explicit or even implied in the texts he cites. Instead, I prefer to see
נר, 'lamp' as the life-force, as seen in the phrase דעך נר 'to extinguish
a lamp' which contextually must mean 'to die'.[40] Thus, נר, 'lamp' and
רוח, 'spirit' which both denote 'life-force', are used of kings. A 'lamp'
is a fitting image for a person's fragile life-force. This metaphor may
have been further encouraged by the ancient Israelite conception of
the afterworld as dark; the 'lamp' thus typifies life.[41] This sense of נר
as 'life-force' is further supported by Job 3:4ff., where the poet uses
imagery of darkness to convey the notion that the day on which he
was born should 'die'. If the interpretation of 'lamp' as life-force is
correct, David's officers are using the 'lamp' metaphorically to
express the primary importance of the king.[42]

Before examining where God is called נר, 'lamp', it is important to
examine the relationship between the graphemes nr and nyr. Most
scholars separate nyr I and nyr II and define nyr II (e.g. Jer. 4:3) in
the agricultural sphere (e.g. Baumgartner, 1983:658 'Neubruch'), and
equate nyr I with nr. Hanson (1968), however, uses morphological,
contextual, etymological and versional evidence to show that nyr I is
'a yoke' or 'dominion', as in Akkadian nīru. His arguments are
convincing. In compiling his examples of nyr = 'dominion', he
correctly omits the occurrence in 2 Sam. 22:29 כי־אתה נירי יהוה,
'You, O LORD are my nyr'.[43] The image of God as ניר, 'lamp' fits in
well with the context in 2 Samuel; he is a lamp in the literal sense,
since he illuminates the psalmist's darkness (v. 29b), but also in the
figurative sense, since he is the psalmist's life-force, giving him

supernatural strength (v. 30). Perhaps this single plene use of *nyr* is intentionally spelled with the *yod* to distinguish it from the non-divine uses of *nr*, 'lamp'.

רוח אפינו, *'Our Life-Spirit'*

The king is called the nation's רוח אפינו, 'our life-spirit' only in Lam. 4:20.[44] This appellation is appropriate to kings, since through their political policies, especially in their role as the commander-in-chief of the army, they were truly responsible for the welfare of the nation.[45] רוח אפינו, 'our life-spirit' is never used as a divine appellation in the Bible,[46] though in Rabbinic Hebrew, רוח הקרש, 'the holy spirit' is a divine name (Marmorstein, 1927:99-100). It is uncertain why the 'spirit' was not used as a divine appellation in the Bible; possibly because the primary use of רוח in the Bible is as 'wind', its use as a divine appellation would have caused too much semantic confusion about whether God or the 'wind' was the referent of an action. Alternately, perhaps in the biblical period, there was an attempt made by certain groups in Israel not to equate Yahweh with specific aspects of nature (1 Kgs 19:11).

מגן, *'Shield'*

The only unambiguous case of מגן, 'shield' referring to a king[47] is Ps. 84:10 מגננו ראה אלהים והבמ פני משיחך, 'O God, behold our shield, look upon the face of your anointed'. As Israel's military leader, מגן, 'shield' is an appropriate term for the king. This figure of speech is similar to Lam. 4:20, 'The breath of our life, the LORD's anointed . . . in whose shade (protection) we had thought to live among the nations'.

מגן, 'shield' is a frequent appellation of God, used almost twenty times, mostly in the Psalms.[48] God's strength is emphasized by using the word 'shield' in conjunction with the substantives חרב, 'sword' (Deut. 33:29), עז, 'strength' (Ps. 28:7), עזר, 'help' (Pss. 33:20; 115:9-11) and רדד, 'subjugator' (Ps. 144:2). This is in marked contrast to the royal use of 'shield' in Ps. 84:10, where it is used ironically, to show the powerlessness of the human 'shield'. In Ps. 84, the psalmist asks God as 'shield' (v. 12) to save the king as 'shield' (v. 10), indicating that although they share the same appellation, that appellation is only fully actualized in God.

צמח, *'Branch'*

צמח, 'branch' is used in several texts of the future Davidic King (Jer. 23:5; 33:15; Zech. 3:8; 6:12).[49] צמח, 'branch' connotes luxuriant growth (cf. Ezek. 16:7), and agricultural imagery was used to describe royalty in biblical period, as evidenced by the detailed allegory in Ezekiel 17, so צמח, 'branch' is an appropriate image for the future Davidic king.[50] As noted by Mowinckel (1956:160), the etymology of Zerubabel's name from Akkadian *zēr bābili*, 'the seed of Babylon', made him a particularly good candidate for the reuse of Jeremiah's oracle by Zechariah. God is never called צמח, 'branch' in the Bible, most likely because it was not a general royal appellation, but a specific designation for the future ideal king.

משל, *'Ruler'*

The root משל, 'ruler' often refers to holding power, a general quality shared by kings and other high officials. The participle משל, 'ruler' is therefore used as a substantive to refer to kings, though it may also be used of high officials (e.g. Joseph in Gen. 45:8). It refers to kings both foreign and domestic as sovereigns over particular territories (e.g. Josh. 12:2, 5; 1 Kgs 5:1), but it is also the general term for king (2 Sam. 23:3; Jer. 22:30; 33:26; Prov. 29:12, 26).

משל, 'ruler' is used of God, but in contexts where it is difficult to determine if the participle is being used verbally, or as an appellation.[51] If משל, 'ruler' in these contexts is an appellation, it is part of a compound appellation where it is followed by a prepositional phrase which usually points to God's supra-human leadership qualities (בגוים, 'the nations' Ps. 22:29; בגאות הים, 'the swelling of the sea' Ps. 89:10; בכל, 'over all' 1 Chr. 29:12; בכל מלכות הגוים, 'over the kingdoms of the nations' 2 Chr. 20:6), thus emphasizing that he surpassed the usual royal 'ruler'.

Rejected Words

Several words which are used in conjunction with or in parallelism to royal appellations are themselves probably not royal appellations. רזן, *rōzēn* which is found seven times in the biblical poetic texts, is one such word. Six times (Judg. 5:3; Hab. 1:10; Ps. 2:2; Prov. 8:15; 14:28; 31:4) it is the B word parallel to מלך, 'king'; once, probably in its latest occurrence, it is the A word, parallel to שפט, 'judge' (Isa.

40:23). The Hebrew usage of *rōzēn* is similar to its single appearance in Phoenician, where it is used in the Karatepe inscription (Donner-Röllig, 1979 #26 iii 13 מלכ במלכם ורזנ ברזנמ) together with מלך, 'king' implying that it is a high royal official, but not the king himself. Thus, Hebrew רזן, *rōzēn* belongs in the semantic field of leadership, and probably refers to a high official (Prov. 8:15; 14:28). In Ben-Sira 44:4 *rōznîm* denote officials rather than kings. Given the likely meaning of *rōzēn* as a 'high official' rather than a 'king', it is not surprising that this appellation is never applied to God.

In many cases, it is difficult to determine the exact sense of a word used in conjunction with or in parallel to a word that is clearly royal. This is because the relationship between A and B words is very complex and has not been investigated fully (Barr, 1968:277-282, Kaddari, 1973, Haran, 1971 and Clines, 1987), especially in light of the innovative studies on biblical parallelism by Berlin (1985). For example, נדיב *nādîb* is used together with מלך, 'king' (Prov. 25:7 and Job 34:18). However, other occurrences of *nādîb* suggest that he was a high official, so the parallelism between *nādîb* and 'king' in Job 34:18 should be seen as heteronymous (Kaddari, 1973:173) rather than synonymous. Similarly, שר, 'noble' may be parallel to מלך, 'king' (e.g. Isa. 49:7), but these too are heteronyms, and the parallelism does not indicate that שר, 'noble' was a royal appellation.

Conclusions

In the previous chapter, we saw that a determinative characteristic of metaphor is the lack of complete correspondence between the tenor and vehicle; e.g. saying 'my love is a rose' does not imply that s/he is green and needs to be watered daily. Only certain characteristics of the metaphor's vehicle are highlighted; unpacking a metaphor involves discovering these characteristics. This chapter illustrated this principle by showing that only certain of the appellations applied to kings were applied to God. The particular appellations applied to God illustrate in what way God was seen as king in ancient Israel.

An investigation of the usage (not etymology) of the human royal appellations משיח, 'anointed', נגיד, 'divine designee' and בחיר יהוה, 'the chosen of the LORD' has determined that these terms indicate the king's relationship *vis-à-vis* God, and thus were not appropriate as divine appellations. It is much more significant that נשיא, 'exalted one' and ראש, 'head', terms that connote inferior royal power, are not applied to God, just as the term שר, 'officer' is never used of God in

Classical Biblical Hebrew.[52] The Bible sees God as the king in the strongest sense of the word, therefore he is only worthy of full-fledged royal appellations, such as מלך, 'king', אדון, 'master' and רעה, 'shepherd'.

The biblical authors were aware that even these full-fledged royal appellations fail to describe God properly. They therefore use two methods to show the inadequacy of the appellations: special morphological or syntactical patterning and the addition of modifiers. A king is a נר, *nr*, but God is a ניר, *nyr*. The king is addressed אדני, *'ădōnî* but God is addressed אדני, *'ădōnāy*. David is called 'our master, David', but God is called 'Yahweh, our master'. These modifications create tension between human royal appellations and their divine counterparts. Furthermore, God is superlative as 'king', 'master' and 'judge'; his extensive power in each of these capacities is emphasized through such phrases as אדון כל הארץ, 'master of all the earth', מלך רב, 'great king' and שפט צדק, 'righteous judge'. Such modifiers are never used with Israelite kings. Indeed, many of these modifiers, by pushing the appellation to the very edge of its acceptable usage, border on creating the semantic contradiction which is the essence of metaphor—can an אדון כל הארץ, 'master of all the earth' still be called merely a 'master'? Furthermore, certain contexts explicitly claim that God as 'king' is also 'creator' and 'maker' of Israel and is a shepherd who uses his rod beneficently. In such cases the metaphor is strained and almost shattered. These discontinuities are central to a proper understanding of God as king, for they show precisely where he fails to be bound by the metaphor. A different type of breakdown of the metaphor is expressed in Ps. 84 through the ironic contrast of vv. 10 and 12; both God and the king are called 'shield', but the power of the human 'shield' is totally dependent on God, the divine, royal 'shield'. The use of particular royal appellations offers general boundaries for understanding God, but through morphological, syntactic and contextual modifications, the biblical authors clarify that God's kinship is qualitatively different from human kingship.

Chapter 3

ROYAL QUALITIES

Introduction

The populace of ancient Israel wanted a king who possessed certain qualities such as longevity, wisdom, wealth and strength, since such a king would foster social stability. No historical king possessed all of these qualities. David, who is often idealized by the biblical historians, comes closest when he is described as (1 Sam. 16:18) 'a stalwart fellow and a warrior, sensible in speech and handsome in appearance'. The future, 'messianic' king is also described in similar idealized terms. This chapter explores how the qualities of long life, wisdom, wealth, strength, majesty and beauty are typically applied to human kings and are projected on to God as king.

Long Life

Royal subjects frequently wished that their king would live a long life, and according to the biblical historiographers this was sometimes accomplished (Malamat, 1982). David lived for seventy years, the full human lifespan according to Ps. 90:10. The monarch's long life is especially prominent in Psalms. In one psalm, the king wanted and received ארך ימים עולם ועד, 'a long life, everlasting' (Ps. 21:5). As noted by Quintens (1978:538-539), עולם, 'everlasting', is hyperbolic in this context; like דור ודור, 'from generation to generation' and נצח, 'unceasing', it indicates a long time and not eternity. These three expressions are similar to English 'always', which is frequently used hyperbolically. This is clearest from 1 Sam. 1:22 וישב שם עד־עולם, literally 'he will reside there forever', which in this context must mean 'he will reside there until he dies'. The claim of North (1932:24; see Healey, 1984:252-253) that the king 'was regarded as endowed with something like immortality' is based on a misunderstanding of these terms. The royal throne is עולם ועד, 'everlasting' (Ps. 45:7), a subject requests from God 'Add days to the days of the king; may his years extend through generations; may he dwell in God's presence forever' (Ps. 61:7-8a) and a subject wants to praise him perpetually (Ps. 45:18 MT). According to Ps. 72:5, the subject wished that the king 'will (reign) long' (following LXX συμπαραμενεῖ) and (v. 17) wanted the king to be as everlasting as the sun and the moon (Paul, 1972). In 1 Kgs 3:14, Solomon is promised a long life. In 1 Kgs 1:31 Bathsheba says to David יחי אדני המלך דוד לעלם, 'May my master David live forever' and Nehemiah introduces his remarks to the Persian king Artaxerxes with המלך לעולם יחיה, 'May the king live forever!' (Neh. 2:3).[1] A similar formula is well-known from the Aramaic sections of Daniel מלכא לעלמין חיי, 'O king, live forever!' (2:4; 3:9; 5:10; 6:7, 22). These phrases serve a double function: they are intended to flatter the king, but also reflect the hopes of the people for stability since chaos often broke out when a king died or was assassinated.

Since human kings cannot attain perpetual life, this wish becomes modified into the desire for an everlasting dynasty (North, 1932:24). This is reflected in various types of divine promises to the Davidic monarchy (see Weinfeld, 1970), where God promises to perpetuate the dynasty forever (Pss. 89:5, 30; 132:12; 1 Chr. 22:10; 28:7; 2 Chr. 13:5), or to make it as stable as the astral bodies (Ps. 89:37-38). Although non-Davidic kings are promised dynasties (1 Kgs 11:38), the promises are never phrased in such superlative terms. Similar dynastic promises to non-Judaean kings probably existed in antiquity, but were not preserved in the predominantly pro-Judaean historiographical texts.[2]

The theological notion that God is eternal would seem to be autonomously true, unrelated to God's kingship. The biblical text, however, by almost always associating God's eternity with the root מלך, 'to reign' or by mentioning it next to terms reminiscent of kingship (e.g. ישב, 'to be enthroned'), suggests that in ancient Israel God's eternal nature was understood within the framework of the metaphor 'God is king'.[3] In contrast, it is rare to find general phrases declaiming God's eternity that are not connected semantically or textually to his role as king such as ואתה־הוא ושנותיך לא יתמו, 'but you are the same, and your years never end' (Ps. 102:28), ומעולם עד־עולם אתה אל, 'from eternity to eternity you are God' (Ps. 90:2) and הלוא אתה מקדם יהוה אלהי קדשי ולא נמות (תמות :read),[4] 'You, O LORD are from everlasting; my holy God you never die' (Hab. 1:12). Instances where God's eternal nature is connected to his kingship outnumber cases where he is generally declared eternal by a ratio of five to one; this suggests that the Israelites understood God's eternal life primarily as an entailment of his kingship.

The human king's longevity in all of its aspects and manifestations is transferred to God with one obvious modification—the human king's longevity becomes God's eternal life. Thus, while jussives are used in phrases such as יחי ארני המלך דוד לעולם, 'May my master David live forever' (1 Kgs 1:31), and kings wish for 'eternal' life, the text frequently notes in the indicative that God is eternal (e.g. Mic. 4:7; Ps. 10:16). Lam. 5:19 אתה יהוה לעולם תשב כסאך לדור ודר, 'But you O LORD are enthroned forever, your throne endures throughout the ages' notes that the divine throne is eternal. As eternal, God will be praised perpetually (Ps. 145:4). God outdoes the human king whose reign is comparable to the astral bodies—the human king or his dynasty may be compared to them (in the vocative) but according to Isa. 60:19-20 (cf. 65:17) God outlasts the present luminaries.[5] Finally, God not only lives eternally, a claim kings may wish to make for themselves or for their dynasty, but he has also lived forever (Ps. 102:25b-27; cf. 29:10), a claim that no human king could make. Thus, by consciously pointing to human kingship when discussing God's eternal nature, the Bible creates a picture of a royal God who outlives any human king. The superiority of God's kingship is greatly emphasized. This is accomplished in a different way when Darius, himself a king, says of God (Dan. 6:27): די־הוא אלהא חיא וקן לעלמין ומלכותא די־לא תתחבל ושלטנה עד־סופא, 'for he is the living God who endures forever; his kingdom is indestructable; and his dominion is to the end of time'.

Wisdom

Kings are חכמים, 'wise', and חכמה, 'wisdom' is necessary for ruling well. The theme of 'wise king' is predominant throughout the ancient Near East (Kalugila, 1980). 'Wisdom' is an inadequate translation of *ḥokmāh*; its connotation is much broader (Fohrer, 1976:63). According to Whybray (1974:12) *ḥokmāh* denotes 'superior mental ability in a general sense, though this is often applied in a particular way'. As applied to kings, this 'particular way' may refer to cunning (1 Kgs 2:9), judicial abilities (1 Kgs 3:12 as understood by 2 Chr. 1:10-12; 1 Kgs 5:9-14; Prov. 8:15), cleverness and perception (2 Sam. 14:20).

Knowledge and curiosity are also depicted as royal qualities (Prov.
25:2-3; 1 Sam. 16:18; 2 Sam. 18:13). *Ḥokāh* enables the ruler of Tyre
to accumulate wealth (Ezek. 28:3-5) and is possibly one factor behind
the depiction of the wise King Solomon as wealthy. Prov. 8:15 states
that *ḥokmāh* is a requisite for ruling well: מלכים ימלכו (בחכמה=) בי,
'Through me (namely, wisdom) kings reign' (cf. Qoh. 4:13-14). The
first qualities enumerated for the future, ideal leader in Isa. 11:2 are
רוח חכמה ובינה, 'a spirit of wisdom and insight'. Most of the narrative
texts discussing royal wisdom are specific to Solomon. This skewed
distribution probably reflects the specific interests of the author of
the Solomon pericope (Liver, 1967) and does not indicate that
Solomon was the only king associated with wisdom in ancient Israel,
since 'wisdom texts' indicate that wisdom was a general royal
necessity.[6]

Ḥokmāh was possessed by many classes of people in ancient Israel
(Whybray, 1974), so there is no obvious reason for seeing divine
ḥokmāh as a projection of specifically royal *ḥokmāh*. However,
several contexts suggest that God's wisdom was associated with his
royalty. For example, in a context replete with royal imagery, Psalm
33 depicts God as wise (v. 11). Jer. 10:7 calls God מלך הגוים, 'king of
the nations', noting in the same verse that there is none like him
בכל־חכמי הגוים, 'among all the wise of the nations'. Such contexts
suggest that God's *ḥokmāh* was often understood as an entailment of
the metaphor 'God is king'.

Although for some reason the Bible is hesitant to call God חכם,
'wise' (see Whybray, 1974:10, esp. nn. 13-14), applying this substantive
to him only once (Isa. 31:2), many biblical texts portray him as
exceedingly wise (see Kalugila 1980:90-101). This is most explicit in
Prov. 21:30 אין חכמה ואין תבונה ואין עצה לנגד יהוה, 'No wisdom, no
prudence, and no counsel can prevail against the LORD'. The same
idea stands behind Job's second response to God in 42:3 לכן
הגדתי ולא אבין נפלאות ממני ולא אדע, 'indeed I spoke without understanding of things beyond me, which I did not know' and is stated in
other wisdom and non-wisdom books.[7] As supremely wise, God
dispenses all types of wisdom to others, including the ability to be a
craftsman (Exod. 28:3 and frequently), to administer effectively
(1 Kgs 5:26) and to be righteous ('religious wisdom'; cf. Ps. 119:27, 34,
66, 73, 125, 144, 169). The Bible also declares God the allocator of
wisdom in its general sense (Prov. 2:6; possibly Job 32:8; 35:11; Ps.
94:10b). In proto-apocalyptic and apocalyptic literature, this

attribute is transferred to the מלאכים, 'the divine messengers' (e.g. Zech. 2:2ff.; Dan. 8:15). God not only dispenses wisdom where appropriate, but can withhold it too (Job 39:17), even from those who are traditionally wise (Isa. 29:14; 44:25[8]). In fact, the text goes out of its way four times to note that Solomon, the wise king *par excellence*, is not 'self-taught', but acquired his wisdom from God (1 Kgs 3:12; 5:9, 21, 26).[9]

The remainder of the texts stress God's wisdom in the context of his creation of the world (Isa. 40:28; Jer. 10:12=51:15; Pss. 104:24; 136:5-9; possibly 147:5 [cf. v. 4]; Prov. 3:19-20; Job 26:12; 38:36-37). The motif of God as creator will be examined in detail later (pp. 116-18); it is sufficient to note that as creator God's capabilities extend beyond any human monarch.

God's wisdom surpasses the wisdom of the king who traditionally was thought of as very wise. No king could claim to be the source of all wisdom or could withhold wisdom from the already wise. Certainly, none using wisdom could embark on as extensive a building project as the cosmos. Even Solomon, wisest of all sages (1 Kgs 5:11), was only wise because God, the ultimate *ḥākām*, 'sage', dispensed wisdom to him.

Wealth

The king's prestige in the ancient Near East was partially determined by his wealth. God's response to Solomon's dream at Gibeon (1 Kgs 3:11) ולא־שאלת לך עשר, 'because you did not ask for riches' indicates that the desire to accumulate wealth typified Israelite kings as well. Israelite kings often controlled vast riches, though unlike the neighboring monarchs, they did not have large land holdings (cf. 1 Kgs 21).[10] The king collected funds internally by levying taxes (see below, pp. 119-20), and externally from booty and by levying tribute on vassals. 1 Kgs 9:26-10:25 narrates in detail Solomon's wealth and its sources. King Hezekiah had sufficient treasures to impress Merodach Baladan (2 Kgs 20:13). The king had control over אוצרות בית יהוה ובית המלך, 'the treasuries of the Temple of the LORD and the royal palace'. These funds could be sufficient enough to pay off foreign powers (2 Kgs 12:19; 16:8; 18:15). Wealth was such an important part of the royal image that one psalmist wishes of the king ויחי ויתן־לו מזהב שבא, 'so let him live, and receive gold of Sheba' (Ps. 72:15).[11] One narrative depicts Saul, the first king, as wealthy (1 Sam. 17:25). Gideon, who in some senses accepts the Israelite offer of kingship, accumulates wealth (Judg. 8:24-27). Foreign kings were also described as rich (Num. 22:17-18; Ezek. 28:4-5; Esth. 1:4). The king's wealth, like all wealth, was normally measured in silver and gold, but could also include (inlaid) ivory palaces (1 Kgs 22:39; cf. Amos), horses (1 Kgs 5:6; 10:25-29), which were extremely expensive in the ancient Near East (Elat, 1977:69-82; Ikeda, 1982:226), trees (2 Chr. 1:15), precious stones and spices, and even rare animals (1 Kgs 10:22; cf. Ikeda, 1982: 219-220). Although Deuteronomy only briefly touches on kingship, it explicitly prohibits the king from accumulating excessive wealth (17:17). This too suggests that the Israelite kings aspired to be wealthy.

Kābôd, usually rendered 'glory' or 'honor', is an extremely polysemic root. However, when used of kings, it usually refers to possessions. This sense is well-attested in the human non-royal sphere.[12] With kings this is certainly its meaning at Esth. 1:4 בהראתו את־עשר כבוד מלכותו, 'when he displayed the vast riches of his kingdom' and is possibly its meaning in 1 Kgs 3:13 (cf. 2 Chr. 1:11,12; 1 Chr. 29:28; 2 Chr. 17:5; 18:1; 32:27). The majority of these cases are post-exilic. In the two other cases where *kābôd* is used with kings, it refers to military strength (see Weinfeld, 1982:25-26, 'Kraft und Macht'). Perhaps *kābôd* began to assume the connotation of strength since it was frequently used in contexts with *hôd* and *hādār* (e.g. Isa. 35:2; Ps. 145:5), which often connote military strength. Alternately, this may be a natural semantic development since other Hebrew words connote both 'strength' and 'possessions'.[13]

Just like any human king, God could accumulate riches through taxation (e.g. tithes, sacrifices; cf. below, pp. 120-22) and booty (e.g. Hag. 2:7-8). However, unlike human kings, God is never portrayed as accumulating wealth in his heavenly storehouses. This is because according to the biblical authors God did not acquire his power through wealth. Verses which indirectly depict God as rich such as Deut. 10:14 הן ליהוה אלהיך השמים ושמי השמים הארץ וכל־אשר־בה, 'Mark, the heavens and their uttermost reaches belong to the LORD your God, the earth and all that is in it' are very infrequent.[14] Instead of emphasizing God's wealth in terms of ownership, the biblical authors typically note both his absolute independence from 'money' and his ability to control it. Thus, unlike human kings who tried to buy off foreign powers (e.g. 1 Kgs 15:19; 2 Kgs 16:8), Zeph. 1:18 notes: גם־כספם גם־זהבם לא־יוכל להצילם ביום עברת יהוה, 'Moreover, their silver and gold shall not avail to save them on the day of the LORD's wrath'. Isa. 52:3; Ezek. 7:19 and Prov. 11:4 express similar notions.

God is often depicted as a wealth-broker, distributing riches to whomever he wishes (Gen. 31:16; 1 Kgs 3:13; Isa. 60:17; Ps. 112:3 Prov. [2:22?;] 30:8; Qoh. 5:18; 1 Chr. 29:12). Furthermore, instead of using his אצרות, 'treasuries' to hold treasures, they are replete with meteorological phenomena (Deut. 28:12), especially רוח, 'wind' (Jer. 10:13= 51:16; cf. Ps. 135:7) or with frightfully powerful weapons (Deut. 32:34). In Job 38:22-23, these two functions of the divine storehouses are combined—they hold meteorological phenomena which are used as weapons.

A polemical tone is evident in the texts claiming that God is not influenced by silver and gold and has no precious metal in his treasuries. They stress that God is owner of all, who controls storehouses with commodities beyond human control. God cannot be bribed by 'additional' wealth. God is wealthy in a very different sense from human kings; he extends beyond the metaphor. Perhaps a similar notion is expressed by the use of *kābôd* with God, since it does not convey 'wealth' in a limited sense.[15] Instead, it may evoke a reaction of awe and reverence (e.g. Lev. 9:23-24). At some point, *kābôd* was seen as so intrinsic to God, that it became a divine appellation (Mettinger, 1982a:107). This contrast in use between *kābôd* with human and divine royal subjects supports the notion that in applying the metaphor 'God is king,' the king's wealth went through substantial modifications when it was used of God.

Strength

The king needed to be strong to be an effective war-leader. The general root used of strength in the Bible is *gbr*. The king is called a גבור, 'warrior' in two royal psalms (45:4 and 89:20; 'warrior' in Isa. 3:2 may also refer to the king). In Ps. 33:16 גבור, 'warrior' is a B word parallel to המלך, 'the king'. Several kings (or future kings) are called (חיל) גבור,[16] 'warriors (with respect to battle)' including Saul (2 Sam. 1:21),[17] Saul together with the crown-prince Jonathan (2 Sam. 1:19, 25, 27), David (1 Sam. 16:18 and 2 Sam. 17:10) and Jeroboam I (1 Kgs 11:28). Perhaps calling a king's ancestor גבור חיל, 'a warrior (with respect to battle)' (1 Sam. 9:1 and Ruth 2:1) sets a type-scene (see Alter, 1981:47-62) which leads to the expectation of the birth of a king. A frequent formula notes that כל־גבורתו, 'all of the valiant acts of a king' are recounted in the royal chronicles is found of ten kings in Kings, ranging from Asa (1 Kgs 15:23) to Hezekiah (2 Kgs 20:20).

It is also used of the post-exilic Persian Ahasuerus (Esth. 10:2). The notion that strength was seen as an intrinsic royal quality is confirmed by Isa. 11:2, where the future Davidic king has רוח עצה וגבורה, 'a spirit of counsel and valor'.

In post-exilic texts, the root *gbr* is no longer used of kings and is replaced by words from the root *ḥzq* or *k(w)ḥ*.[18] For example, 2 Chronicles narrates that when Rehaboam and Jeroboam became strong (*wb/kḥzqtw* [12:1; 26:16]) they abandoned God. Of the two cases where *gbwrtw* is used in the concluding formula of Judaean kings (1 Kgs 15:23; 2 Kgs 20:20), Chronicles omits it once (2 Chr. 16:11) and once changes it to *ḥsdyw* (2 Chr. 32:32).[19] Various Greek kings show excessive *kḥ* (Dan. 8:6, 22, 24; 11:25; cf. 11:2). This shift in terminology away from *gbr* is especially striking since the root *gbr* and the noun גבורה, 'strength' remained productive in non-royal contexts throughout the post-exilic and rabbinic periods. This suggests that the root was intentionally avoided in human royal contexts.

Other words from the semantic field of strength are either rarely or never used of kings. At most the adjective עז, 'mighty' is used with the king twice (Isa. 19:4 and Dan. 8:23), both of non-Israelite kings.[20] The substantive עז, 'might' is related to kings in 1 Sam. 2:10 and possibly Ps. 28:8. In both cases the king's עז, 'might' is bequeathed to him by God. The royal מטה עז, 'mighty rod' of Ezek. 19:11-14 withers and is destroyed by God. Similarly, מעוז, 'protection' is used of the Egyptian king in Isa. 30:2-3 in a context which points to his inadequacy; it is never used of an Israelite king. Thus, words from the root *'wz/'zz*, a very productive biblical root, are never used to describe the strength of the Israelite monarch, and are rarely used of non-Israelite kings.

The major Aramaic terms for royal strength are *tqp'* and *ḥsn'* (Dan. 2:37; 4:27). The cognate Hebrew *tqp*, an Aramaic loanword in Hebraized form (Wagner, 1966:120), is used of royalty in post-exilic books (e.g. Esth. 9:29; 10:2; Dan. 11:17). Dan. 2:37 די אלה שמיא מלכותא חסנא ותקפא ויקרא יהב-לך, 'to whom the God of heaven has given kingdom, power, might and glory' follows the earlier Hebrew tradition, which emphasizes that these powers are given to the king by God.

A large number of biblical words from other semantic fields have been absorbed into the field of strength. Some, such as סלע and צור, 'rock,' metaphorically come to mean strength. Only once, in Isa. 31:9 וסלעו ממגור יעבור וחתו מנס שריו, 'His rock shall melt with terror, and his officers shall collapse from weakness' may 'rock' refer to a king (see Dillmann, 1898:283), the Assyrian monarch. צור never refers to a king. Words related to 'fortress' and 'protection' may also be used metaphorically to indicate strength. These include משגב, 'haven,' מנוס, 'refuge,' מחסה, 'shelter' and מצודה, 'fortress,' none of which is applied to kings. Most words in the *qaṭṭîl* pattern, which perhaps indicated substantives that 'possess a quality in an intensive manner' (Gesenius, 1974 §84^{b}f) are strength related: אביר, אמיץ and כביר, all typically translated as 'mighty'. *'addîr*, often translated as 'majestic' (BDB; Baumgartner, 1967:13 'gewaltig, prächtig'; cf. the various translation equivalents in the LXX), is best related to the strength field. This is clear from contexts such as Exod. 15:10 and Ps. 93:4, and from Nah. 2:6 where it has the same reference as (v. 4) גבריהו, 'his warriors'. Of these *qaṭṭîl* nouns, only *'addîr* is used of human kings, but never in contexts that stress their strength. In fact, in Ps. 136:18 God slays מלכים אדירים, 'mighty kings'. The difficult Jer. 30:21 calls the king of restored Israel *'addîrô*. *'addîr* is also used in late literature to designate a type of royal official (Jer. 14:3; 2 Chr. 23:20; Neh. 3:5; 10:30), a development similar to *nāgîd* (pp. 33 and 173, n. 7). The lack of use of *'addîr* with Israelite kings is especially striking when compared to the use of this term in Phoenician. Phoenician *'dr* (which is usually properly rendered as 'strong' by Semitists) is attributed to kings (Karatepe; cf. KAI I,5-6 #26 A III;) and appears two or three times as a royal appellation (Eshmunazar [KAI I, 4 #14] and Kilamuwa [KAI I, 4 #24, I 5-6] and possibly in the Ma'ṣūb inscription [KAI I, 4, #19^{21}]). Given the meagre extent of the Phoenician corpus, this contrasts sharply with the reticence of biblical authors to use this term of human kings.

Arm imagery can often be used metaphorically of strength. This is true of יד, 'arm, hand' (e.g. Josh. 8:20 ידים לנום, 'strength [literally hands] to flee') and ימין, 'right (hand)', but especially of זרוע, 'arm'. זרוע, 'arm' is used of kings in exilic and later contexts—in Ezek. 30:21 it is used of Pharaoh, in 2 Chr. 32:8 Sennacherib has זרוע בשר, 'an arm of flesh' and in Dan. 11:6 it refers to a future king's strength. The first two texts explicitly note the superiority of divine strength to the human 'arm'. Similarly, Ezek. 30:24-25 depicts God as strengthening or weakening the זרעות, 'arms' of kings. Only in Ezek. 22:6 is זרוע, 'arm' (in the sense of power) an Israelite royal quality. This verse however, does not use זרוע, 'arm' in its usual neutral sense, but shows how the Israelite king abuses his power to spill blood. Twice in royal psalms the king's ימין, 'right hand' is cited (21:9 and

45:5), but in each case the king's power is contingent on his past or future righteous behavior (21:8; 45:3, 8). Elsewhere, the Bible is more explicit, describing how it is God who holds a king's right hand (Isa. 45:1; Ps. 89:26), implying that no king, Israelite or foreign, is strong independently of the divine will.

The words *hôd* and *hādār* properly belong in the semantic field of strength. *Hôd* is usually translated as 'glory' or 'splendor'[22] and is often connected to Akkadian *melammu* (e.g. Mulder, 1972:104); however, it rightfully belongs in the field of strength. It is largely used in poetry to describe great strength, which is usually possessed by God or the king. 'Splendor' is especially misleading, since *hôd* is typically heard rather than seen.[23] *Hôd* is used together with or in parallelism to words for strength in Pss. 45:4; 96:6 (cf. 1 Chr. 16:27); 145:5 and Prov. 5:9-10. 'Strength' is the most plausible rendering in verses such as Isa. 30:30 הוד קולו ('his strong voice') and Job 39:20. In Num. 27:15-23, Moses asks God to appoint a new military leader for Israel; God expresses the transferring of Moses' power to Joshua in v. 20 in terms of transferring Moses' *hôd* to Joshua. The expression 'to be clothed with *hôd*' (Ps. 104:1; Job 40:10) is syntactically parallel and perhaps semantically parallel to 'be clothed with strength' (Isa. 51:9; 52:1). Finally, whenever *hôd* is used without reference to God or king, it clearly denotes strength. Thus, in Dan. 10:8 and Prov. 5:9-10 (MT), *hôd* is used adjacently to כח, 'strength'. Finally, in Hos. 14:7, *hôd* refers to the produce (of a tree) which is elsewhere called כח, 'strength' (Gen. 4:12; Job 31:39). These contexts suggest that *hôd* is certainly related specifically to 'strength' and should not be translated 'glory'.

Dan. 11:21 and 1 Chr. 29:25 specifically mention הוד מלכות, 'royal *hôd*', implying that *hôd* is a specifically royal quality. The pre-exilic dirge הוי הרה/הדו הוי, 'Ah, his *hôd*' (Jer. 22:18) indicates that the *hôd* was intrinsic to royalty in the pre-exilic period. The importance of *hôd* as a royal quality is also stressed by (post-exilic) Zech. 6:13, where the power of the future king is stressed by saying והוא-ישא הוד, 'he will assume *hôd*'.

Although textual difficulties sometimes obscure our understanding of *hādār*, its frequent association with other words from the strength field[24] indicate that it is strength related. *Hādār* refers to the military might of kings in Pss. 21:6 and 45:4-5.[25] Similarly, the feminine *hadrāh* in Prov. 14:28 ברב-עם הדרת-מלך, 'A numerous people is the *hadrāh* of the king' most likely refers to the military power given to the king through a sufficiently large army. Ps. 110:3 is in too obscure a verse to be interpreted with any certainty,[26] but even there, the military terms in vv. 2-3 suggest that *hādār* probably refers to military strength. Thus, especially when used of kings, *hādār* like *hôd* belongs in the semantic field of strength.

Although the semantic field of strength is very rich in Biblical Hebrew, terms from it are rarely applied to human kings, especially to Israelite monarchs. When we consider that kings play a major role in the historiographical books and that there are some royal psalms and several prophetic passages concerned with kings, the paucity of references to the Israelite kings' strength, even in polemical or negative contexts, is especially striking. A comparison to the use of cognate terms of kings in Phoenician makes the lack of these terms in the Bible even more noteworthy. This suggests that God as king has usurped many 'strength' terms from the human sphere.

According to the biblical evidence, the ancient Israelites applied to God all of the strength terminology used of human kings, but used these terms in new ways and incorporated special strength terms for God to distinguish him from human kings. Ps. 24:8, where the question מי זה מלך הכבוד, 'who is the king of *kābôd*?' is answered יהוה עזוז וגבור יהוה גבור מלחמה, 'the LORD, mighty and valiant, the LORD, valiant in battle', suggests that God's strength could be an entailment of his portrayal as king. Ps. 145:11-12, where מלכות, 'kingship' and גבורה, 'strength' are chiastically balanced in two verses at the center of the psalm further supports this contention.[27] This parallelism persists, and is found in Ben Sira (MS. B) 44:3. God is called גבור, 'strong, warrior' in his depiction as a 'divine warrior,' especially when he appears in the Day of the Lord (e.g. Zeph. 1:14). Sometimes he is compared to a 'warrior' in a simile rather than a metaphor[28] (Isa. 42:13, where the *Hitpaʻel* is durative [cf. Speiser, 1955]; Jer. 14:9 [MT]; 20:11; Ps. 78:65; Job 16:14). In Aramaic, *gĕbûrtāʼ*, 'power' is one of the two qualities of God singled out by Nebuchadnezzer in Dan. 2:20. The image of God's strength was seen as so central that this divine royal attribute eventually became incorporated into a formula: Deut. 10:17 האל הגדל הגבר והנורא,[29] 'the great, the mighty, the awesome God' > Jer. 32:18 האל הגדול הגבור יהוה צבאות שמו 'the great mighty LORD, the LORD of hosts is his name' > Neh. 9:32 האל הגדול הגבור והנורא שומר הברית והחסד, 'the great, mighty and awesome God, who stays faithful to his covenant'. This formula survived into the post-biblical period and became incorporated into the daily *ʻămîdāh* prayer. The association between

God and גבור, 'strong, warrior' is strengthened by noting that his מלאכים, 'messengers' or the members of his heavenly council are called גבורים, 'warriors' (Judg. 5:23, cf. 13; Joel 4:11; Ps. 103:20). If divine messengers either originate from demoted gods (Rofé, 1969:63-78) or if they represent hypostasized aspects of God (cf. 2 Sam. 24:1 and 1 Chr. 21:1), their naming as גבורים, 'warriors' may reflect an originally divine attribute that was transferred to them.

God as king possesses גבורה, 'strength' in a measure unparalleled by humans (cf. Jer. 10:6-7; Ps. 66:7; 2 Chr. 20:6). The most vivid illustration of the total power incorporated into the divine strength is in Job 12:12-25: 'with him are wisdom and strength. . . whatever he tears down cannot be rebuilt; whomever he imprisons cannot be set free. . . with him are strength and resourcefulness. . . he undoes the belts of kings. . . and loosens the belts of the mighty. . . he exalts nations, then destroys them, he expands nations, then leads them away'. This divine גבורה, 'strength' is explicitly mentioned over twenty-five times in the Bible. Its importance is clarified by its narrative placement—in Ps. 21:14 it climactically concludes the psalm, and הללוהו בגבורתיו, 'Praise him for his mighty acts' appears in Ps. 150:2 as part of the climactic conclusion of the psalter as a whole. After seeing God's גבורה, 'strength' a person may know that his name is Yahweh (Jer. 16:21); thus strength is an intrinsic part of the divine essence. This divine גבורה, 'strength' is manifest throughout time; God showed his גבורה, 'strength' in 'mythical time' (Job 26:14), in 'historical time' (Ps. 66:7) and a new manifestation of it may be anticipated in the future (Isa. 63:15). The connection between God and the root *gbr* is further strengthened by the use of the plural form גבורות, 'mighty acts' solely of God in the Bible (Ginzberg, 1961:154-155).

This close association of *gĕbûrāh* and God continues throughout the biblical period. It is evident in the Aramaic of Daniel (2:20) and in the Hebrew fragments of Ben-Sira (e.g. 15:18; 33:3; 43:12-15). This connection between God and *gĕbûrāh* reaches a new stage of development in the rabbinic period when *gĕbûrāh* becomes a divine name (Marmorstein, 1927:82; Kosmala, 1975:371), usually used in connection to God's epiphany at the giving of the Torah. By using different vocalization to accomplish semantic differentiation, Hebrew gains the following words out of the root *gbr*: *geber* of people, *gebîrāh* of royalty and *gĕbûrāh* of God. To summarize: the root *gbr* and the word *gĕbûrāh* have a strange history—they were appropriated by ancient Israel from human kingship for God, and eventually became more intimately attached to divine than to human kingship. This explains why in post-exilic biblical literature, the root *gbr* is very rarely used of human kings (cf. the cases noted above, p. 58, where the Chronicler intentionally avoids the term), and by the tannaitic period, only God himself could properly be called *gĕbûrāh*. This clearly discernable diachronic development suggests that certain other 'strength' terms may not be used of human kings in the Bible because they have been appropriated by God the king.

As we saw earlier, although human kings' strength (from the root *ḥzq*) is directly related to their ability to reign (cf. 2 Kgs 12:2; Hag. 2:4; 2 Chr. 17:1), no king is ever called the substantive חזק, 'strong'. In contrast, חזק, 'strong' is used several times of God (in order of certainty: Jer. 50:34; Prov. 23:11; Isa. 40:10; 28:2 and Ps. 18:2). A much more central word indicating God's power is כח, 'strength' used from early (Exod. 15:6) to late (1 Chr. 29:12; 2 Chr. 20:6) literature. The divine כח, 'strength' is more far-reaching than its human counterpart; the creation (Jer. 10:12=51:15; 27:5; 32:17), God's defeat of the mythological creatures, his control over the heavenly court (e.g. Isa. 40:26), his deliverance of Israel from Egypt (Deut. 4:37; 9:29; 2 Kgs 17:36; probably Neh. 1:10) and his future trouncing of the nations (Isa. 63:1) are all be attributed to his כח, 'strength'. Paradoxically, his כח, 'strength' is evident not only in his ability to fight, but also in his forgiving nature (Num. 14:17). God also dispenses כח, 'strength' to others (Deut. 8:18; Isa. 40:29), therefore ultimate כח, 'strength' does not lie with people (1 Sam. 2:9; Ps. 33:16), not even the 'great king' of Assyria (cf. Isa. 10:12-13). Only God is ישגיב בכחו, 'beyond reach in his power' (Job 36:22). The centrality of God's כח, 'power' is seen in Nah. 1:3 where the divine attributes known from Exod. 34:6-7 and the decalogue are modified to יהוה ארך אפים וגדול/וגדל-כח, 'The LORD is slow to anger and of great power'.[30]

The reticence of the biblical text to say that kings have עז, 'might' stands in marked contrast to the ascription of this quality to God.[31] God as king is girded with עז, 'strength' in Ps. 93:1, a psalm that is infused with royal imagery; he is called מלך עז, 'a mighty king' in Isa. 19:4. God himself states כי עז לאלהים, 'might belongs to God' (Ps. 62:12). Early (Exod. 15:2, 13) and late (Isa. 45:24; 1 Chr. 16:27-28) texts ascribe עז, 'might' to God. God could even be invoked with the vocative עזי, 'my might' (Ps. 59:18). Using his עז, 'might', God defeated mythological creatures in the past (Isa. 51:9; Ps. 89:11) and conquered Canaan (Exod. 15:13). Knowledge of God's עז, 'might' provides tremendous security (Isa. 12:2; Pss. 28:7; 118:14). עז, 'might' was such a central attribute of God that it could be used to denote the ark in the Temple, a symbol of the divine presence (Pss. 63:3; 78:61; 105:4= 1 Chr. 16:11; Ps. 132:8>2 Chr. 6:41). The superiority of the divine עז, 'might' to the human עז, 'might' is the theme of Psalm 21. This is a royal psalm which nevertheless opens יהוה בעזך ישמח־מלך, 'O LORD, the king rejoices in your might' and closes רומה יהוה בעזך נשירה ונזמרה גבורתך, 'Be exalted, O LORD, through your might; we will sing and chant the praises of your mighty deeds', effectively bracketing the human king's power with God's. Similarly, God's מטה־עז, 'mighty scepter' (Ps. 110:2) is powerfully effective in saving the human king, a stark contrast to the withered and scorched 'mighty scepter' of the human king (Ezek. 19:11-14). Perhaps the unique strength of God is emphasized through the word '*ĕzûz* which only has God as its subject in the Hebrew Bible (Isa. 42:25; Pss. 78:4; 145:6). Finally, it is noteworthy that God's power which is unknowable in its vastness (Ps. 90:11) is not exclusively destructive, as is typical of עז, 'might' as possessed by humans; it incorporates the love for משפט, 'justice' (Ps. 99:4; cf. Isa. 45:24) and even the granting of peace (Ps. 29:11). This paradox befits the divine king only.

Metaphors of strength based on rock and fortress imagery are often applied to God. He is called סלע, 'crag' four times (2 Sam. 22:2 = Ps. 18:3; Pss. 31:4; 42:10; 71:3),[32] always in the form סלעי, 'my crag', and צור, 'rock' over twenty times,[33] all in poetic texts. The personal names אליצור, צורישדי, צוריאל and פדהצור, all of which ascribe 'rock' elements to God, are ascribed by P to Israelites in the period of wandering (Num. 3:35; 1:5, 6, 10; cf. the hypocoristicon צור in 1 Chr. 8:30). In Ps. 89:27, the Israelite king is instructed to call God צור, 'rock', emphasizing that such a term might be inappropriate to the Israelite king since it belongs to God.

Many 'fortress' and 'protection' words are also used of God. He is a מחסה, 'shelter', fifteen times, משגב, 'haven', twelve times (משגב is only used in the Bible fifteen times!), מעוז, 'stronghold', five times,[34] מצודה, 'fortress' four times and מנוס, 'refuge', twice.[35] In Ps. 48:3-4 this image of God as 'fortress' is explicitly connected to his role of royal protector of Jerusalem: קרית מלך רב אלהים בארמנותיה נודע למשגב, 'city of the great king, through its citadels, God has made himself known as a haven'.

All *qaṭṭîl* verbs of strength are applied to God. He is '*ābîr*, 'mighty' (a morphologically differentiated form of '*abbîr*),[36] אדיר, אמיץ and כביר, all usually translated as 'mighty'. In 1 Sam. 4:8, even the

Philistines recognize God as אדיר, 'mighty'. Psalm 8 has God's
אדירות, 'mightiness' or 'majesty' as its theme—it opens and closes
יהוה אדנינו מה־אדיר שמך בכל־הארץ, 'O LORD, our master, how majestic
is your name throughout the earth' and claims that even babes
recognize God's strength (v. 3). In Isa. 33:17-24, God's kingship is
connected to his being אדיר, 'mighty' (vv. 17, 21, 22). Two other
words related to strength are used only of God: מפלט, 'deliverer'
(Sawyer, 1972:108) and זמר II, 'might'.

God's overbearing strength is further emphasized through 'arm'
terms. His זרוע, 'arm' is mentioned over thirty times, in early (Exod.
15:16) to late (Isa. 53:1) texts, his ימין, 'right (hand)' is noted over
twenty times, and the phrases יד חזקה, 'a strong hand' and בחזק יד,
'with a strong hand' are used of God over thirty times. Sometimes יד,
'hand' unmodified is used of God (e.g. Jer. 16:21). Some of these
terms are used in contexts where God's kingship is explicit, such as
Ezek. 20:33-34, Pss. 44:4-5 and 74:11-12. Although God's זרוע, 'arm'
is anthropomorphic, it is supra-human, as indicated by God's
challenge to Job (40:9) ואם־זרוע כאל לך, 'Have you an arm like God's?'
In Isa. 62:8 נשבע יהוה בימינו ובזרוע עזו, 'The LORD has sworn by his
right hand, by his mighty arm', the image of God swearing by raising
his arm is conflated with the image of his destructive power, creating
a complex powerful picture of an unbreakable, ever-powerful vow.
However, in contrast to human 'arm-power', which is only
destructive, Second Isaiah follows an image of God's destructive arm
with כרועה עדרו ירעה בזרעו יקבץ טלאים, 'Like a shepherd he pastures
his flock: he gathers the lambs in his *arms*' (Isa. 40:11). Similarly in
Isa. 41:10, God supports Israel with ימין צדקי, '[his] victorious right
hand'. God's power can also be gentle and beneficial.

We saw previously how God's supra-human power is conveyed by
reserving certain terms in the semantic field of 'power' for him,
implying that his strength is qualitatively different than human
strength. This exaltation is also accomplished by stringing together
words from this field, either through conjunctive *wāw*s, poetic
parallelism or 'synonymous' constructs.[37] This is most common in
the phrase יד חזקה זרוע נטויה, 'with a mighty hand and an outstretched
arm', used five times in Deuteronomy in reference to God the
redeemer of Israel from Egypt (cf. Jer. 32:21 and Ps. 136:12).
Elsewhere, God is עזי ומעזי ומנוסי, 'my strength and my stronghold;
my refuge' (Jer. 16:19), צור מעוז, 'a rock, a stronghold', ... לבית מצודות
סלעי ומצודתי, 'a citadel... my rock and my fortress' (Ps. 31:3-4)
and חסדי ומצודתי משגבי ומפלטי לי מגני ובו חסיתי הרודד עמי(ם) תחתי, 'my

faithful one, my fortress, my haven and my deliverer, my shield, in whom I take shelter, who makes peoples subject to me' (Ps. 144:2). The opening verses of 2 Samuel 22 are even more extensive (the parallel Psalm 18 is slightly shorter): 'O LORD, my crag, my fastness, my deliverer, O God, the rock wherein I take shelter: my shield, my mighty champion, my fortress and refuge, my savior, you who rescue me from violence!' Such collections of terms are frequently applied to kings in Mesopotamian royal inscriptions (Seux, 1967), but are nowhere applied to reigning or dead Israelite kings in the Bible.

The terms *hôd* and *hādār* are also used of God's strength (e.g. Isa. 2:19, 21; 30:30; Hab. 3:3; Pss. 8:2; 29:4[38]), sometimes in contexts which specifically call God a king (Ps. 96:6, cf. v. 10, 145:12). Sometimes, the divine *hôd* and *hādār* surpasses the human *hôd* and *hādār*—no person could match God's power as storm god (Ps. 29), nor does any human *hôd* and *hādār* allow a king to control nature, creation or mythological creatures. When humans have *hôd* and *hādār*, it is often granted them by God (Pss. 8:6; 21:6 of a king). Finally, a human king could have power over parts of the earth, but could never say (Ps. 148:13) הורו על־ארץ ושמים, 'his *hôd* covers heaven and earth'.

The centrality and extraordinary nature of God's power is further indicated by the large number of strength roots used in theophoric names. These names, many of which appear on seal rings or seal impressions, offer an important extra-biblical control for understanding Israelite religion (Tigay, 1986:5-9). Particularly striking are the עז names, including the biblical עזא, עזה, עזי, עזיא, עזיאל, עזיהו, all of which ascribe strength (עז) to God (Noth, 1928:160; for extra-biblical attestations, cf. Tigay, 1986:59-60, 83). The name יהועז is known from three separate epigraphic sources from the eighth and seventh centuries (Heltzer-Ohana, 1978:49). Other biblical names describing divine strength are: חזקי, חזקיה(ו) (Noth:160), מחסיה (Noth:158, also at Elephantine), מעזיהו (Noth: 157, also Elephantine) אמצי, אמציה (Noth:190; cf. אלאמץ on an Ammonite seal in Heltzer-Ohana:31), אחיהוד[39] and עמיהוד, הוד, הודיהו (Noth:146). מעוזי, מחסה, מעוז and מעוזיה are known from Elephantine (Noth:157-158; cf. מחמיהו in Avigad, 1986 #14). אל(י)עז, אלירם and זמריהו are found on pre-exilic seals (Heltzer-Ohana:33, 44; Avigad, 1986 #17, 18, 28, 29, 55, 71, 72, 73, 90, 117), and בעלזמר, a Northern Israelite name, is known from the Samaria ostraca (Heltzer-Ohana:37).[40] No other semantic field incorporates the variety and number of theophoric names found here.

Certain metaphors, similes and attributes which characterize divine strength are rarely or never used of human kings, showing that God's strength is qualitatively superior to human strength, even royal strength. However, it is difficult to evaluate these skewed ratios and to determine whether they reflect the socio-linguistic realities of ancient Hebrew in general, or if they only reflect the interests of the biblical authors. The answer will determine the extent to which we may speak of the metaphor 'God is king' in the Bible or in ancient Israel. No general solution to this problem is obvious, although the predominance of divine strength terms *vis-à-vis* royal, human strength terms is so extensive, it probably reflects to some extent ancient Israelite (and not just biblical) reality. This impression is seconded by the predominance of theophoric names which emphasize God's strength. For example, in the corpus of bullae from the late pre-exilic period published by Avigad (1986), one person is named מחסיהו בן פלטיהו, literally 'the LORD is a shelter son of the LORD delivers', and the personal name פלטיהו, 'the LORD delivers', is used of six different individuals. Until more epigraphic material is found, including Israelite royal inscriptions, no definitive decision on this issue is possible.[41]

Exodus 15 and Psalm 29, two early literary compositions, portray God's strength within the context of his kingship, suggesting that at an early point in Israelite religion, God's strength and kingship were seen as interrelated. Although it is unlikely that every instance God was called strong was intended as an entailment of the kingship metaphor, texts from a wide variety of periods, e.g. Ps. 24:8, which is generally considered pre-exilic, and Psalm 145, which Hurvitz (1972:70-107) shows must be post-exilic, specifically connect divine kingship and strength, implying that God's strength was perceived as an entailment of his kingship throughout the biblical period.

The images of the king as strong and of God as strong are not fully parallel. Many terms are only applied to God as king (e.g. צור, 'rock', משגב, 'haven', מצודה, 'fortress', מפלט, 'deliverer', מנוס, 'refuge', מחסה, 'shelter', חזק, 'strong' and אמיץ, כביר and אביר, all 'mighty'), and relate back to the human king by being in the general semantic field of 'strength', while other terms predominate in divine rather than royal usage (e.g זרוע, 'arm', סלע, 'crag' and עזז/עוז, 'to be mighty'). This synchronic feature of the language, where a word is 'disinfected', that is becomes applied only to God (Sawyer, 1972:53 and 103), stresses God's supra-royal power. This process can also be seen diachronically, as God takes over the royal attribute גבורה, 'the strength' by the post-exilic period, and it is no longer used of human kings. If images from different contexts may be meaningfully combined, the Israelite king's broken מטה עז, 'mighty rod' (Ezek. 19:11-14) contrasts powerfully with God's 'mighty rod' (Ps. 110:2), which can save the people. Also, specific contexts stress the superiority of God's power by noting that he supplies kings with power (e.g. Isa. 45:1; Pss. 21:6; 89; Dan. 2:20, 23), and can even kill מלכים אדירים, 'mighty kings' (Ps. 136:18). God can deliver the people (an active act of control) with a יד חזקה, 'strong hand', but the only time this phrase is used of a human king is when Pharaoh will release them and will chase them out (Exod. 6:1), in a sense mocking Pharaoh's 'strong hand'. God's supra-human qualities are also reinforced by showing how his power incorporates his role as creator, deliverer (past, present and future), controller of weather and subduer of mythological creatures. Biblical language further stresses the excessive divine power by combining in single contexts many power terms of God, a feature absent with Israelite kings, in sharp contrast to the Mesopotamian royal tradition. A short list of royal qualities is used in describing the ideal king in Isaiah 9:5 and 11:2, but the descriptions of God's qualities and strength far surpasses these. God's power is sometimes evident in beneficent actions, such as his love for משפט, 'justice', his forgiving nature, and his granting peace; this ability to use power beneficently is limited to the divine king.

Majesty

In English, the most general royal quality is 'majesty', which is etymologically related to 'major' in the sense of 'great'. If the Hebrew semantics of kingship were similar, we might expect גדול, 'great' to be a common royal quality. This is not the case with Israelite kings. גדול, 'great' is used with foreign kings; for example, Sennacherib is called המלך הגדול, 'the great king' (2 Kgs 18:19, 28= Isa. 36:4, 13), a calque of Akkadian *šarru rabû*. In a tantalizing, very broken ivory inscription found at Nimrud, the phrase ממלך גדל, 'from a great king' appears, possibly referring to the Assyrian king (Gibson, 1971:19-20). According to the common emendation of Hos. 5:13 and 10:6, מלך רב refers to the Assyrian king (Wolff, 1974b:104). גֹּדֶל, 'greatness' is attributed to Pharaoh in Ezek. 31:2, 7, in a context that describes his diminution. In post-exilic texts, the גדולה, 'greatness' of Ahasuares is noted in Esth. 1:4 and the root גדל, 'to be(come) great' is applied to various foreign kings in Daniel 8 and 11.

The propensity for calling foreign rulers גדול, 'great' contrasts with Israelite kings. One narrative in Samuel emphasizes that David, who might be considered the paradigm of a 'great' king, is הקמן, 'the small or young one' (1 Sam. 16:11). No Israelite king is called גדול, 'great', although David had a שם גדול, 'a great name' (2 Sam. 7:9) and Solomon was 'great' in respect to wisdom and wealth (1 Kgs 10:23; cf. 2 Chr. 9:22). The post-exilic 1 Chr. 29:25 claims ויגדל יהוה את־שלמה למעלה 'the LORD made Solomon exceedingly great' (cf. 2 Chr. 1:1), connecting Solomon's greatness to God and avoiding the adjective גדול, 'great'.[42] Only of the future king could it be said in unqualified terms (Mic. 5:3) כי־עתה יגדל עד־אפסי־ארץ, 'for he shall wax great to the ends of the earth'.

The small Biblical Aramaic corpus generally conforms to this picture—foreign kings are 'great' or 'majestic', but never Israelite kings. Dan. 5:20 and 7:14 indicate that *yqr* was a general royal attribute. Nebuchadnezzer (Dan. 2:37; 4:27, 33) and Belshazzar (5:18, 20) possessed it.[43] *Hdr*, used only of royalty in Biblical Aramaic (Dan. 4:27, 33 and 5:18; cf. the calque in Hebrew *hdr mlkwt* in 11:20) and in its only other pre-Late Aramaic attestation (Ahiqar 108; cf. Jean-Hoftijzer, 1965), is best translated 'majesty'. Similarly, *rbw* (determined *rbwt'*) is only used of kings in Biblical Aramaic (Dan. 4:19, 33; 5:18, 19; 7:27). Sennacherib is called אסנפר רבא ויקרא, 'the great and glorious Asnapar' (Ezra 4:10) and in Dan. 2:10 the magicians refer to any מלך רב, 'great king'. Although the Aramaic sections of the Bible represent a small corpus which must be used cautiously, it tentatively suggests that various terms for 'grandeur' or 'majesty' were applied to foreign kings in the post-exilic period. Furthermore, Ezra 5:11, where Solomon is called by the returnees from exile מלך לישראל רב, 'a great king of Israel' indicates that in the post-exilic period, Israelite kings began to be called great (cf. 1 Chr. 29:25 and 2 Chr. 1:1, also of Solomon).

Although Hebrew kings are not generally called great, we may infer from many contexts that they were considered to be great. Laws and narratives which juxtapose the king to God reinforce the king's greatness. Oaths are taken by both their names (2 Sam. 15:21), both are cursed together (1 Kgs 21:10, 13) and both must be feared (Prov. 24:21). An attack against Israel may be perceived as an attack against God and king (Ps. 2:2), people bow down to 'God and king' (1 Chr. 29:20; cf. Hos. 3:5) and the Second Temple was completed under the aegis of God and the Persian kings (Ezra 6:14). However, biblical texts maintain the bounds between God and the king and never call the king divine (see above, pp. 39-40).

Actions performed by the king reflect his importance. He sits at the head of the table (1 Sam. 9:22). He was expected to behave with certain decorum (2 Sam. 6:20). He entered Jerusalem through a special gate (Jer. 17:19; Ezek. 44:3). If 'exalted one' in Lev. 4:22 refers to the king, he offered a special חטאת, 'purification offering' when he inadvertently sinned (Lev. 4:22-26). According to 2 Kgs 16:15 and Ezek. 46:13-15, he also provided a regular daily offering. Ideally, nations bless themselves in his name (Ps. 72:17). 2 Kgs 5:6 presupposes that some people attributed healing powers to the king (see North, 1932:12). Finally, places were named after him; the Bible mentions עמק־המלך, 'Valley of the King' (2 Sam. 18:18), and גבעת שאול, 'Gibeah of Saul' (1 Sam. 11:4 and others), עיר דוד, 'City of David' (2 Sam. 5:9 and others) and possibly עמק יהושפט, 'the Valley of Jehoshapat' (Joel 4:2, 12).[44]

The king's central importance is especially reflected in texts that narrate his death. His death during battle caused panic and retreat (1 Sam. 31:7). Having no king is compared to birth pangs (Mic. 4:9), a biblical image for extreme pain. Special funerary rites, including fasting and ritual wailing, were observed after Saul's death (1 Sam. 31:8-13; 2 Sam. 1:12, 24) and special incense was burned at the royal funeral (Jer. 34:5; 2 Chr. 16:14; 21:19). The king's continued existence was so central to the nation that any threat to his well-being, e.g. by cursing him (1 Kgs 21:10, 13; cf. Exod. 22:27) or by failing to guard him properly (1 Sam. 26:16), was considered a capital offense.

The special status of the king derives to an extent from the people's dependence on him for orderly leadership in times of war and peace. This dependence is reflected in the royal appellation רוח אפינו, 'our life-breath' (see above, p. 46) and in the nation's claim that David should not fight כי־עתה כמנו עשרה אלפים, 'but you (reading אתה) are worth ten thousand of us' (2 Sam. 18:3). Ultimately, this notion became extended so that the king could be viewed as responsible for the welfare of the population as a whole.[45]

There is a clear disparity between the narrative, which in many different ways stresses the Israelite king's greatness and centrality, and the biblical reticence to call kings גדול, 'great'. An examination of גדול, 'great' and the root גדל, 'to be great' as they were applied to God may explain this disparity. A predominant theme of the Bible, studied in detail by Labuschagne (1966), is God's incomparability. One way this idea is conveyed is by describing as 'great' or 'majestic' only God as king and not the Israelite king. As incomparable divine king, God is מלך גדול על־כל־אלהים/הארץ, 'great king over all the gods/earth' (Pss. 47:3; 95:3), מלך גדול, 'great king' (Mal. 1:14), מלך הגוים, 'king of the nations' (Jer. 10:7), מלך רב, 'great king' (Ps. 48:3; cf. above, p. 32) and רב, 'great' (Ps. 89:8 emended with some versions; cf. Kraus, 1961:614). His greatness is mentioned in other contexts which describe his kingship (Pss. 99:1-3; 145:3; 1 Chr. 29:11). The adjective גדול, 'great' is applied to God[46] over thirty times. In Dan. 2:45, God is called אלה רב, 'great God'. גדול, 'great' is such an important attribute of God that by the post-exilic period it becomes incorporated into a formula אדני האל הגדול (הגבבור) והנורא (שומר הברית והחסד), 'LORD, great and (strong and) awesome God (who stays faithful to his covenant)' (Dan. 9:4; Neh. 1:5; 4:8; 9:32). Finally, it is noteworthy that גדול, 'great' is often used of God in contexts that stress his absolute greatness, such as Jer. 10:6: מאין כמוך יהוה גדול אתה וגדול שמך בגבורה, 'O LORD, there is none like you! You are great and your name is great in power' (cf. e.g. Pss. 77:14; 86:10; 96:4). Thus, when applied to God, גדול, 'great' approaches the sense of the English superlative 'most majestic'.

Other forms of the root גדל, 'to be great' are also applied to God. *Gōdel*, 'greatness' is specific to Deuteronomy (4 times) and Ps. 150:2; *gĕdûlāh*, when applied to God, is its post-exilic equivalent (1 Chr. 29:11; Ps. 145:3, 6). In its verbal usage, it is clear that people praised God by claiming that he should be 'made great'. This is reflected in the declarative (or delocutive; see Hillers 1967) *Piel* of Ps. 34:4 גדלו ליהוה אתי ונרוממה שמו יחדו, 'Exalt (make, or declare great) the LORD with me; let us extol his name together' (cf. Ps. 69:31). Perhaps this declaration is reflected in Pss. 35:27; 40:17; 70:5 where the faithful worshipper will always proclaim יגדל יהוה, 'Extolled (great) be the LORD'. The personal name גדליה, 'God has become great' (Baumgartner, 1967:172) is used of five people from the late pre-exilic to the post-exilic period and is attested to in the pre-exilic seal corpus eight times (Tigay, 1986:49). The superlative nature of God's greatness is reflected in 2 Sam. 7:22 על־כן גדלת יהוה אלהים כי־אין כמוך, 'You are great indeed, O LORD God, there is

none like you' and in Ezek. 38:23 והתגדלתי והתקדשתי. . . וידעו כי־אני יהוה,
'Thus I will manifest my greatness and my holiness. . . and they shall know that I am the LORD'.

Several words which originated in the sphere of 'height' and moved into the sphere of 'greatness' are also used of God. He is called עליון, 'most high' in biblical poetry over twenty times, from a relatively early period (Num. 24:16 and Deut. 32:8) through the exilic period (Lam. 3:35, 38), usually as a B word parallel to a divine name.[47] He is רם, 'exalted' (in the *Qal*) or is requested to manifest himself as רם, 'exalted' (e.g. Ps. 21:14) over ten times.[48] The name אל(י)רם, God is exalted' is known from the pre-exilic seal corpus (Avigad, 1986 #29). He is called נשגב, 'exalted' four times in First Isaiah (2:11, 17; 12:4; 33:5), once in Ps. 148:13 and in some personal names.[49] None of these terms is ever applied to human kings.

This evidence suggests that throughout the biblical period, terms of greatness were an intrinsic part of the description of God. These terms are often explicitly connected to God's royalty, but were not applied to Israelite kings. This terminological absence is especially surprising when we examine the narrative and legal sources which suggest various ways in which the king was seen as great or majestic. The evidence indicates that at some point God the king totally appropriated the terms that normally belonged in the 'greatness' or 'majesty' sphere of Israelite kingship.[50] As far as this area of the lexicon is concerned, God has become king at the expense of human kings.

Beauty

Physical beauty was ascribed to several kings. Saul was handsome and tall (1 Sam. 9:2; 10:23) and David was ruddy and handsome (1 Sam. 16:12, 18). The good looks of Absalom (2 Sam. 14:25) and Adonijah (1 Kgs 1:6) are described in passages that emphasize their potential royal legitimacy. Although all of this narrative evidence concerns kings of the united monarchy, prophetic and Psalms texts indicate that beauty was a general royal quality, extending to later Israelite kings as well (Ezek. 16:13-15; Ps. 45:3). Foreign kings were also given this attribute (Ezek. 28:12, 17; 31:8-9). The origin and significance of this tradition is unclear, although it is probably connected to the notion that the king is superlative in all respects[51] or that a physically desirable person should be a leader (cf. Lev. 21:16-21). This tradition that kings are beautiful persisted into rabbinic times (Leiter, 1973-74:140).

The only place where God is portrayed as beautiful is in Isa. 33:17 מלך ביפיו תחזינה עיניך, 'your eyes behold a king in his beauty'. The reticence of the biblical text to project this human royal quality on to God contrasts sharply with what we have seen elsewhere of royal qualities, where God is generally portrayed as having greater royal powers than the human king. Thus we might have expected God to be portrayed as most beautiful. It is likely that after Israelite worship of God became aniconic,[52] God was not called handsome since this attribute would encourage visualizing God (Hallo, 1988:64). In contrast God's attributes of יד חזקה, 'a strong hand' or זרוע נטויה, 'an outstretched arm' were very limited in extent, and were probably processed linguistically as expressions, rather than literally, and therefore did not foster the visualization of God with limbs. The study of royal trappings in the next chapter bolsters the connection between the iconic prohibition and the lack of texts describing God as beautiful.

Conclusions

A metaphor draws similarities between different entities, but does not equate them. This is particularly evident in comparing the royal qualities of God the king to those of the Israelite king. A full synthesis of this material is difficult due to the limited biblical corpus and problems in dating specific biblical texts. Furthermore, it is not always clear in each case that God's attributes specifically build on human *royal* attributes.[53] Nevertheless, certain conclusions may be offered.

If a royal quality projected on to God would have clashed with Israelite religious principles, it is not used of God. For example, God is not called 'handsome', although this was a common royal attribute, because this might have encouraged the plastic depiction of God, which was inappropriate once Israelite religion became aniconic. Likewise, God, unlike human kings, is not depicted as possessing silver and gold since this might suggest that God attains his power and prestige through bartering his wealth—a principle that would undermine the omnipotent God generally depicted in the Bible. God's royal wealth could only be depicted in a modified form which would not raise this association.

In other instances, God as king rarely merely mimics the king; his royal attributes are often depicted as quantitatively or qualitatively superior to those of people. The *wish* of the loyal royal subject that the king should live 'forever' becomes a *statement* that God has reigned and will reign forever, and is more eternal than the luminaries themselves. God's wisdom incorporates his ability to create the world, and although wisdom texts stress the importance and greatness of human wisdom, they state that God dispenses royal wisdom and that his wisdom exceeds human wisdom. The divine wealth, when mentioned, is qualitatively different from royal wealth; God owns all of creation, and holds in his storehouses elements such as the wind, which are far beyond human control. The semantics of the word *kābôd* make a similar point—although both kings and God possessed *kābôd*, the ancient Israelite must have realized that the *kābôd* possessed by God far exceeded the *kābôd* (=merely wealth) of the human king.

Although the divine attributes originated as projections of royal attributes, these divine attributes shaped the lexicon of human kingship. This is especially evident of 'strength' and 'majesty'. Certainly kings were expected to be strong and great, and indeed they are called גבור, 'strong' and the verb חזק, 'to be strong', is used of them. However, the Israelite kings are almost never called גדול, 'great' and only a small number of 'strength words' are used of them. This lack cannot be completely ascribed to a deficiency of strength or greatness of all Israelite kings; it is best explained by assuming that the Hebrew lexicon had appropriated these terms for God as a way of indicating the superiority of the divine king. This process is clearest in the history of the root *gbr*, which is shared by the human and divine king in pre-exilic sources, becomes applied exclusively to God in post-exilic sources, and by the rabbinic period is so clearly attached to God that he may be called *hgbwrh*, 'the strong one'. The large number of personal names declaiming God's strength and majesty in biblical and extra-biblical sources further reflects the centrality of these royal attributes as they are possessed by God in their supra-royal sense. The extra-biblical personal names are especially significant, since they indicate that the emphasis on God's strength extended beyond the circles that composed the Bible. The evidence suggests that one result of God becoming king was the dethronement of certain aspects of the human king.

The tension which is central to any metaphor is particularly evident in viewing the royal attributes of God the king. Although he clearly shares many qualities with human kings, in almost every case he surpasses the human quality. A king may be relatively wealthy, wise, moderately strong and the narrative sources might depict him as great; God owns all, gives kings wisdom and has created the world with wisdom, has an exceedingly large number of strength terms applied to him and is called incomparably 'great'. In some instances God possesses a royal quality in a paradoxical fashion; for example, by using his strength to grant peace and to show a love for justice. The metaphor 'God is king' helped to shape the ancient Israelite perceptions of God while allowing sufficient flexibility for God's incomparability to be expressed.

Chapter 4

ROYAL TRAPPINGS

Introduction

A series of objects worn or used by kings distinguished them from
other members of Israelite society. The items worn include a crown,
special royal jewelry (the אצעדה) and royal clothing. Other objects
closely associated with royalty are the scepter, the throne and the
royal platform (עמוד). This chapter examines the function of these
items, and the extent to which these trappings are projected on to
God.

Crown

One of the characteristic elements of the Israelite king's wardrobe
was the crown, called *nzr*, *ṭrh*, *ktr* and *mṣnpt*. No chronological,
geographical, dialectical or source-critical differences appear to
distinguish the *nzr* and *ṭrh*, though the evidence is sparse and it is
possible that they had different shapes or functions. The crown was
such a central symbol of royalty that in biblical poetry and narrative,
it can represent kingship itself as in Lam. 5:16 נפלה עטרת ראשנו,
literally, 'the crown of our heads has fallen', which means 'our king
has died'. It is difficult to know the exact role the crown played in the
royal rituals. In 2 Kgs 11:12 (=2 Chr. 23:11), the crown (נזר) has a
prominent role in Joash' coronation. Similarly, the handing over of
Saul's crown (נזר) to David in 2 Sam. 1:10 might have represented
the transfer of the kingdom from Saul to David. The crown (עטרה)
continued to be an important Israelite royal symbol in the post-exilic
period as evidenced by the manufacturing of a royal crown[1] for
Zerubbabel (Zech. 6:11-15). In poetic texts, removing the crown
represented loss of kingship (Ps. 89:40; Jer. 13:18; Ezek. 21:31).
Conversely, a crown placed on the king's head by God (Ps. 21:4) and

a shining crown (Ps. 132:18)[2] are signs of royal success. The material and construction of the crown are unclear; it is sometimes of gold (Ps. 21:4), or of silver and gold (Zech. 6:11—post-exilic), and was probably jeweled (Zech. 9:16 and 2 Sam. 12:30//1 Chr. 20:2[3]). Israelite tribute-bearers must have seen Mesopotamian kings wearing crowns,[4] and the biblical authors knew that Persian kings wore crowns (כתר, e.g. Esth. 6:8).[5] The scant biblical evidence suggests that the queen and the queenmother also wore crowns (Esth. 1:11; 2:17; Jer. 13:18; Ezek. 16:12; cf. Greenberg, 1983b:279).

Although the evidence is not equally strong for all periods, it is clear that Israelite kings and foreign kings with whom the Israelites came into contact wore some sort of distinguishing headgear throughout the pre-exilic and post-exilic periods. In contrast, God is never pictured wearing a crown on his head.[6] Perhaps portraying God with a crown would have caused God as king to resemble the human king too closely. As pointed out by Professor Irene Winter (oral communication), in Mesopotamia, where Gods and kings are often depicted in a similar manner, during any one time-period each wore a distinct head-dress (Hallo, 1988:56). Although literary texts describe both Mesopotamian gods and kings having crowns, allowing the royal and divine to be conflated, this conflation would be corrected by pictorial scenes. Therefore, in Israel, where pictorial depiction of God was prohibited, the verbal and written descriptions might structurally parallel the Mesopotamian pictorial depictions, so it was necessary to distinguish on the literary level between the divine and royal clothing. Alternately, depicting God literarily with a crown might have encouraged creating an image of him with a crown. In either case, the iconic prohibition might be responsible for the lack of parallel in the divine and human spheres. However, in the period of rabbinic Judaism when the danger of the population creating plastic images of God had passed (Urbach, 1959:154), God's garb, including his crown, were described, especially in certain mystical circles (Scholem 1956:56-64).

The Royal Bracelet

The *'ṣ'dh* or *ṣ'dh*,[7] some sort of royal armband or bracelet, is mentioned only in 2 Sam. 1:10, along with the crown which the Amalekite transferred from Saul to David. Perhaps it is mentioned again as a royal symbol in the coronation of King Jehoiada in 2 Kgs

11:12, if we emend הערות, 'the testimonies' to צעדות, 'the royal armbands'.[8] Comparative evidence offers no parallels of armbands playing a significant role in royal ritual. Although Mesopotamian reliefs show both kings and gods wearing armbands (e.g. Reade 1983:59 plate 87; Paley 1976:38, and plates 4 and 6; ANEP #533 and Frankfort, 1977:163, plate 188), these armbands are not limited to them, and are generally worn by most members of the upper-class (Irene Winter, oral communication).

The אצעדה, 'royal bracelet' is never associated with God. Since it is difficult to evaluate the use of the אצעדה, 'royal bracelet' with human kings, the significance of its absence with God is uncertain. However, it is possible that like the crown, it was not projected on to God because it conflicted with the iconic prohibition.

Clothing

Almost nothing is known about the clothing that the king wore. The only descriptions of royal garments in the Bible are post-exilic or describe foreign kings. Esth. 8:15 describes לבוש מלכות תכלת וחור ועטרת זהב גדולה ותכריך בוץ וארגמן, 'royal robes of blue and white, with a magnificent crown of gold and a mantle of fine linen and purple wool'. According to Jon. 3:6, the king of Assyria wore an אדרת, a type of overgarment (Hönig, 1957:66-69). According to Judg. 8:26, the Midianite kings wore ארגמן, 'purple' and had jewelry called נטפות, 'crescents' and שהרנים, 'pendents'. It is unclear whether these descriptions of foreign royal attire are accurate or reflect Israelite royal garb (see pp. 25-26). The Israelite queen's garments are described in detail in Ezek. 16:10-13 (Greenberg, 1983b:279). To the extent that we may extrapolate from these texts, it is likely that the Israelite king wore an outer garment of fine dyed material (שש, תחש, רקמה, משי). Ps. 45:9 implies that the royal garb was perfumed, but it is uncertain if this was generally true or is specific to the royal wedding which this psalm describes.

Nowhere in pre-exilic literature is God described bedecked in royal clothing. The detailed portrayal of God and what surrounds him in Ezekiel chapter one (esp. vv. 26-27) shows a complete lack of interest in the issue. In Isa. 6:1, God is clearly wearing a garment since ושליו מלאים את-ההיכל, 'the skirts (of his robe) filled the Temple' (see Keel 1977:62-70). The only detail of the garment emphasized is its extra-ordinary size (Greenfield, 1985 and Smith, 1988); nothing of its color or style is noted. Thus, the two pre-exilic texts which we might have expected to detail God's garments as royal are silent.

Post-exilic literature is slightly less reticent about describing the divine garb. This is parallel to the way rabbinic literature felt comfortable depicting God with a crown (above, p. 78)—what was taboo in an early period became permissible, probably because there was no real danger of fostering iconic worship of God. Isa. 63:1-3 describes God the warrior dressed in a blood-stained garments (לבוש, מלבוש and בגד). These are all general terms for clothing, and provide no details on the royal garb. It is possible that these bloodstained garments could reflect a red royal garment which is known from pre-exilic texts, but the text does not seem to be self-consciously pointing out that connection. Only Dan. 7:9 specifies what God's clothing looked like: in a context depicting him sitting on a throne it says לבושה כתלג חור, 'his garment was like white snow'. No text describes human royal garb in such terms, although it is possible that Daniel reflects an unknown Hellenistic royal custom.[9] It is more likely that the white symbolized absolute purity (see Brenner, 1982:180), and the writer has mixed metaphors, combining 'God is royal' and 'God is pure'.

Scepter

שבט, 'scepter', could be used as a general non-royal term for power (e.g. Isa. 10:24 and Zech. 10:11) and was typically used by several types of people, including fathers (Prov. 13:24) and shepherds (Lev. 27:32). It was also an important royal implement and can be used to represent specifically royal power (Isa. 11:4; Ezek. 19:11). Oddly enough, the royal scepter is never mentioned in the historical books nor is it found in any description of the coronation ritual. The scepter was especially associated with the royal role of meting out justice (Isa. 11:4; Ps. 45:7; see Olivier, 1979). With non-Israelite monarchs 'wielding the scepter' (Amos 1:5, 8) symbolizes rulership. In Esther the king's golden scepter (שרבים[10]) (4:11; 5:2; 8:4) determined the subject's access to the king. Although the paucity of references to the Israelite king's scepter might suggest that it played a minor role, the fact that 'scepter' (שבט and מחקק) is used metonymically for 'king' in two poetic passages (Gen. 49:10 and Num. 24:17[11]) suggests that the scepter was an important royal symbol.

It is difficult to know if the depictions of God having a scepter are related to God's royal authority since the scepter was used for many purposes, such as striking or beating a person or animal (cf. esp. Isa.

28:27). It never appears in contexts which harp on God's kingship such as Isa. 6:1ff. or in the 'enthronement' psalms. It is most frequently used to indicate divine punishment, in which case it might be a weapon rather than the specifically royal scepter (Isa. 10:5, 26; 30:31; Ps. 110:2; Job 9:34; 21:9; Lam. 3:1).[12] None of these contexts is infused with God's royalty. A second context in which God wields a scepter is where he is depicted as a shepherd (Mic. 7:14 and Ps. 23:4). Although the depiction of God as a shepherd is related to his kingship (see above, pp. 36-37), it is unclear if each time the shepherd image is used, it is meant as a submetaphor of the kingship image.

The royal scepter is not projected onto God. The only exception may be Isa. 33:22, כי יהוה שפטנו יהוה מחקקנו יהוה מלכנו הוא יושיענו, 'For the LORD shall be our ruler, the LORD shall be our scepter/ prince, the LORD shall be our king: He shall deliver us'. It is uncertain if מחקקנו reflects God carrying a royal staff (cf. Gen. 49:10) or if it is a royal official (Dillmann, 1898:298). If the first choice is correct, God would be exceptional in two ways in this unit—he is beautiful (see above, p. 73) and has a royal scepter. If this unit in Isaiah predates the iconic prohibition in Israel (see below, p. 181 n.52), these two exceptions might be inter-related. The lack of scepter imagery with God the king is especially surprising since the scepter was associated with royal justice, and as we shall see next, the royal כסא, 'throne', which has similar associations, is frequently projected onto God.

Throne

The Biblical Hebrew vocabulary for 'seat' and 'sitting' is much more general than its English counterpart. *Ks'* encompasses at least 'seat', 'throne' and 'chair'[13] and *yšb* may be 'to sit' or 'to be enthroned',[14] aside from its sense 'to reside'. Only context clarifies which object or action is being designated, although several cases remain ambiguous.

The throne (כסא) is an important symbol of royalty. Sitting on the throne is equivalent to reigning; thus in Jer. 22.30 ישב על־כסא, 'to be enthroned', is parallel to משל, 'to reign', in 2 Sam. 3:10 להקים את־כסא דוד, 'to establish the throne of David' is equal to להעביר הממלכה, 'to transfer the kingship' and the question 'who will reign next?' is phrased in 1 Kgs 1:20 and 27 מי ישב על־כסא אדני־המלך אחריו, 'who will sit on the throne of my master the king after him'. Loss of kingship is expressed through the image of overturned thrones (Hag. 2:22; Ps. 89:45), with the king left sitting on the floor (Ezek. 26:16). A king's or dynasty's success is expressed figuratively through a high throne (Isa. 14:13), a firm (כון) throne (Prov. 16:12; 2 Sam. 7:13; 1 Chr. 22:10 etc.) or an everlasting throne (Ps. 89:5, 30, 37). Although כסא, 'throne', often appears in construct with דוד, 'David', מלוכה or ממלכה, 'kingship' and יהוה, 'the LORD' or מלכות יהוה על־ישראל, 'the LORD's kingship over Israel'[15] to denote the throne, the word כסא, 'chair' alone may refer to a throne (e.g. Judg. 3:20; 1 Kgs 1:13). The verb ישב, 'to sit' may be elliptic for ישב (ב)כסא, 'to sit on the throne', and may refer to the royal enthronement (e.g. Ps. 61:8; Isa. 10:13). The future ideal king is also described as enthroned (Isa. 16:5).

Solomon's throne is described in 1 Kgs 10:18-20 and 2 Chr. 9:17-19. If we may judge from Syrian, Egyptian, Ugaritic, Hittite and Persian evidence,[16] a footstool must have accompanied this throne, but it is not mentioned in 1 Kings 10. Although in the ancient Near East much of the royal business such as receiving royal delegations took place while the king was seated on his throne,[17] in Israelite sources the throne is particularly associated with the king's role as judge. The throne room is called (1 Kgs 7:7) אולם הכסא אשר ישפט שם אלם המשפט־, 'the throne portico, where he was to pronounce judgment—the hall of judgement', and the pilgrim thinking of Jerusalem notes (Ps. 122:5) כי שמה ישבו כסאות למשפט כסאות לבית דוד, 'There the thrones of judgment stood, thrones of the house of David'. This association is particularly strong in Proverbs, where the throne is called כסא־דין, 'throne of judgment' (20:8), and where the king's just behavior assures a firm throne (20:28; 25:5; 29:14). This connection between כסא, 'throne' and justice further indicates the role the king played in meting out justice in Israel (see below, p. 112).

God as king reigns from his throne: מלך אלהים על־גוים אלהים ישב על־כסא קדשו, 'God reigns over the nations; God is seated on his holy throne' (Ps. 47:9; cf. 93:1-2; 97:1-2; 103:19). He may even be called the appellative יושב, 'the enthroned one' (Ps. 22:4).[18] God's enthronement is an early concept, and is probably already mentioned in Exod. 15:17 מכון לשבתך, 'the place you made to sit in'.[19] It is found in early classical prophetic literature (Isa. 6:1), frequently in the Psalms, and in late pre-exilic (Jer. 14:21), exilic (Lam. 5:19) and post-exilic (Ps. 103:19—cf. Hurvitz, 1972:107-130; Dan. 7:9) literature. As with its earthly archetype, God's throne is specifically associated with his role as judge (Jer. 49:38; Joel 4:12; Pss. 9:5, 8; 89:15; 97:2); however God's justice is an accomplished fact, not a royal ideal. This notion is probably also reflected in the very difficult Isa. 28:6 which states that in the future God will be ולרוח משפט ליושב על־המשפט, 'a spirit of judgment for him who sits in judgment'—as the ultimate source of judgment, God can assure that the future enthroned earthly king will carry out justice fairly.

In Isa. 6:1 the prophet sees God יושב על־כסא רם ונשא, 'seated on a high and lofty throne/seated high and lofty on a throne'. As reflected in the translation, the Hebrew is ambiguous—it may describe a throne which is located high in the heavens, a throne which itself is of unusually large size or both. To the extent that this points to the large size of God's throne, it parallels the oversized royal garment worn by God in the same verse. The cherubim throne depicted in the Solomonic Temple (1 Kgs 6:23-28) was also of enormous proportions (Smith, 1988). A description of the throne itself is in Ezek. 1:26 (and 10:1) where it is כמראה אבן־ספיר, 'in appearance like lapis lazuli' (Köhler–Baumgartner, 1958:664; Baumgartner, 1983:722; Keel, 1977:255-260 and Zimmerli, 1979:155-160). Lapis, an imported luxury item in the ancient Near East, could be used for (the inlay of) a royal throne of great sumptuousness.[20] The Ezekiel tradition may also be based on Exod. 24:10, where the divine palace has a floor of lapis, probably reflecting a partial etiology of the sky's blueness.[21] Finally, a set of texts, most of them pre-exilic, describe God as י(ו)שב (ה)(כר(ו)בים, 'enthroned on the cherubim' (1 Sam. 4:4; 2 Sam. 6:2; 2 Kgs 19:15; Isa. 37:16; Pss. 80:2; 99:1; 1 Chr. 13:6). Most of these texts refer to God's Temple throne, made of the cherubs whose wings formed a seat for the divine (Mettinger, 1982b:113-116 and Metzger, 1985, vol. 2). Such thrones are known from the Ahiram sarcophagus from Byblos, an ivory plaque from Megiddo and several other places (Keel, 1977:15-35). It is noteworthy that the designation 'enthroned on the cherubim', used throughout much of the biblical period in both Southern and Northern (Psalm 80) texts, does not project onto God the Solomonic-type throne; rather it uses a throne-type well known from Israel's northern neighbors. This raises the possibility that this depiction of God may originate from the pre-monarchical period, or was imported from Phoenicia via Northern Israel. The possible pre-monarchical origin of this image agrees with other scholarly arguments that the designation יושב כרובים, 'enthroned on the cherubim' originated at the Shiloh sanctuary (Mettinger, 1982b:128-130, based on Eissfeldt 1966; cf. Metzger, 1985, vol. 1:309-352).

The notion that God has a throne in his Temple may be complemented by the notion that he has a footstool there. Haran (1978:255) follows earlier scholars in claiming that the ark served this function, but Fohrer (1972:109-110) claims that the position of the ark in the Solomonic Temple precludes this possibility (cf. Metzger, 1985, vol. 1:352-365). Görg (1977) posits that the *kprt*, 'the ark cover' reflects the Egyptian *kp rdwy*, 'footstool', a suggestion tentatively accepted by Mettinger (1982b:116-117). However, it is unclear why this particular word should be borrowed from Egyptian, especially given the limited range of Egyptian loanwords in Hebrew (see Lambdin, 1953). Furthermore, there are alternative suitable internal Hebrew etymologies for *kprt*. Thus, the question exactly what, if anything, serves as the representation of God's footstool in the Temple remains open.

The relationship between God's earthly throne in the Jerusalem Temple and his heavenly throne is unclear. Even the phrase ישב כרובים, 'enthroned on the cherubim' in some contexts is ambiguous—the cherubim may refer to the Temple cherubs or to living celestial cherubs described in Ezekiel's visions. The ambivalence about whether God has an earthly or a heavenly abode is clearly reflected in 1 Kings 8, Solomon's prayer. This chapter is clearly composite (Levenson, 1981); in v. 13, a pre-exilic section of this prayer, God's abode is clearly on the earth בית זבול לך מכון לשבתך עולמים, 'a stately house, a place where you may sit/dwell forever', while the exilic additions polemically pick up the phrase מכון לשבתך, 'a place where you may sit/dwell', and use it in the phrase השמים מכון שבתך, 'the heaven, the place where you sit/dwell' (vv. 39, 43, 49), as if to correct v. 13. The texts which depict God as enthroned on the earth are in the minority and are largely associated with the traditions surrounding the building of the Jerusalem Temple (2 Sam. 7:5-6; 1 Kgs 8:13; Ps. 132:14; Ezek. 43:7 and possibly Jer. 17:12 MT; Ps. 91:1).

Theories which explain how God is enthroned on both heaven and earth by suggesting that the Temple was founded on a 'cosmic mountain' where 'the heaven and earth meet' and 'that the Jerusalem cultic tradition... was profoundly influenced by this mythical concept of space' (Mettinger, 1982b:119-123) are based on antiquated syntheses of ancient Near Eastern material (Clifford, 1972). More probable is the suggestion of Haran (1978:257; cf. Levenson, 1987:38-39), that 'the throne in the holy of holies is but a model of the throne on high'. A similar type of conception is described in greater detail in the treatment of Egyptian religion by Hornung (1982:229):

> But for the Egyptians an image is not 'merely' an image; it constitutes a reality and a physical presence. The temple is a 'sky' on earth, which contains the efficacious image of the God and may serve as an abode for the god himself. . . . There, in his shrine on earth, the god can be reached and addressed at any time, even though his true abode may be far away in the sky. Therefore one, and by no means the least, of the aims of the cult is to make the earth an attractive place for the gods to live, to create in the temple a worthy residence for the god's image and a likeness of the sky, and to tend the cult images so well that it is happy to live among men.

This may provide a model for understanding the residence of God in both heaven and in the temples in Israel. However, in Israel at a certain point clear polemical tendencies developed which note that God is not confined to the earthly Temple. Jer. 3:17 claims that in the future people יקראו לירושלם כסא יהוה, 'will call Jerusalem the throne of the LORD', making it clear that God's presence will not be confined to the Temple or to the ארון, 'ark' (see v. 16; cf. Ezek. 48:35b for a related notion). Some texts stress the Temple's inability to contain God (1 Kgs 8:27). Isa. 66:1 makes a similar claim: השמים כסאי והארץ הדם רגלי, 'the heaven is my throne and the earth is my footstool'. All of these texts are exilic or later[22] and probably reflect traditions that developed in response to the absence of the Temple ark.

God's throne and enthronement are entailments of his kingship. However, his throne is larger and more luxurious than the human throne (1 Kgs 6:23-28; Ezek. 1; Isa. 6:1) and is associated with absolute justice. The divine throne takes many forms, perhaps related to different contexts, to varying conceptions of God's transcendence, and to different historical periods: it may be cherub-like, in the Temple, near enemies (Joel 4:12), in heaven, or it may even incorporate the entire 'world' (Isa. 66:1). Each of these portrayals reflects a different way of applying the submetaphor 'God is enthroned' to describe God's kingship.

The Royal Platform

It is unclear what role the עמוד, 'the platform' played in royal ceremonies. A king standing (עמד) on the platform (עמוד) is mentioned twice, in connection to Joash (2 Kgs 11:14; cf. 2 Chr. 23:13), and with Josiah's reform (2 Kgs 23:3; but cf. 2 Chr. 34:31). Neither text sufficiently clarifies the nature of this platform. Von Rad has suggested that it is a 'pillar-like platform' (1966b:224), while others have connected it to the Jachin and Boaz which stood in the Solomonic Temple (Gray, 1976: 575 n. e). Some have even claimed to have found ancient archaeological evidence for such a royal column (Kutschke–Metzger, 1972:162-166). However, its exact shape, nature and purpose remain unclear.

The עמוד, 'royal platform' has no role among the heavenly furniture of God. Although an עמוד, 'pillar' is connected with God's theophany in the desert (e.g. Exod. 13:21-22; Num. 12:5; Deut. 31:15), it does not have the same function as the royal עמוד, 'platform', and should not be treated in conjunction with it.

Conclusions

It is difficult to fully evaluate the relationship between the human and divine royal accouterments since many royal trappings which are not reflected in the Bible must have existed in ancient Israel. Even the form and function of some of those mentioned (e.g. the royal bracelet and royal platform) are unclear. Describing royal garb was not an interest of the biblical authors, in marked contrast with at least one author's interest in describing the priestly vestments. If we should unearth texts describing royal rituals or royal reliefs, our understanding of these royal accouterments would greatly improve, possibly extending our understanding of the metaphor 'God is king'.

Nevertheless, the limited descriptions of royal trappings which we do have offer an interesting contrast with the qualities associated with God. In previous chapters we have seen how human royal qualities and appellations were often applied to God in a magnified fashion; here, this is not generally true—with the exception of the throne, none of the trappings are projected on to God. God as king has no crown, no *royal* scepter, no bracelet, no platform, no detailed royal garb. One factor may explain all of these absences—explicit descriptions of God the king with his royal trappings might have encouraged pictorial representations of God, breaking the iconic proscription in ancient Israel, and perhaps leading to visual and even perceptual confusion between the human and divine kings.[23] The exceptions to this theory further support its plausibility. The one place where the royal scepter might be mentioned in conjunction with God may predate the iconic prohibition (Isa. 33). In the rabbinic period, when there was little danger of Judaism becoming iconic, God is frequently described with a כתר מלכות, 'royal crown'. Only in Dan. 7:9, a late text, is God's clothing described in some detail. Although God is described in the biblical period as sitting on his throne, this is a trapping which he only uses passively, i.e. unlike clothing which is worn or a scepter which is grasped and would be dropped if released, a throne is an autonomous object which does not become part of God. Thus, it may only peripherally be called a trapping, and in the conscious absence of descriptions of God's garb, crown or scepter, the throne alone need not encourage visualizing and then pictorially depicting God. The throne acts just like God's royal qualities—it is a quantitatively superior projection of the human royal throne onto God. If we may conflate various biblical verses, it was of supra-human dimensions, of unusually elegant and costly material, and pure justice was associated with it. In a word, it was divine.

Chapter 5

THE KING AND DOMESTIC AFFAIRS

Introduction

A person living in the ancient Near East might have been subject to two kings: the king of his or her country, and an overlord, to whom the king of his or her country was subservient. This first type of king may be called 'sovereign', the second, 'suzerain' (Levenson, 1985:70-75). Since kings often dealt with foreign and domestic subjects differently, each of these roles could imply different sets of relationships between subject and king. It is therefore important to distinguish between the king and domestic affairs, which will be studied in this chapter, and the king and foreign affairs, which is beyond the compass of this work. This chapter examines the extent to which God is patterned after the king in his domestic role, in other words, as 'sovereign'.

The following issues will be examined: the palace, access to the palace, the king's interrelationship with his subjects, the royal court officials, the king as judge, the king as builder and royal resources. This chapter does not attempt a complete summary of the king's role in domestic affairs, which has been the subject of several monographs; each of these areas will be examined in the realm of human kingship (the vehicle) only to the extent that it fleshes out the human realities and conventions which might be projected on to God as king (the tenor).

Two areas that are part of the king and domestic affairs are not treated in this chapter: the enthronement ritual and the king as warrior. The rites surrounding becoming king are very complex, and are examined in detail in the next chapter. The king certainly had a major role leading the Israelites into war (e.g. 2 Sam. 12:26ff; 1 Kgs 22), but it is very difficult to glean sufficient information from the biblical account to create an informed picture that would help us

understand God's depiction as a warrior. For example, it would be
interesting to know if the image of Ps. 97:3, אש לפניו תלך ותלהט סביב צריו,
'Fire is his vanguard, burning his foes on every side', might reflect an
image of royal bodyguards who surrounded the king during battle, an
institution well-known from Assyria (Saggs, 1984: 253). However,
the Bible is silent on such matters, and, contrary to common practice
(e.g. Miller, 1973 and Weinfeld, 1984), we may not use Near Eastern
images to automatically fill in the biblical picture of the king as
warrior. The inability to develop a picture of the human king's role
as military leader is especially unfortunate since God's role as
warrior is a major entailment of his kingship (Miller, 1973:174), so it
would have been interesting to see how closely it is modeled after
human kings as warriors.

The Palace

The only royal palace described in some detail in the Bible is
Solomon's (1 Kgs 7:1-12). This description is very brief and technical
and it is difficult to deduce many architectural features from it.
Although other royal palaces are mentioned or presumed in several
texts (e.g. 2 Sam. 7:1; 1 Kgs 12:25; 21:2; 22:39; 2 Kgs 7:11), none of
these give substantial architectural details; it is unclear, for example,
if later Judaean kings might have renovated the Jerusalem palace or
if Northern Israelite kings followed the outlines of the Solomonic
palace. To the extent that the structure of Solomon's palace may be
discerned from a careful reading of 1 Kings 7, it is reasonable to
assume that it is patterned after the *bit-ḥilāni*, known primarily from
Zinjirli (Ussishkin, 1966b). The *bit-ḥilāni* contained several rooms
connected in a non-linear fashion, with the throne-room as the
largest room. Its structure was determined by purely pragmatic
considerations—many rooms were needed to house and support the
palace personnel. For propagandistic purposes the throne-room was
the largest—it reflected the king's significance. David's palace at
Megiddo may have had a similar structure (Aharoni, 1978:181),
although archaeological evidence suggests that other royal palaces,
especially late ones, might have broken with this pattern.

In contrast to other Semitic languages, there was little semantic
specialization of terms for the royal palace. It is usually called
בית המלך, 'the house of the king' (e.g. 1 Kgs 9:1), or בית, 'house of'
with a personal pronoun (e.g. 2 Sam. 7:1; 1 Kgs 21:2; cf. the royal
official who was called אשר על הבית, 'appointed over the house';

Avigad, 1986:21-22). Only twice is the Israelite palace called *hykl*
(1 Kgs 21:1; Ps. 45:16). This is particularly surprising since etymologically *hykl* reflects the very common Sumerian word *É.GAL*, 'big
house', which was borrowed into Akkadian (*ekallu*), where it is very
frequently used to refer to the 'palace' (CAD E 52b-62b and
Ottosson, 1978). As 'palace' it entered Northwest Semitic, where it is
attested in Ugaritic (Gordon, 1965, III:390) and Imperial Aramaic
(Ahiqar 9, 17, 23, 44; cf. Cowley, 1967:212-213). The two biblical
uses of *hykl* for palace suggest that this Northwest Semitic usage was
known in Hebrew, but was generally avoided; a reason for this will
be adduced below.

The overlapping terminology used to refer to the Temple and the
royal palace suggests that the Temple was clearly perceived as a royal
palace. The usual name for the Temple is בית יהוה, 'the house of the
LORD', which is frequent in the Bible (less often: בית אלהים, 'the
house of God') and is even attested to in one of the Arad letters
(inscription 18, line 9 בית יהוה; see Aharoni, 1975:35 and esp. 39-40).
It is also used of pre-Jerusalem temples (e.g. Judg. 19:18 [MT]; 1 Sam.
3:15) and a syntactically parallel phrase is used of pagan temples
(2 Kgs 5:18 בית-רמון, 'the house of Rimmon' and 2 Kgs 10:21, 25, 26,
27 of בית-הבעל, 'the house of the Baal').

Relatively often, *hykl* is used to designate the entire Temple or a
specific portion of it (e.g. Isa. 6:1; Neh. 6:10), a sharp contrast to the
'secular' use of the word *hykl* as 'palace' elsewhere in Northwest
Semitic. This suggests that *hykl* existed in Hebrew as a general
designation for palace, then became applied to the Temple as God's
palace, and eventually became so closely attached to this sacred
usage that the potential for using it secularly was largely lost. Like
various terms describing the king's strength and majesty (see above,
pp. 57-72) the term became 'disinfected' (see above, p. 67). The use
of *hykl* as 'Temple' in Ben-Sira (50:1, 2, 7) and at Qumran (4Q400 i
13; Newsom, 1985:89; cf. 11QŠŠ 2-1-9, 7, esp. p. 377) shows how
entrenched the use of *hykl* in the divine, rather than human royal
sphere became.[1]

The architecture of the Jerusalem Temple was not modeled after
the architecture of the royal palace. The layout of Solomon's and
Ezekiel's Temple (1 Kgs 6; Ezek. 40-43) is clearly described. Its
central section is quite different from the floor-plan of the palace; it is
essentially a long rectangular room divided into three parts. The
innermost room (קדש קרשים, 'the most holy section' or דביר, 'shrine')

which housed God's cherubim throne is the smallest room, in contrast to the royal throne-room. Studies have suggested that the structure of the Israelite Temple is borrowed from Syrian Temples (Ussishkin, 1966a) rather than patterned after secular palaces. The lack of patterning of Israelite temples (divine homes) after Israelite palaces (royal homes) reflects the different functions of each. In general, the palace operations were more complex than those of the Temple, so it needed to be larger and structured differently. In particular, the human throne-room needed to be large enough to hold and impress large delegations of visitors, while God's throne-room in the Temple according to some sources was inaccessible to the public (see below, pp. 94-95 and Haran, 1978:175-185) and was therefore small. Pragmatic considerations prevented the metaphor from operating on the architectural level. It is noteworthy, however, that in certain periods Mesopotamian temple architecture mirrored palace architecture.

The submetaphor 'God as king has a palace' was realized on the literary level, but ignored on the architectural level. Utilitarian considerations inhibited the metaphor of the Temple as God's palace from achieving architectural realization. However, the metaphor continued to function on the literary plane: God's palace is called a בית, 'house', and evidence from other Semitic languages suggests that the Temple largely stole the term היכל, 'palace' away from the human royal palace. The superiority of the Temple to the royal palace is expressed in various ways. Architecturally, the palace is lined with fine wood, while gold is used to plate the inside of the Temple. On the literary level, the palace is a plain בית, 'house' while the Temple is a בית זבל (1 Kgs 8:13=2 Chr. 6:2; cf. Isa. 63:15), an 'exalted (Held, 1968:90-92) house/palace'. Divine sovereignty has been strengthened at the expense of human sovereignty.

Access to the King

Although several texts indicate that the average Israelite had access to the king (2 Sam. 14 and 1 Kgs 3), these are all in the context of judicial parables (Simon, 1967), whose historicity is questionable. 2 Sam. 15:1-4, the introduction to Absalom's revolt, clearly implies that in practice David could not accept all cases brought to him. Various judicial systems were instituted throughout the monarchic period (Weinfeld, 1972:233-236 and Wilson, 1983) precisely because the king could not see all plaintiffs who wanted to see him. The king could even ban his son from appearing in royal court (2 Sam. 14:24). To the extent that particular non-Israelite practices recorded in the Bible might be projections from the Israelite court, it is noteworthy that neither the viceroy (Gen. 50:4) nor in one case the queen (Esth. 4:11) had automatic access to the king. If a king could control who resided in royal cities (Amos 7:12-13), he certainly could decide who entered into the palace. Even those with free access were encouraged to stay away from the powerful king (Prov. 25:6-7a).

Two concerns probably motivated these limits to royal access. The king could not perform his normal administrative duties if outsiders constantly flocked in. Furthermore, the king's life would constantly be endangered if everyone had free royal access. This concern was addressed by the royal guards who protected the palace entrance. These guards could be called שרי הרצים השמרים פתח בית המלך, 'officers of the guard, who guarded the entrance of the royal palace' (1 Kgs 14:27; 2 Chr. 12:10), שמרי משמרת בית המלך, 'guards of the royal palace' and כרי, 'Carites' (2 Kgs 11:4, 19; see J. Gray, 1976:571). In Esth. 2:21 and 6:2 they are called שמרי הסף, 'guards of the threshold'. Although this term for palace guards is attested to only in Esther, there is no linguistic reason to assume that it was unknown in pre-exilic Hebrew.

There is no uniform conception reflected in the Bible concerning who had access to God the king. In most non-priestly texts, all had easy access to the Temple. This is reflected in Psalms where the worshipper wants to or promises to visit the Temple (5:8; 23:6; 27:4-5; 66:13; 73:17), in laws which imply that the Israelite had unhindered access to the altar (Exod. 21:14) and in some prophetic texts (e.g. Zech. 14:16). These texts imply that the average person could enter the Temple (divine palace) precincts. The narrative in 2 Kings 11 implies that there were not an abundance of guards around the Temple precincts. According to this chapter, when Jehoida the priest wanted to ensure the safety of young King Joash who is about to be crowned in the Temple, he took royal guards from the palace and imported them into the Temple. This suggests that there was not a large armed presence in the Temple at that point. The contrast between easy access to the general precincts of the Temple and very limited access to the royal palace is not surprising— unlike the human king, God's life would not be threatened by human visitors nor would his 'administrative efforts' be disturbed by them.

It is more difficult to evaluate what access the individual had within the Temple; i.e. could the worshipper see God the king himself or was his or her access limited, excluding the throne room? 1 Kgs 8:8 (=2 Chr. 5:9), a verse that might show Priestly influence (J. Gray, 1976:210) implies that in Solomon's Temple the throne room was hidden away in the *dbyr* (see Montgomery-Gehman, 1976:189). However, other texts imply that a worshipper is supposed to ראה (נפעל) את/אל פני יהוה, 'to appear before the LORD' (Exod. 23:17; 34:23; Deut. 16:16; 1 Sam. 1:22; Isa. 1:12; Ps. 42:3). This phrase is peculiar, in that a *Niphal* of ראה, 'to see', which is generally passive, is being used actively. Various solutions to the grammatical anomaly have been suggested, with the most popular explanation that an original *Qal* has been piously altered to a *Niphal* (Geiger, 1928:237-238; cf. Levenson, 1987:44-46). If this is correct and the reconstructed phrase ראה את פני יהוה, 'to see the LORD's face' could be taken literally and is not simply an idiom for coming to the Temple, then we might deduce that all had access directly to the throne room.[2] At some point, the *Qal* might have been revocalized to a *Niphal* to reflect a later custom (also known in P) of severely limited access to the Temple.

This picture of relatively unrestricted access to God in the non-priestly sources contrasts sharply with P. According to the detailed analysis of Milgrom (1970; cf. Spencer, 1984), the function of the Levites was to assure that no זר, namely an 'unauthorized person' would 'encroach' upon the precincts of the Tabernacle (Milgrom, 1970:5-59). This exactly parallels the function of the guards of the royal palace. The patterning of the Levites after the royal guards is made explicit by the terminology associated with them: they are שמרי משמרת (Milgrom, 8-16), 'doers of guard duty', a secular term borrowed from the royal court. They were armed and would have enforced the prescription הזר הקרב יומת, 'the unauthorized encroacher shall be put to death' (pp. 5-59). The historical reality of these armed Levites according to Milgrom (pp. 13-15) is reflected in 1 Chr. 9:27 and 2 Chr. 23:4-8. Despite its attestation only in post-exilic literature, Milgrom contends that this function of the Levites dates from the pre-exilic period (pp. 46-59).

A similar picture to the one depicted of the Levites in P is found in sources about the הכהנים שמרי הסף, 'the priestly guards of the threshold', who served at the entrance to the Temple (2 Kgs 12:10; 22:4), controlling access to the Temple grounds. It is difficult to know when these functionaries came into being; they are first mentioned in Kings and in Jeremiah and are attributed to the late ninth century (2 Kgs 12:10). They were important enough to be singled out in an exile list alongside the high priest and his assistant (2 Kgs 25:18=Jer. 52:24). They must be equivalent to the Levites who are depicted in P as שמרי משמרת, 'doers of guard duty'. This is implied by 2 Chr. 34:9 which cites 2 Kgs 23:4 ואת־שמרי הסף, 'the guards of the threshold' as הלוים שמרי הסף, 'the Levites, the guards of the threshold'.

This is not the place for a discussion of the date of P, its place of origin,[3] the function of its legislation[4] and its model for the משכן, 'Tabernacle'.[5] It is sufficient to note that in ancient Israel there were two contradictory views concerning the access of the individual to God. P drew a close analogy of God to the king,[6] and as a result developed a God who could not be approached directly. The biblical evidence for שמרי הסף הכהנים, 'the priestly guards of the threshold' suggests that P's conception had some basis in reality, at least by the (late?) pre-exilic period. Other groups in ancient Israel did not extend the kingship metaphor to the same extent as P, thereby creating a less royal but much more approachable God.

The Interrelationship between King and Subject

The king was extremely powerful; anyone who made him unhappy could anticipate banishment (Amos 7:12), imprisonment (Jer. 37:21; 38:5), or at worst, could be killed (1 Sam. 22:16; 1 Kgs 1; 2 Kgs 21:16; Ezek. 22:6; 22:25 LXX). This power encouraged the prudent subject to approach the king with fear. This is reflected in Prov. 20:2 נהם ככפיר אימת מלך מתעברו חוטא נפשו, 'The terror of a king is like the roar of a lion; he who provokes his anger risks his life' and Prov. 25:6-7 אל־תתהדר לפני־מלך ובמקום גדלים אל־תעמד כי טוב אמר־לך עלה הנה מהשפילך לפני נדיב, 'Do not exalt yourself in the king's presence; do not stand in the place of nobles. For it is better to be told, "Step up here", than to be degraded in the presence of the great'. The correlation between royal power and fear of his subjects is explicit in Dan. 5:19: כל עממיא אמיא ולשניא הוו זאעין/זיעין ודחלין מן־קדמוהי די־הוה צבא הוא קטל, 'all the peoples and nations of every language trembled in fear of him. He put to death whom he wished'. The only place in the historiographical texts where this attitude might be reflected is in 1 Sam. 21:2: ויחרד אחימלך לקראת דוד, 'Ahimelek trembled before David'. In contrast, no text associates joy with approaching the king.

The physical actions connected with appearance before the king may be easily reconstructed. 2 Sam. 24:20 is a typical text: ויצא ארונה וישתחו למלך אפיו ארצה, 'So Araunah went out and bowed low to the king, with his face to the ground'. Even the queen partakes in this gesture (1 Kgs 1:16; Ps. 45:12). 2 Sam. 16:4, which reads ויאמר ציבא השתחויתי, 'and Ziba replied, "I bow low"' is particularly instructive; it shows that השתחוה,[7] 'bowing', is equivalent to recognizing the king's sovereignty. Often in royal contexts, השתחוה 'bowing', is supplemented by ארצה אפים or ארצה, 'to the ground', or אל/על־פניו or על אפיו, 'on his face', or נפל, 'to fall', or with the verbs כרע, 'to kneel' or קדד, 'to bow low'. Although an absolute generalization cannot be made, the addition of these complements to השתחוה, 'to bow' often indicates a more severe gesture, indicative of more intense subjugation of the subject to the king. Often this is entreaty (e.g. 2 Sam. 14:4; 19:19; Esth. 8:3) or submission (e.g. 1 Sam. 24:9; 2 Sam. 9:6; 14:33) or thanks for granting a special request (2 Sam. 14:22; 1 Kgs 1:31). 2 Sam. 14:22 ויפל יואב אל־פניו ארצה וישתחו ויברך את־המלך, 'Joab flung himself face down on the ground and prostrated himself and Joab blessed the king' suggests that while the subject bowed, he might bless the king. The content of the blessing is unclear; 1 Kgs 1:31 suggests that it might have been יחי המלך לעולם, 'May the king live forever!' However, it is possible that the 'blessing' was the general greeting recited to any acquaintance whom a person encountered (2 Kgs 4:29; 2 Kgs 10:15; 2 Sam. 19:40). This might have been ברוך אתה ליהוה, 'Blessed are you of the LORD' (1 Sam. 15:13; for the feminine Ruth 3:10), or one of the 'greeting formulae' known from the corpus of Hebrew epistles (Pardee, 1982:148-149). Perhaps there was no one standard blessing, and special blessings were created for special situations. Thus, although we may surmise that a 'blessing' from the subject to the king was part of the royal greeting, it is impossible to know if it was unique to royalty or if it came from the usual set of ancient Israelite greetings.

Especially in the Northern kingdom, subjects often decided not to show obeisance to the king and rebelled. Although the roots פשע, מרד and קשר, 'to rebel' are often considered together in discussing rebellions, only קשר, *qešer* refers to an internal revolt, while the other two refer to renouncing an overlord.[8] According to Israelite historiography, the fear of *qešer*, 'rebellion' appears in the beginning of the monarchy (1 Sam. 22:8, 13), actual rebellions already appear against David (2 Sam. 15:31), and the verb קשר, 'to rebel' (sometimes with its accusative cognate), appears with several internal revolts against Judaean and Israelite kings (e.g. 1 Kgs 15:27; 16:9,16, 20; 2 Kgs 10:9; 12:21; 14:19; 15:10, 15, 25; 21:23-24; Amos 7:10). The result of a successful rebellion is inevitably the monarch's murder. Only in the post-exilic 2 Chr. 24:21 is the verb קשר, 'to rebel', used of anyone other than the king. The noun *qešer* in the sense of 'revolt' is more difficult to evaluate; it appears in texts with textual problems and is a polysemic root, conveying both 'rebellion' and 'conspiracy', but in reference to 'rebellion', it too may refer specifically to internal revolts.[9]

The interrelationship between God and people is more variegated than that between the king and people.[10] This is because various sources project the submetaphor on to God to differing extents. These differences are particularly obvious in examining the different attitudes that people are described as having when they (physically) approach God the king. In ritual contexts, we saw that there was a distinction between texts that allow free access to God and those that limit it (above, pp. 93-95). Several texts that encourage free access (esp. Deut. 16:16) indicate that 'seeing' God is accompanied by joy, not fear (v. 11). Indeed, the general Deuteronomic idiom ושמחת/ושמחתם לפני יהוה אלחיך/אלהיכם, 'and you shall rejoice before the LORD your God' (12:12, 18; 16:11; 27:7) suggests that joy typified visits to God. In contrast, P had a very different idea of who had access to God, limiting it only to the high-priest on the tenth day of the seventh month, the Day of Atonement (Leviticus 16). This visit to God is fraught with danger and demands careful preparation and proper attire, so that God will not kill the high priest (v. 2; see Milgrom, 1970:5-8). Lev. 16:1 as it now stands as an introduction to the ritual of the Day of Atonement might suggest that Nadab and Abihu were killed for just such an improper visit (see Shinan, 1979:206). The complex procedure of disassembling the Tabernacle in Num. 4:1-20 (esp. 5-6, 19-20) assures that no one may see the royal king's throne.[11] The differences between D and P are consistent with their respective attitudes about approaching the Temple: ritual texts which do not model access to the Temple after access to the palace do not project fear onto the worshipper who approaches God (so Deuteronomy), while those that do not allow free access, implying that the Temple is a palace, also project the danger implicit in coming before the king (so P).

The same two images exist in (non-royal) narrative texts which describe God outside of the Temple precincts. Both attitudes are particularly evident in Exodus 19-24, chapters which defy source analysis because 'the author appears to have been reluctant to exclude any scrap of data from this momentous occasion' (Greenberg, 1972:1056).[12] One set of texts depicts the fear of the people at God's sudden appearance (Exod. 19:16); a related set of texts implies that such fear is appropriate since seeing God might cause death (19:21, 22, 24 and 20:18-19). 1 Sam. 12:18, where God 'shows himself' through thunder and lightening, with the result וייַרא כל־העם מאד, 'the people were greatly afraid' is similar. In Hab. 3:10 and Psalm 114, the image of people trembling in fear is transformed to various geological objects trembling. Perhaps the tradition that anyone who sees a מלאך אלהים, 'divine messenger' will die is an extension of this principle. However, another set of texts records no fear, and implies that the people may ascend the mount (Exod. 19:13b; 24:9-11). Thus narrative texts reflect the same differences in the attitude of a worshipper toward God that were seen in the cultic texts.

The gestures of greeting performed by a subject before God mirror those performed before a king. When God appears וקם כל־העם והשתחוו איש פתח אהלו, 'all the people would rise and bow low, each at the entrance of his tent' (Exod. 33:10). This gesture of bowing so characterized the greeting to the divine that השתחוה, 'bowing' widened semantically to refer to worship in general, as reflected by its LXX translation equivalent προσκυνεῖν and the related Vulgate's *adorare* (Gruber, 1980:94-95). Sometimes submission (e.g. 1 Sam. 15:30) or thanks (Gen. 24:26) is specifically indicated by this gesture. Psalm 95, where the Israelite is called to (v. 6) באו נשתחוה ונכרעה נברכה לפני־יהוה עשנו, 'Come, let us bow down and kneel and bless the LORD our maker' because he is king (v. 3) indicates that this gesture could be recognized as patterned after the (domestic) royal greeting. As we surmised in the human sphere, certain exceptional circumstances such as a theophany or extreme supplication are reflected by exceptional bowing, as indicated by the idioms נפל אל/על פנים, 'fall on one's face',[13] or by התנפל, 'to throw oneself down' (Deut. 9:18, 25 [2×]; Ezra 10:1) which is used in this sense only of entreaty to God. The recognition that bowing to God reflects a specifically royal gesture persisted into the post-biblical period, as indicated by the prayer: ואנו משתחוים [לפני] מלך מלכי המלכים ברוך הוא עלינו, 'while we bow down before the king-of-kings' King, blessed is he' (Kugel, 1981:306-307).

After bowing to God the king, but before reciting a prayer to him, another feature was taken from the human, possibly royal sphere—the ברכה, 'blessing'. Ps. 95:6 באו נשתחוה ונכרעה נברכה לפני־יהוה עשנו, 'Come, let us bow down and kneel and bless the LORD our maker' makes this progression of actions clear. It is also reflected in Gen. 24:26-27, where upon the initial fulfillment of his mission, the anonymous servant of Abraham performs the following: ויקד האיש וישתחו ליהוה ויאמר ברוך יהוה, 'The man bowed low in homage to the LORD and said, 'Blessed be the LORD. . .''. We do not have enough evidence to know if this divine blessing was specifically modeled after the royal blessing, or followed the general human pattern (see Greenberg, 1983a:31-36).

Although rebellion against God (apostasy) was quite common in ancient Israel, it does not reflect the vocabulary of domestic rebellions. The verb *qšr*, 'to rebel (domestically)' is never used in the religious sense of apostasy. This may also be true of the noun's use, depending on the interpretation of *qešer* in Jer. 11:9. The text reads נמצא־קשר באיש יהודה ובישבי ירושלם, 'A rebellion/conspiracy exists among the men of Judah and the inhabitants of Jerusalem'. Ancient and modern commentators are split, with some preferring 'conspiracy' (LXX; NJPS; Bright,1965; Rudolph,1968; Holladay, 1986; McKane, 1986) and others 'rebellion' (TJ, Qimhi, RSV). In any case, the absence of the verb קשר, 'to rebel' and the rare or non-use of the noun קשר, 'rebellion' to refer to rebellions against God implies that apostasy was not not seen as parallel to domestic rebellions against a sovereign. Rather these rebellions against God use the terms for 'rebellion against an overlord' (פשע or מרד). Two factors might be responsible for this patterning: (1) the power of God is increased by depicting him as an overlord rather than a sovereign king and (2) קשר, 'domestic rebellion' usually involved the death of the monarch, which is inappropriate as applied to God.

In a sense, this section has been an exception to the usual structure of this work. Instead of finding cases where the divine sphere was patterned after the royal sphere, I have examined one component of the royal sphere, namely the interrelationship between the king and his subjects, and have shown that the metaphor God is king is *not* generally applied to this subarea. For example, although some texts show signs of projecting fear of approaching the king on to God, there is a clearly countervailing tendency of שמחת לפני יהוה, 'rejoicing before the LORD'. Rebellions against God are terminologically not connected to rebellions against the domestic king. Only in terms of gestures (bowing) was patterning operative, but even here it might be based on the vassal-overlord or commoner-high status person and not specifically on the subject-king analogy. Two opposing tendencies explain the lack of parallelism between interrelationships between king and subject in the royal domestic sphere and God. On the one hand, the king's role on the international plane provided him with more power than his domestic role, so God, who is most powerful, might have been modeled more on the international model. On the other hand, at least one group in ancient Israel thought of God as very approachable. This is consistent with neither the king's domestic nor international role, so to the extent that God may be approached by all Israelites, and joy accompanies seeing him, God must break free from the expected entailments of the metaphor.

The Royal Court

The composition of the royal court and the precise function of each royal official at specific time-periods are complicated issues, which have been studied in detail elsewhere (e.g. Mettinger, 1971, Ahituv, 1973, Clements, 1973, Yeivin, 1971, Macholz, 1972 and Redford, 1972:141-144). It is sufficient to note that a royal bureaucracy existed, as reflected for example in the lists of royal officials under David (2 Sam. 8:16-18; 20:23-26) and Solomon (1 Kgs 4:2-6). Indeed, according to משפט המלך, 'the practice of the king' (1 Sam. 8:11-13), Samuel assumed that the establishment of a bureaucracy is concurrent with establishment of the monarchy. The officials of the royal court that are important for understanding God's kingship are the שר הצבא, 'the army commander' (e.g. 1 Sam. 17:55; 1 Kgs 1:19; cf. Judg. 4:7) and the מלאכים, 'messengers', who played an important role in conveying or making public the royal word (e.g. 1 Sam. 16:19; 2 Kgs 1:2; 14:8; cf. 19:9). Royal bureaucrats had certain general roles and responsibilities: they might volunteer for important royal missions (cf. 1 Sam. 26:6)[14] or might act as middlemen, giving commoners access to the king (cf. 2 Kgs 4:13 and Macholz, 1972:314-316). Finally, it is noteworthy that although the king traditionally possessed wisdom, he would ask a counselor for advice on important matters (2 Sam. 17:5).[15]

There is no general collective term in Hebrew equivalent to 'cabinet', the assemblage of royal officials. This assemblage is designated by various general plural nouns. The most common general term is שרים, 'officers'. Several texts mention the king and his

royal officers (e.g. Jer. 36:21; 49:38; Hos. 13:10; Qoh. 10:16-17) in the
sense of the king and those who facilitate his leadership by carrying
out his commands. A royal official may also be called עבד המלך,
literally 'the servant of the king' or 'the servant of King X' (e.g. Gen.
21:25; 1 Sam. 16:15; 2 Sam. 15:15; 2 Kgs 19:5; Esth. 3:2). Many seals,
some of extraordinary craftsmanship, also attest to this title's use in
the pre-exilic period (Clermont-Ganneau, 1888:33-38; Albright,
1932:79-80; Hestrin and Dayagi-Mendels, 1978:16-18; Avigad,
1986:23-24). This title covers all types of officials (Westermann,
1976:186) and reflects the officers' relation to the king, whom they
heed as their royal master.[16] At the end of last century, Clermont-
Ganneau (1888:36), argued that בן־המלך, literally 'the son of the king'
may be used as a title of royal officials. This contention has been
debated, but is probably correct.[17] The title probably reflects a period
when many members of the royal family were involved in running
the government. A late designation for royal officials is משרת,
'attendant' or המשרתים את־המלך, 'the royal attendants' (1 Chr. 27:1;
28:1; 2 Chr. 17:19; 22:8; Esth. 1:10).[18]

Very little is known about the relationship between the king and
his court. Royal officials would stand before the king while attending
him (1 Sam. 16:21-22; Jer. 36:21; Dan. 1:19; 2:2), therefore they
could be called הזקנים אשר־היו עמדים את־פני שלמה, 'the elders who
stood before Solomon' (1 Kgs 12:6; cf. 8) or עבדיך אלה העמדים לפניך,
'these servants who stand before you' (1 Kgs 10:8; cf. Gen. 41:46).
Occasionally, a royal official would bow to the king (e.g. 2 Sam.
14:22; 18:28; see Gruber, 1980:182-201, esp. 191-197; for ancient
Near Eastern parallels see 201-257), but this action was not peculiar
to royal officials but was part of the general court ceremony (see
above, p. 96).

Little is known about the relationship between the king and the
royal officials. Ideally the officers were supposed to heed the king's
command, and when the king was powerful, this was done out of fear
(cf. Qoh. 8:2-4). However, royal officers could gain great power and
did in cases subvert the king's direct order (e.g. 2 Sam. 18:14). This is
particularly reflected in narratives about the North where ranking
royal officials rebelled against or sometimes assassinated the king
(1 Kgs 16:16ff.; 2 Kgs 15:25). Few positive actions of the officials
toward the king are recorded, though occasionally an official may
bless (ברכ) the king or praise (הלל in the *Piel*) him (2 Chr. 23:12).[19]
The biblical authors had few opportunities to show the regular
working of the royal court, so our general picture is incomplete.

It is also very unclear how declarations were promulgated via the royal court. A statistical study of the the messenger formula (Westermann, 1967:100-115) X כה אמר, 'thus says X', where X is not God, suggests that this formula was frequently used with proclamations deriving from the king via a messenger.[20] The lack of the phrase כה אמר, 'thus says' in the extant Hebrew epistolary corpus (see Pardee, 1982), none of which derives from kings, may further support the contention that it was a very formal, largely royal formula. The possibility that כה אמר, 'thus says' is of a high register and primarily royal is further suggested by the only certain use of אמר, 'says' with כה, 'thus' in the Aramaic epigraphic corpus, which is in Sefire ICl כה אמרן וכה כתבן, 'so we spoke, and so we wrote', which appears at the end of a royal treaty (Fitzmyer, 1967:18, 73). Non-royal proclamations may have been introduced differently, perhaps by דברי, 'the words of', which is well attested to as an introductory formula to prophetic books and other works (Jer. 1:1; Amos 1:1; Prov. 30:1; 31:1; Neh. 1:1).

Several texts such as 1 Kings 22, Isaiah 6 and Daniel 7:9-14 clearly depict a heavenly royal court which is analogous to a human royal court. This section will examine the composition of this court and the terminology associated with it and will explore the extent to which it corresponds to the human royal court.

Before investigating whether the heavenly court is based on an earthly royal archetype, it is necessary to make a methodological observation concerning the synchronic versus diachronic study of Israelite religious institutions. Two major studies of heavenly beings by Rofé (1969) and Mullen (1980) explain these beings by showing how they originate as demoted gods. This is stated explicitly by Rofé who claims categorically, 'The belief in many gods became angelology' (p. 89).[21] In an earlier study, Heidt (1949:27) proposed a similar notion:

> The sacred author was merely utilizing the artistic and religious concepts of pagan neighbor nations and infusing into them higher spiritual meanings. The bottles were old but the content was new.

Rofé and Mullen bring extensive lists of comparable terms for ancient Near Eastern minor gods (especially from Ugarit) and the terms for heavenly beings or their assemblage in the Hebrew Bible.

They tacitly assume that this borrowing 'explains' the heavenly beings in the Bible. The evidence that they muster may explain the *origin* of certain heavenly beings, but does not explain how these beings *functioned* once they were integrated into Israelite thought. It is especially striking that Rofé (24) claims that in Ugarit, 'The appearance of מלאכים, 'angels, messengers' in the mythical texts is nothing but a projection of parallel human customs into the divine sphere...', but he does not make any such consideration for ancient Israel.

This type of methodology was criticized in Morton Smith's classic article 'The Common Theology of the Ancient Near East' (1952). Talmon (1977 and 1978) has also argued that internal biblical parallels, whether lexical, literary or socio-political should be examined before applying external (ancient Near Eastern) parallels. In the vein of Talmon's critique, I will examine the extent to which the arrangement of the divine council parallels its earthly counterpart. I do not mean to deny that Israelite religion at various stages of its development had knowledge of polytheistic religions, and that 'angels' may have their *origin in part* in demoted gods. I do however want to assert that internal Israelite factors, especially the tendency to project royalty and many of its entailments on to God, could be constructively applied here to foster an 'internal' explanation for the *function* and *composition* of the divine council. This non-comparative methodology is especially pertinent here since it is unclear to what extent we may use the Ugaritic mythological texts to explicate the Bible. The exemplars of the texts known to us were mostly written down in the fourteenth century but are generally considered a few centuries earlier (Coogan, 1978:11); it is unknown whether they represent the Canaanite religion(s) that might have shaped Israelite beliefs in their formative stages.

The clearest and most detailed pre-exilic depictions of the Israelite heavenly council are in 1 Kings 22 and Isaiah 6. In both cases, God is seated (1 Kgs 22:19; Isa. 6:1), and is surrounded by the members of the heavenly court who stand about him (1 Kgs 22:19; Isa. 6:2), an exact parallel to the human court. Like its human counterpart, the members of this council could try to help (God) the king solve a difficult political problem (1 Kgs 22:20) and God, like the king, would accept the most suitable advice (vv. 21-22). God could also ask for and get a volunteer to fulfil a particular royal mission (Isa. 6:8). The notion of a heavenly middleman or intercessor (Job 33:23 and probably 9:33-35; 16:19-21; 19:25; cf. Pope, 1973:251 and Mullen, 1980:253) is probably based on a human model.

The heavenly council also performed actions that showed God the king's superiority. Heavenly beings would bow down before him (4QDeut[a] 32:43 [Skehan, 1954], הרנינו שמים עמו והשתחוו לו כל אלהים, 'rejoice, O heavens with him; bow down to him all heavenly beings'[22]; cf. Neh. 9:6). Ps. 29:1-2 is similar: השתחוו... הבו ליהוה בני אלים ליהוה בהדרת-קרש, 'ascribe to the LORD, O divine beings. . . bow down to the LORD, majestic in holiness'. These beings also sing the king's praise (4QDeut[a] to 32:43; Isa. 6:3; Ezek. 3:12 (MT); Ps. 103:20-22; possibly 19:2-3; 148:1-3; Job 38:7). Here too no exact analogy in the human sphere is known from the biblical sources, although it is possible that the royal officials who are מהללים את-המלך, 'praising the king' during Joash' coronation according to 2 Chr. 23:12 (cf. Ps. 148:1-3) are reflecting a general royal practice.[23] Perhaps the male singers and female singers (nârî [LÚ.NAR.MEŠ] and nârāti [MI.NAR.MEŠ]) sent as tribute by Hezekiah to Sennacherib performed this function in the Judaean royal court.[24] It is also unclear how, where and how often this royal song was sung and if it contained the terms which are all commonly used to indicate the praise of God. The heavenly beings were also considered to be wise (2 Sam. 14:20), probably a projection of the ideal qualities of a member of the earthly royal council. Thus, there are substantial similarities between the heavenly and human royal courts, suggesting that many aspects of the royal court were projected on to God's court.

There are also substantial differences between the heavenly and earthly councils. In pre-exilic texts, the members of the heavenly council are not generally differentiated. The only exception is the שר-צבא יהוה, 'the LORD's army commander', who is mentioned in Josh. 5:13-15, a very strange and truncated literary unit. The councilors generally all have the same role and are unnamed. This contrasts sharply with the human court. This lack of correspondence is theologically significant—there is no complex heavenly bureaucracy to correspond to the earthly bureaucracy. A heavenly bureaucracy could have diminished God's sovereignty by suggesting that he is not in full control. It might have implied that God is not ultimately responsible for the world's events. This prevented the heavenly court from developing to be fully parallel to the earthly court.

In almost all biblical texts, the power of the divine court is limited by God. Unlike the human court, there is no possibility that God's decision could be subverted by a member of his council. This is explicit in Job 4:18 הן בעבדיו לא יאמין ובמלאכיו ישים תהלה, 'indeed he cannot trust his own servants, and casts reproach on his heavenly beings', and in Job 15:15, 25:5 and Isa. 24:21 (Rofé, 1969:80 and Mullen, 1980:232) and is implied by Job 1:12 and 2:6. In Psalm 82 the members of the divine council are demoted by God to be like (mortal) human councilors (שרים, v. 7) because they do not adequately fulfil their job of rendering justice.[25] The only possible exception in biblical literature to this notion of the limited power of the divine court is in the post-exilic 1 Chr. 21:1 where שמן, 'Satan' (no definite article!) or 'accuser' seems to be acting on his own accord. Even there, however, it is ultimately God who takes charge of the situation.

In post-exilic literature, the role and the structure of the court changes. One member is השמן, 'the accuser', found in Job 1-2 (see Hurvitz, 1974) and Zech. 3:1. According to Tur-Sinai (1967:38-45), Pope (1973, 9-11) and Luzzatto (cf. Oppenheim, 1968:175-177), the שמן, *śāṭān* is modeled after a member of the Persian royal court, who is *šṭ b'rṣ*, 'wandering about the land'. However, this suggestion assumes an interchange between *š* and *ś*, which is very unlikely since these represented distinct phonemes throughout the biblical period (Blau, 1979: 59-61). Although the term עיר, 'watcher', used in Daniel and in roughly contemporaneous Aramaic writings (see Fitzmyer, 1971:80-81 and Fitzmyer-Harrington, 1978:332, 352 s.v. עיר) is unknown as a designation for a human court official, in function, the 'watcher' may reflect the officially appointed spy who was central to the functioning of the royal court (Teixidor, 1967:634). In the post-exilic period, angels began to acquire names: גבריאל, 'Gabriel' and מיכאל, 'Michael' are named in Daniel (8:16; 9:21; 10:13, 21; 12:1). Gabriel's role as a dream interpreter has no certain parallel in the human court[26] while Michael's title of השר הגדול, 'the great officer' suggests that he is modeled after a vizier. In non-canonical literature roughly contemporaneous with Daniel, a hierarchy of angels is presented (*Jub.* 2:2) and angels are assigned specific functions (*1 Enoch* 20:1-8; see Mullen, 1980:276), though these are not based on earthly archetypes. שרים, 'officers' of the nations which are explicit in Daniel (10:13, 20) and are explicit in non-Massoretic versions of Deut. 32:8 (see LXX and Qumran; see Rofé, 1969:66-68, 98ff.) do not mirror functions in the human court. Dan. 7:10 breaks the pre-exilic model in a different way. While largely consistent with earlier images (e.g. the council members *stand* before God), it says that the members of the council number אלף אלפים/אלפין, 'thousands upon

thousands' and רבו רבוא/רבבן, 'myriads upon myriads'. This multitudi-
nousness reflects an effort to show that the heavenly court
surrounding God is quantitatively, and thus qualitatively superior to
the human court. If we may conflate these various post-exilic images,
an interesting paradox emerges—the size and specificity of the
bureaucracy begins to develop, which could suggest a diminishment
of divine control over the world,[27] but this is counteracted by the
image of God's great hosts which suggest his great majesty and
control over all.

Another way to examine the extent of influence of the earthly
court on its heavenly counterpart is to compare the terminology used
of them. In doing this, it is important to distinguish between two
types of nouns: collective nouns, appearing in the singular which
denote the divine council as a whole, and (non-collective) nouns in
the plural used of the assembly. The following collective nouns are
used of the heavenly assembly: עדת (אל-), '(divine) assembly' (Ps.
82:1), קהל (-קרשים), 'assembly of (holy beings)' (Ps. 89:6), סוד,
'council' (Jer. 23:18; Amos 3:7; Ps. 89:8; Job 15:8), perhaps דור,
'assembly' (Amos 8:14 emended; cf. Neuberg, 1950 and Ackroyd,
1968) and צבא, 'host' or צבא השמים, 'heavenly host'[28] (1 Kgs 22:19
[=2 Chr. 18:18], Isa. 24:21; Pss. 103:21; 148:2; Dan. 8:10; Neh. 9:6).
None of these terms were applied to the earthly royal council; some
might have been borrowed from pre- or non-Israelite nations where
they were used of the council of gods (so e.g. Mullen, 1980:118-119).
The others, with the possible exception of צבא, 'host' (see below,
pp. 107-108), are applications of designations for general gatherings
of people to this heavenly group. Thus, for reasons that are unclear,
the biblical sources suggest that several collective nouns were used to
designate the divine council, while not one such noun is attested for
the human council. However, almost all of these divine terms are
general nouns rather than technical terms only denoting the council,
and they are all found in poetic texts which have no clear
corresponding parallels in the human sphere, so no conclusions may
be drawn from this disparity between the human and divine royal
spheres.

Many of the same non-collective nouns are used of the members of
the earthly and divine councils. שר, 'officer' which is a very common
designation around the human court, for some reason is rare and late
of the divine council (Dan. 10:13, 20, 21; 12:1). They are called God's
עבדיו, 'servants' in Job 4:18, and the post-exilic term משרתיו,
'attendants' is used of them in Ps. 103:21, a post-exilic psalm

(Hurvitz, 1972:107-130, Qimron, 1978:144). Instead of being called בני־המלך, 'sons of the king' they are called בני אלים, 'sons of divine beings' (Psalm 29:1; 89:7; possibly 4QDeut[a] 32:8), possibly בני אלהים, 'sons of God' (possibly 4QDeut[a] 32:8 and Deut. 32:43 emended [cf. Rofé, 1969:69-75]) and בני (ה)אלהים, 'sons of the God' (Job 1:6; 2:1; 38:7; cf. Dan 3:25) (Tsevat, 1969-70:126 n.9). They are also called מלאכים, 'messengers' (Ps. 103:20; 148:2), and as such are supposed to deliver 'royal' messages (see Cross, 1953 on Isa. 40:1) and might have other roles which parallel human messengers (Ross, 1962:105).

In pre-exilic texts the prophet is depicted as standing in the divine סוד, 'council' (see esp. Jer. 23:18, 22); indeed the prophets Isaiah and Ezekiel stand in God's heavenly council (Isaiah 6 and Ezekiel 1), and the מגלת־ספר, 'written scroll' given to Ezekiel (2:8–3:3) closely parallels a ספר 'letter' which might be sent via a human royal official acting as a מלאך, 'messenger' (e.g. 2 Sam. 11:14). Although I would not go as far as Baltzer (1968) who claims that the prophet is specifically God's vizier, the prophet is depicted as a member of the divine council. This explains the designation of a prophet as a מלאך, 'messenger' in post-exilic literature (see Ross 1962; 2 Chr. 36:15, 16; Isa. 44:26 [Rofé 1969, 117-118]; Hag. 1:13 and Mal. 1:1[29]; 3:1).[30] Thus, although some terms are used for heavenly beings which have no corresponding human equivalents, most of the terms for heavenly beings are clearly projections of the human royal bureaucracy heavenward. This inner-Israelite terminological equivalence suggests that 'angels' should not be studied exclusively as 'fallen' or 'demoted' gods, as is typical of the approaches of Rofé (1969) or Mullen (1980), but should be examined as they interrelate to human royal officials.

It is impossible to discuss the heavenly court without at least some attention to the divine name יהוה צבאות, which is traditionally rendered 'LORD of hosts'. Even in an era before Ugaritic studies could complicate the issue, an entire monograph was devoted to the problems of this designation (Wambacq, 1947). A limited survey of literature on this problem (see esp. Tsevat, 1965, Ross, 1967 and Mettinger, 1982b) suggests that no general consensus will be reached on the name's interpretation. The first unresolved (and perhaps unresolvable) problem is the syntax of the phrase. While the most natural tendency is to parse the phrase as personal (divine) name in construct + noun, Tsevat, on the basis of a detailed evaluation of the biblical evidence, carefully shows that this is impossible in Biblical Hebrew, since personal names of this type may not be used in a construct chain. However, Tsevat's conclusions may be questioned given the evidence of ליהוה.שמרנ, 'to Yahweh of Shomron' and יהוה.תימנ, 'Yahweh of Teman' in the Kuntillet 'Adjrud inscriptions.[31] Others try to circumvent this problem by assuming that יהוה צבאות is derived from a shortened formula, e.g. צבאות X יהוה, 'Yahweh, X of hosts' or that it evolved from אל צבאות, 'God of hosts' (Mettinger, 1982b). The underlying problem with this methodology is that if we must reconstruct an earlier term to understand יהוה צבאות, there is no way of verifying or falsifying this term's existence or meaning. The suggestion of Cross (1973:65-75), that יהוה has a verbal force is problematic for the same reason. A second unresolved issue concerns what Mettinger (p. 111) calls 'contextualization'—judging the term's meaning by its use in various contexts. Here too unresolvable problems emerge, as is clear from the studies of Ross, Tsevat and Mettinger, all of whom use contextualization to arrive at different conclusions. The central problem is deciding which contexts are determinative. Tsevat and Ross opt for the earliest occurrence, but the differences between their conclusions indicate how difficult this evaluation might be. Mettinger (p. 112) opts for the most frequent associations, but even this judgement is uncertain since at some stage the designation might have become a personal name, and might be used for stylistic rather than semantic reasons. Since these underlying problems do not allow for a clear resolution of the issue, it will suffice to note that many commentators including Mettinger conclude that the צבאות, 'hosts' in the phrase יהוה צבאות, 'LORD of hosts' refer to the 'heavenly beings', such as those which are described in 1 Kgs 22:19. If this is correct, then this name is a further indication of the centrality of the image of the divine court in ancient Israel.

The phrase כה אמר יהוה, 'thus says the LORD' has been the subject of study by the leading form critics. In his classic study, Westermann (1967:100-115) claims that it is based on the human messenger formula. Koch (1969:89) also sees it as a *'messenger formula'* and claims that it must have introduced *all* oral prophecies. However, these studies, along with newer studies of the formula (e.g. Bjørndalen, 1974 and Hoffman, 1976-77) seem unaware of the high, primarily royal register of the phrase. Thus, by using כה אמר, 'thus says' the prophet is not only reflecting that he serves as God's messenger, but also suggests that the message originates with God the king.

The following three observations derive from the study of the heavenly court in relation to the earthly court. First, the metaphor

'God is king' associates the heavenly and earthly courts, but does not equate them. Both courts have officials called מלאכים, 'messengers', עבדים, 'servants' and בנים, 'sons'. Both depict courtiers standing around a seated king, and both share the כה אמר, 'thus says' message formula. However, unlike the human king's court, God's courtiers always obey him and the heavenly court has few differentiated officers. This is consistent with the tensive view of metaphor. Second, it is possible to see how the metaphor remains vital, and continues to function diachronically. As the earthly court or its terminology changed, parallel changes entered the heavenly court. For example, in the post-exilic period, משרתים, 'attendants' and possibly (ה)שטן, 'Satan', or 'the adversary' and the עיר, 'watcher' became part of the divine court. This mirrored corresponding changes in the human court. Finally, a study of the metaphor has indicated that Israelite kingship can to a large extent explain the structure and function of the divine court. This suggests that current biblical scholarship, which often pays great attention to external cultures or the precursors of a biblical institution, should pay more attention to possible internal explanations for Israelite religious beliefs and institutions.

Judge

The use of שפט, 'judge' as a royal appellation (see above, p. 44) indicates the important role of the king in the judicial system. Exactly what role he had remains unclear. Whitelam, 1979, an extensive study of this problem, concludes (217), 'the king was probably the greatest contributor to the developing system of law necessary in such a dynamic society as that of monarchical Israel'. Wilson (1983:240) claims, 'judicial authority ultimately lay in the hands of the king'. These claims may be overstated; although all genres of biblical literature show the king's involvement in meting out justice, other officials such as the שפטים, 'judges' and כהנים לוים, 'levitical priests' (Deut. 17:8-13) played major roles in the judicial system.[32] In contrast to ancient Near Eastern law 'codes', such as Hammurabi, no text explicitly mentions the Israelite king as the promulgator of an extensive body of law. It is quite possible that the Pentateuchal law collections, which show remarkably little interest in the royal court, developed independently of the king.[33] Zedekiah's emancipation of the slaves recorded in Jer. 34:8ff. does not point to royal involvement in the promulgation of laws; this text does not describe a new royal decree, but royal enforcement and interpretation (see Sarna, 1973) of pre-existent Torah legislation. Whitelam (1979:217-18) correctly notes, 'there is little unambiguous evidence to suggest that monarchical judicial authority extended to the promulgation of law'.

It is difficult to reconstruct the role of the king within the judicial system because the sources which portray him as an arbiter or judge are few in number, and information which may be gleaned from judicial parables (Simon, 1967:220-25), or is imbedded in prophetic stories, or is in wisdom collections may only be used with great difficulty to reconstruct history. Nevertheless, these sources are important because they reflect various popular perceptions of the king's judicial role, and it is these popular perceptions rather than the actual practice that would have influenced the conceptions of God the king as judge.

It is unknown when a person could bring a particular case before the king; was he only a court of last resort, or did specific types of cases come before him initially? In 2 Sam. 15:4, Absalom, in his attempt to unseat David his father plays king, states ועלי יבוא כל־איש אשר־יהיה־לו־ריב ומשפט והצדקתיו 'everyone with a legal dispute would come before me and I would see that he got his rights'. Although this seems to imply that any case could be brought before the king, it really indicates the opposite, namely that the real king, in this case David, did not have the time to adjudicate all of the claims his subjects wanted to bring before him. The author of the Absalom story implies that this was a serious enough problem to help foment a rebellion. The case of the two harlots coming before Solomon (1 Kgs 3:16-27) and of the cannibalistic mothers coming before the king of Israel (2 Kgs 6:24-31) seem far-fetched and folktale-like (Long, 1984:70); indeed, it is impossible for practical reasons that all claimants could have free access to the king. These texts probably reflect a wish that the king would be more involved in helping the problems of the oppressed. 2 Chr. 19:4-11 describes King Jehoshaphat's role in establishing a national system of justice. The historicity of this unit has been hotly debated, with polar views presented by Wellhausen (1973:191) claiming that the entire unit is a late etiological midrash on the name יהושפט, literally 'the LORD judges' and Albright (1950) using Egyptian parallels to show that the historicity of the account is plausible, thus the biblical account is likely. No consensus has been reached concerning its historicity; in any case, the narrative reflects a tradition that the king at some point established local judicial systems. Perhaps the king was also involved in certain types of appeals, in cases concerning property (Whitelam, 1979:138) and in pardons (2 Sam. 14:10-11; cf. Whitelam, 1979:133). The emphasis of the importance of a just king (see below) is consistent with the picture of a king as a supreme court, who relegated lessor matters to others. Ps. 122:5 כסאות למשפט כסאות לבית דויד, 'thrones of judgement, thrones of the house of David' may refer to courts established by the Davidic king and under his control. Also, scholars have suggested that Moses is patterned after royalty in the Bible (see below, p. 174, n. 14). It then becomes significant that Moses is credited with establishing a judicial system in which he only decided cases which were too difficult for local magistrates (Exod. 18:13-26; Deut. 1:9-17).

The general responsibility of the king for establishing justice may be inferred from Judg. 17:6 and 21:25: בימים ההם אין מלך בישראל איש הישר בעיניו יעשה, 'In those days there was no king in Israel; every man did as he pleased'. Key words in the demand that the king be just are משפט, 'justice', צדקה and צדק, 'equity' and אמת, 'truth'[34] and it is often emphasized that the king had a particular responsibility to protect the downtrodden. For example, Jeremiah addresses the monarch (22:3) כה אמר יהוה עשו משפט וצדקה והצילו גזול מיד עשוק וגר יתום ואלמנה אל־תנו אל־תחמסו ודם נקי אל תשפכו במקום הזה, 'Thus says the LORD: do what is just and right; rescue from the defrauder him who is robbed; do not wrong the stranger, the fatherless and the widow; commit no lawless act and do not shed the blood of the innocent in this place' and states concerning Josiah (vv. 15b-16a) ועשה משפט וצדקה אז טוב לו דן דין עני ואביון אז טוב, 'he dispensed justice and equity—then all went well with him; he upheld the rights of the poor and needy—then all was well'. Similar sentiments are reflected in Ps. 45:5, רכב על־דבר־אמת וענוה־צדק, 'ride on in the cause of truth and meekness and right' and v. 8 אהבת צדק ותשנא רשע, 'You love righteousness and hate wickedness' and in Ps. 72:1-4 and 12-14. In Psalm 101, which is entitled by Kenik (1976) 'Code of Conduct for a King', the king tells God how he destroys evildoers (vv. 4-5, 7-8) and rewards the righteous. Some wisdom texts share a similar ideal: the king who follows משפט, 'justice' and אמת, 'truth' has a stable reign (Prov. 29:4, 14). Most texts concerned with royal justice are either in contexts of rebuke, noting the king's lack of adherence to general judicial standards or to specific judicial norms (1 Kings 21), or are conditional, stating that if the king is righteous, all will go well (e.g. Ps. 45:8; Prov. 25:5). Prov. 16:10 קסם על־שפתי־מלך במשפט לא ימעל

‏פיו-‏, 'There is magic on the lips of the king; he cannot err in judgement' is *sui generis*, and may reflect popular notions or a particular 'court wisdom ideology' concerning the king's superlative wisdom.

The hollow verb ‏דנ‏, 'to judge,' which is often used with an Israelite king as its subject, reflects the important association between kings and justice.[35] It conveys the same ideas as ‏שפט‏, 'to judge'—it is used in admonishing kings to be just (Jer. 21:12; Ps. 72:2; Prov. 31:9), and to note that when a king is ‏דן דין־עני ואביון‏, 'upholds the rights of the poor and the needy' it is 'good' (Jer. 22:16). Its use often stresses the gap between the ideal of royal justice and the actual performance of Israelite kings.

Only the future ideal ruler (Thompson, 1982) will sit (Isa. 9:6) ‏על־כסא דוד ועל־ממלכתו להכין אתה ולסעדה במשפט ובצדקה‏, 'upon David's throne and kingdom, that it may be firmly established in justice and equity'. His description in Isa. 12:3-5 is brimming with idealized judicial terminology. Similarly, Isa. 16:5 notes of the future Davidite: ‏והוכן בחסד כסא וישב עליו באמת באהל דוד שפט ודרש משפט ומהר צדק‏, 'And the throne shall be established in goodness in the tent of David, and on it shall sit in faithfulness a ruler devoted to justice and zealous for equity'. Jeremiah, who names the future king ‏יהוה צדקנו‏, 'the LORD is our integrity' (23:6) says of him ‏ועשה משפט וצדקה בארץ‏, 'and he shall do what is just and right in the land' (v. 5=33:15). To some extent, these ideals are projected backwards on to David, who ‏עשה משפט וצדקה לכל־עמו‏, 'executed true justice among all his people' (2 Sam. 8:15). Most prophecies concerning the future king have justice as one of their central themes; these prophecies reflect the hope for a new world order, with true royal justice.

As the supreme judicial official, the king had the power to execute his royal sentences. This is expressed in an extreme fashion in Daniel's words to Belshazzar (Dan. 5:19): ‏די־הוה צבא הוה קטל‏ ‏ודי־הוה צבא הוה מחא ודי־הוה צבא הוה מרים ודי־הוה צבא הוה משפיל‏, 'He put to death whom he wished, and whom he wished he let live; he raised high whom he wished and whom he wished he brought low'. This power is not limited to post-exilic foreign kings. The power to put a person to death is related of Pharaoh (Gen. 40:19, 22; Exod. 2:15; 10:28), Saul (1 Sam. 11:13 MT), David (2 Sam. 11:15; 21:6), Joash (2 Chr. 24:21), Jehoiakim (Jer. 26:21) and Darius (Ezra 6:11). This royal power to effectively execute judgement stands behind the warning in Qoh. 8:2-4 that it is important to act properly before a king lest you are punished; Prov. 16:15 ‏באור־פני־מלך חיים ורצונו כעב‏

מלקוש, 'the king's smile means life; his favor is like a rain cloud in spring' expresses the opposite notion—the power of the king to help those whom he favors. The king could carry out lesser punishments too, e.g. Zedekiah had Jeremiah imprisoned (Jer. 37:21; cf. 36:26 and 38:5); such lesser punishments, however, are rarely mentioned.

It is difficult to determine the extent to which God's role as judge may be studied within the metaphor 'God is king'.[36] As we just saw, the sub-vehicle is unclear—we do not know the exact role the king had within the judicial system. Furthermore, most texts in which God is depicted as a judge or in which he acts justly do not specifically call him king or evoke kingship images. The image of God as judge is a projection from the human sphere (Niehr, 1987:226-227). However, since the role of judging was never confined to the royal sphere, and most texts connecting judgement to God do not mention his kingship, we may not assume that all texts which use juridical terminology of God are a projection of *royal* justice on to him. Therefore, in the following section, I confine myself to texts in which God is specifically depicted as king, either through the use of the root מלך, 'to reign' or through a clustering of clearly royal terms or images. For example I exclude from the following discussion the chapters in Exodus and Deuteronomy which describe the giving of the law. Although Buber claims (1967:126; cf. 121-135), 'The Sinai covenant is a kingly covenant', the contexts describing the lawgiving have few kingly reminiscences, so it may not be assumed that they are patterned after the human king's judicial role. This lack of royal imagery in the Sinai pericope is not surprising, since as we saw earlier, the Israelite king did not promulgate law, therefore, Israelite kingship could not serve as a suitable vehicle for God's revelation of law.

Cases where God as king is explicitly depicted as a judge often stress the rectitude of his judgement. In Ps. 9:5 a worshipper calls him שופט צדק, 'righteous judge' and says of him והוא ישפט־תבל בצדק ידין לאמים במישרים, 'it is he who judges the world with righteousness, rules the peoples with equity' (v. 9). The phrases שפט צדק, 'righteous judge' and מישרים, 'equity' are unique to God as royal judge, never appearing as realized qualities of human kings. In Ps. 10:18 God the king fulfills the human royal *ideal* of judging the downtrodden fairly. Pss. 96:(11-)13 (cf. 1 Chr. 16:33) and 98:(7-)9 poetically reflect on the uniqueness of God as a royal judge—because he renders judgement באמונתו, 'faithfulness', בצדק, 'justly' and במישרים, 'with equity', all unbiased observers, namely the natural world, rejoice at his arrival.

As judge the Israelite king was supposed to judge justly and with equity; this would assure him a firm throne. However, as we saw, this remained an ideal, fulfilled only to some extent by the idealized David and by the future Davidic leader. God as king fulfills this ideal. He executes משפט, 'justice' (Pss. 9:17; 99:4), especially for the downtrodden who should have been protected by human kings (Pss. 103:6; 146:7-9; cf. Deut. 10:17-18). God's superiority as royal judge over human royal judges is explicit in Ezekiel 34, which has as its central image a comparison between the Israelite kings as רעים, 'shepherds', God as רעה, 'shepherd' and a future ideal רעה, 'shepherd'. God's superiority to his human counterparts is expressed by God's claim (v. 16) ארענה במשפט, 'I will tend them with justice'. God the judge's superiority to human kings is expressed differently in Ps. 146:7-9. This psalm, in trying to adduce reasons not to trust human rulership (v. 3), but rather to have God as king (v. 10), gives an unusually long list of downtrodden groups whom God helps and states in the midst of this list (v. 8) יהוה פקח עורים יהוה זקף כפופים, 'The LORD restores sight to the blind; the LORD makes those who are bent straight'. In other words, because of God's vast power, his ability to rectify wrongs and unfairness vastly exceeds that of any mortal. We saw that the verb דן, 'to judge' is predominantly used with kings in the Bible; its use with God stresses his overwhelming power in a different way—it is usually used with God's judgement over all nations (Gen. 15:14; 1 Sam. 2:10; Isa. 3:13 (MT); Pss. 7:9; 9:9; 96:10; 110:6). This power of the divine judge is further emphasized by the depiction of God standing in judgement (Tsevat, 1969-70:127), in contrast to human kings who usually sit. God's inherent quality of absolute righteousness is behind the image of Ps. 89:15 צדק ומשפט מכון כסאך, 'Righteousness and justice are the base of your throne' (cf. Pss. 9:5, 8; 97:2).[37]

Not every ancient Israelite believed in the superiority of God the royal judge. We earlier saw the *sui generis* Prov. 16:10 ('There is magic on the lips of the king; he cannot err in judgement'). However, the message of this proverb, which did not fit 'standard proverbial theology' was modified by an editor of Proverbs by following it with פלס ומאזני משפט ליהוה מעשהו כל־אבני־כיס, 'Honest scales and balances are the LORD's; all the weights in the bag are his work'. This second proverb is probably placed here as a corrective to the first, to declaim that justice belongs to the divine rather than to the royal king.[38]

It is impossible to address the question of God the just king without mentioning Israelite literature which raises the question of theodicy. Already Abraham is depicted as wondering if God as judge really executes משפט, 'justice' (Gen. 18:25). This issue persisted into the post-exilic period; Mal. 2:17 quotes the people saying איה אלהי המשפט, 'Where is the God of justice?'[39] If we read Job as a vindication of Job's position at the expense of his friends' (42:8), the friends' contention of God's משפט, 'justice' (e.g. 8:3; 34:12; 37:23) is corrected by Job's claim (19:6-7): דעו־אפו כי־אלוה עותני ומצודו עלי הקיף הן אצעק חמס ולא אענה אשוע ואין משפט, 'Yet know that God has wronged me; he has thrown up siege works around me. I cry, "violence!" but I am not answered; I shout, but can get no justice'. However, in no text which questions God's justice is he depicted as a king. This is curious—the capriciousness with which the human king meted out justice in a self-interested manner could have offered a suitable model to justify God's inexplicable behavior. We saw earlier how the royal bureaucracy was not projected on to God, even though this would have been theologically useful; similarly, the unfair aspects of human kingship were intentionally not projected onto God the king. The ancient Israelites eschewed such a simple solution to theodicy, preferring to think that God is just ('traditional' wisdom; Job's friends), is about to be just (Second Isaiah) or that his justice is paradoxical (the book of Job read as a whole).

The few texts which show God the royal judge punishing the accused (see Good, 1985), emphasize his great power. Nations tremble in anticipation of his judgement (Pss. 96:9; 97:5, 7a; 99:1) which is total and final (Ps. 9:6). Conversely, when God the judge vindicates Israel (Ezek. 34:16), he shows great care and tenderness toward them; this is unusual behavior by the acquitting judge toward the former accused.

God as royal judge fulfills the same functions as human judges, but does a perfect job. משפט צדק and מישרים, 'justice' and 'equity' are accomplished through him, rather than with the human king. That justice is so intrinsic to him that it can be called מכון כסאו, 'the base of his (=God's) throne'. God's justice is so powerful that the accused tremble in fear before it, while the objective onlooker rejoices in its fairness. Unlike royal 'justice', God the judge is not capricious. As judge, God's justice so surpasses that of the human king that a worshipper could ask (Ps. 72:1) אלהים משפטיך למלך תן וצדקתך לבן־מלך, 'O God, endow the king with your judgements, the king's son with your righteousness', explicitly pointing to the superiority of the divine king's justice.

Builder

According to the biblical text, the Israelite king was the master builder. He built (בנה) palaces (e.g. 1 Kgs 7; 22:39), temples (e.g. 1 Kgs 6; Zech. 6:13) and even cities (e.g. 1 Kgs 12:25; 2 Kgs 14:22). Aside from the general verb בנה, 'to build,' other verbs are used to describe different stages and types of royal construction: הקים, 'to set up' (1 Kgs 7:21; 16:32; 2 Kgs 21:3), יסד, 'to found' (Zech. 4:9), חזק in the *Piel*, 'to strengthen' (2 Chr. 11:11, 12; 26:9; 29:3)[40] and possibly כון, 'to establish' (in the *Polel* in Hab. 2:12 and *Hiphil* in 1 Kgs 6:19, but these texts present exegetical and textual difficulties). There is certainly some exaggeration involved in this picture of the king as builder. Perhaps, as in Mesopotamia, the king served in a 'supervisory capacity' (Ellis, 1968:20; cf. pp. 20-26), or performed a symbolic or ritual activity connected to the building and was therefore credited with it. The importance of the Mesopotamian king as builder is reflected in the so-called 'historical inscriptions', which are usually really building inscriptions which follow a very long 'introduction' about the king's general achievements with a description of a particular royal building project (Reade, 1975:189 on Sennacherib's inscriptions). In Israel as well, the king is credited with work that he could not and did not accomplish. This is explicit from a comparison of Ezra 3:10 ויסדו הבנים את־היכל יהוה, 'When the builders had laid the foundation of the Temple of the LORD' to Zech. 4:9 ידי זרבבל יסדו הבית הזה, 'Zerubbabel's hands have founded this house'.

God's role as 'builder' or creator became so central to Israelite belief that it was used by P and J to open their account of history. The notion of God as creator is part of ancient Near Eastern religious thought[41] and it must have entered Israel as part of what Morton Smith (1952) calls 'The Common Theology of the Ancient Near East'. However, as we previously saw in connection to the divine cabinet (above, pp. 102-109), the origin of a religious institution or belief should not be confused with how it was understood and depicted once it was incorporated into a religious system. The important issue therefore becomes: since Israel used the image of kingship to understand its God, was the role of the king as builder used in depicting God the creator? This problem is especially acute since other strong metaphors, such as 'God is father', could also provide a solid grounding for depicting God as creator, as seen from Mal. 2:10 הלוא אב אחד לכלנו הלוא אל אחד בראנו, 'Have we not one father? Did not one God create us?' The extent to which the king as builder shaped the Israelite notion of creation must be examined by seeing the extent to which God's role as creator is described in specifically royal contexts.

Several texts attribute creation to God the king, and use the same construction terminology that we saw above with the king as builder. God as creator is central to some of the יהוה מלך, 'The LORD is king' psalms. Psalm 93, whose introduction has as its theme God's kingship says (1b) אף־תכון תבל בל־תמוט, 'the world is established firmly, it cannot be shaken'. In Psalm 96, God's role as creator is spoken of at two distinct points,[42] in v. 5b ויהוה שמים עשה, 'but the LORD made the heavens' and v. 10 אף־תכון תבל בל־תמוט, 'the world is established firmly, it cannot be shaken'. The first section of Psalm 89, which has as its theme God's kingship says (vv. 12-13a): לך שמים אף־לך ארץ תבל ומלאה אתה יסדתם צפון וימין אתה בראתם, 'The heaven is yours, the earth too; the world and all it holds—you established them. North and south—you created them'. In a doxology of sorts following the mention of God as king in Jer. 10:10, we find (v. 12) עשה ארץ בכחו מכין תבל בחכמתו ובתבונתו נטה שמים,[43] 'He made the earth by his might, established the world by his wisdom, and by his understanding stretched out the skies' (cf. Jer. 51:15). In Isa. 43:15, Deutero-Isaiah combines God's kingship and creation, although there the creation of Israel as a people (and not the world) is referred to. Weinfeld (1981) argues that Gen. 1:1-2:3 is suffused with royal imagery. It is possible that the plural verbs used of God in Genesis chapter one reflect his role as the head of the divine council, informing his councilors of his decision.[44] If this is correct, God's role as creator in Gen. 1:1-2:3 might have royal reminiscence. This would be particularly likely if it could be proven that the first creation story in Genesis is based on Enuma Elish (Heidel, 1963:82-140 and Speiser, 1964:10), which has as its theme the kingship of Marduk (Jacobsen, 1976:183-86). Although in some of these texts the association of God's kingship with his role as creator is clearer than in others, the connection is explicit in a sufficient number of texts to suggest that in ancient Israel, God as creator could be understood within the submetaphor 'God the king is royal builder'.

Other contexts suggest that God's role as creator is in part based on that of the king as builder. For example, the frequent description of God as builder of Zion/Jerusalem (Isa. 14:32; 62:7; Jer. 24:6; Ezek.

36:36; Amos 9:11; Pss. 102:17; 147:2, 13) is probably a projection from the royal realm. God, like any king, has built himself a palace in his (heavenly) abode (Amos 9:6). God's image as royal builder stands behind the literary conceit of Ps. 78:69 ויבן כמו-רמים מקדשו, 'He built his sanctuary like the heavens' (cf. Exod. 15:17).[45] In contrast to the historiographical texts (e.g. 2 Samuel 7; 1 Kings 5-6; Ezra 3-6), but following the royal pattern, God is portrayed here as building his earthly Temple/palace. However, God's role as builder goes far beyond that of constructing his palace or capital city. As sovereign of the world he has created the world (e.g. Isa. 40:26, 28; 43:7; 45:7, 8, 12, 18,[46] Jer. 33:2; Amos 4:13; Pss. 8:4; 24:2; 104:5, 8; 119:90; Prov. 3:19; 8:27). His role as royal builder explodes even beyond his creation of the world, which still fits the extended metaphor of God as royal builder of cities. God has not only created his city, his palace and even the world, but has even fashioned Israel into a people (Isa. 43:1; cf. Deut. 32:6; 2 Sam. 7:24); indeed he has created people in general (e.g. Gen. 1:27; 5:1-2; Isa. 45:12; Ps. 89:48). He is the superlative royal builder. He even created abstractions such as מישרים, 'equity' (Ps. 99:4). Also, although God is sometimes 'merely royal' in that his building involves typically royal qualities like wisdom and strength (e.g. Jer. 10:12=51:15), often his building involves qualities to which kings could only aspire. For example, God's structure is perfectly constructed so it never totters (Ps. 93:1; 96:10; 104:5; cf. 1 Chr. 16:30) and God does not tire after building (Isa. 40:28; cf. Weinfeld, 1968:121-26). God's building involves certain aspects or techniques which are absent from human kings—only God is *br'*.[47] Thus, to the extent that the picture of God as builder continued to be informed by royal archetypes, God surpassed these models.

This position of God as the superlative royal builder, capable of projects and quality which far exceed any human king, can be expressed in a different way. As part of royal *rhetoric* the nation's building projects were attributed to the king, who might have initiated or supervised these projects. This rhetoric was transformed into a reality as it was applied to God: God actually did build and create all, even certain abstractions. In God, the royal hyperbole has been literally realized. This is similar to the way in which the wish for the king's long life was projected on to God as an accomplished fact (see above, pp. 52-53).

Royal Resources

The king was frequently a wealthy man who had control over the אצרות המלך, 'the royal treasuries' (see above, p. 55). Though not all kings were as wealthy as Solomon or Hezekiah, all needed income to support the palace dependents (2 Sam. 19:34) and to fund building projects. No single system was used throughout the half millennium of Israelite monarchy to raise funds. I will synchronically examine the various systems of domestic taxation commonly used to raise capital; exceptional methods, such as royal theft of property (1 Kings 21) will not be included.

By the time of Solomon, a regular system of נצבים, 'prefects' who acted as tax collectors was established (1 Kgs 4:7), possibly following an Egyptian model (Redford, 1972). The details of how these taxes were exacted, at what percentage various goods were taxed and whether this institution predated Solomon or continued beyond the united monarchy are unknown. Corvée or statutory labor (Soggin, 1982) (מס [עבד]) was another important source for royal 'income'. The evidence for this institution is largely confined to the early monarchy. 1 Sam. 8:11-13, 16 part of משפט המלך, 'the practice of the king' refers to various officials who will be 'drafted' (יקח) by the king. Mendelsohn (1956) has claimed that this document reflects the practices of the early monarchy, but this is not certain (Rainey, 1970:193-198 and Mettinger, 1976:81, esp. nn. 6-7). The practice of Israelites serving in corvée is explicitly mentioned in 1 Kgs 5:27-30; 1 Kgs 9:20-22 and 2 Chr. 2:16-17, which exempt Israelites from this practice, are apologetic attempts to exonerate Solomon from using forced Israelite labor and are historically inaccurate, as indicated by the biblical account of Jeroboam's rebellion. The corvée was controlled by an official who was על-המס, 'in charge of forced labor' (2 Sam. 20:24; 1 Kgs 4:6; 5:28; 12:18 =2 Chr. 10:18). Temporary levies of Israelites for building projects might have been carried out in the later monarchy (1 Kgs 15:22; possibly Jer. 22:13).

Reconstructing details of the tax system is very difficult. The tithing of agricultural products and sheep by the king is mentioned in 1 Sam. 8:15, 17. Although these tithes are not mentioned elsewhere in the Bible, they must reflect the historical reality of some period. Other possible references to taxation are uncertain philologically (e.g. Amos 5:11 and 7:1) or refer to extraordinary events. 1 Kgs 10:24-25 might suggest that visitors to the royal court brought gifts with them.[48] Song of Songs 8:11-12 may presuppose some form of royal sharecropping; however כרם, 'vineyard' in this context might only be functioning metaphorically (as a woman), in which case these verses offer little insight into Israelite economic history (Pope, 1977: 688-689).

Evidence concerning taxes paid to non-Israelite kings in the post-exilic period is much more abundant. The terms used are מס, 'tribute', (Esth. 10:1 etc.), מנדה־בלו והלך, 'tribute, poll-tax and land-tax' (Ezra 4:13), three Akkadian terms borrowed via Aramaic, and מרת המלך, 'king's tax' (Neh. 5:4); we even find references to excessive taxation (Neh. 9:37) and tax refunds (Esth. 2:18). However, these sources do not illuminate the pre-exilic Israelite tax structure; the generalization of de Vaux (1965:139) still stands: 'Little is known about the fiscal system of Israel or the resources at the disposal of the state'.

It is extremely difficult to evaluate the extent to which God's image as king incorporates receiving resources from his (domestic royal) subjects. Several factors contribute to this difficulty. We have seen that the subvehicle (the king obtaining royal resources) is particularly unclear, making it difficult to evaluate the subtenor (God the king obtaining royal resources). Second, most gifts to God are not given directly to him, but are given to the priests who are functionaries in his Temple; it is unclear if these should be considered as gifts to God. Finally, it is difficult to evaluate whether the phrase נתן ליהוה, 'to give to the LORD', which is often used with gifts given at the Temple, implies a direct gift to God or refers to a gift to the Temple personnel, who are acting as intermediaries. The second and third questions are interrelated and can probably be resolved. We have previously seen that the Temple was considered the royal palace of God (above, pp. 91-92). The cultic officials there are משרתים, 'attendants', paralleling the function of palace attendants or heavenly councilors. Therefore resources given to them, or given (נתן) to God through them, allow the Temple, God's earthly royal palace, to function properly. This is analogous to the gifts given to the king which are used to support the royal palace. Thus, these gifts given to the Temple functionaries should be considered in conjunction with the royal resources given to the earthly king.

The clearest parallel between God and the king is in the institution of tithing. This is reflected in the narrative of Gen. 28:22, where Jacob promises after his dream וכל אשר תתן־לי עשר אעשרנו לך, 'and all that you give me, I will set aside a tithe for you'. The law in Lev.

27:30, 32 mandates tithing agricultural products and cattle. How and when these tithes were collected is not indicated in that chapter. Num. 18:24 and 26 specify that God is giving his מעשר, 'tithe' to the Levites; perhaps this implies that originally the tithe was burned as an offering to God, like a sacrifice. Deuteronomy treats the tithes differently. According to Deuteronomy, the donor must eat it in the divine presence (לפני יהוה אלהיך) instead of giving it to God (12:6-7, 12, 18; 14:23); only once in every three years is given to the Levites (14:28 and 26:12). The sarcastic Amos 4:4 indicates that some sort of tithe was given in the eighth century.[49] Post-exilic texts indicate that the tithe continued to be collected by the Levites, although Nehemiah (10:38, 39; 13:5, 12) implies that it was only from produce while Chronicles (2 Chr. 31:6) assumes that it was also of cattle.[50] The post-exilic sources suggest that in this period, the tithe served an economic function, allowing the Levites (the Temple/palace personnel) to survive. Therefore, the rhetoric of (post-exilic) Mal. 3:8-10 is particularly interesting since in castigating the people for neglecting the tithe, it claims that *God directly* is being robbed and is left hungry. This implies that even in the post-exilic period when the tithe was given to the Levites, it was still viewed as given to God, perhaps on analogy to the royal מעשר, 'tithe' described in 1 Samuel 8.

Other gifts to God are mentioned in the Bible, but too little is known about the gifts the Israelite king received to know if they are parallel. The injunction ולא־יראו פני ריקם, 'none shall appear before me empty-handed' appears in Exod. 23:15 and in the parallel 34:20 in connection to חג המצות, the Mazzot festival, and is extended in Deut. 16:16 to all festivals. This may have been equivalent to the subject bringing display gifts before the king to predispose him to act kindly. The Akkadian term for such gifts is *tāmartu*, from the root *amāru*, which is similar in meaning to the root ראה, 'to see, to appear' which is used in these festival texts in Exodus and Deuteronomy. Other types of gifts to God seem to have had no parallel in the human sphere, such as the gift of the first-fruits (e.g. Exod. 23:19a=34:26a), the firstborn of livestock and humans[51] (Exod. 13:2, 12-13; 22:28b-29; 34:19-20; Deut. 15:19; Ezek. 20:25-26; Micah 6:7) and animal sacrifices. No parallel to the royal corvée was exacted by God, unless we consider the priests or the life-long nazirites[52] to have served this function, although no corvée terminology is associated with them. It is also possible that the half-shekel levy for the building of the Tabernacle reflected some type of levy for a royal building project and that the annual levy for Temple maintenance mentioned in Neh. 10:33-35 reflected a similar secular tax. Here too, too little is known of the vehicle to fully appreciate the extent to which the metaphor is functioning.

This section could do little more than probe some ways in which God's resources paralleled those of the human king. The nature of the data makes all conclusions extremely tentative. The references to God collecting resources are especially problematic since they do not appear in contexts that are explicitly royal, so it is uncertain whether the Israelites connected God's collection of resources to the collection of resources by the Israelite king. The most striking overlap is that both God and king collect tithes, but it is noteworthy that no explicitly royal text describes God receiving tithes. The structure of donations to God does not seem to change diachronically to parallel different royal taxes; this contrasts with the structure of the heavenly council, which was modified to keep up with changes in the human royal court (see above, p. 105). The general lack of parallelism between the description of how God and the king collect resources fits the picture that was developed earlier with divine wealth; the Bible is hesitant to call God the king wealthy because his wealth is qualitatively unlike royal wealth (see above, pp. 56-57). It is therefore not surprising that the depiction of God collecting resources is not analogous to the human king since the metaphor 'God is king' does not function extensively in the area of royal wealth.

Conclusions

The study of 'the king and domestic affairs' shows that in certain areas the metaphor 'God is king' strongly shaped the Israelites image of the divine, while other areas remained largely independent of the metaphor. For example, the terms used for the royal palace or royal officers had a decisive influence on descriptions of the divine realm, to the extent that the structure of the heavenly council changes diachronically to match changes in its royal counterpart. On the other hand, the institutions associated with raising money by the king had little influence on the Israelite's portrayal of God. The ability of certain aspects of God to closely parallel those of the king while others differ markedly from him, is typical of the way metaphors function.

Previous chapters illustrated how the metaphor 'God is king' grounds God within royal behavior or attributes, while allowing him to surpass the human king. This is true as well when comparing God to 'the king and domestic affairs'. As judge, God functions as a full-time, fair judge, a צדק שפט, 'just judge' who possesses מישרים, 'equity', This is only paralleled on the human sphere by the idealized David or the ideal future king. Similarly, as a royal builder, God's 'building projects' include the creation of the world and the 'building' of humanity and nations. The power of God as king is also seen through the 'disinfecting' nature of the metaphor: kingship adheres to God to the extent that he 'steals' the term היכל from the human sphere, stressing that he is more kingly than the Israelite monarch.

In other areas, however, there is a stricter correspondence between the vehicle and tenor. For example, both human and divine courts contain מלאכים, 'messengers' and officials called בני־המלך or בני־(ה)אל(הים), 'sons of the king' or 'sons of God', and both human king and royal God typically introduce their official proclamations using the כה אמר, 'thus says' formula. Both God and king have a שר צבא, 'an army commander'. The Temple is called 'the house of the LORD', after the palace which is called 'the house of the king'. A person entering the Temple used rituals borrowed from the royal ceremonies. Similarly, according to P's conception, the access to the divine palace (namely the Temple) is limited by שמרי משמרת, 'doers of guard duty', a conception borrowed from the human royal sphere. However, other ancient theologians seem to have made a self-conscious attempt not to pattern God after the Israelite king.

This lack of patterning is evident in several areas and has different causes. Deuteronomic literature emphasizes free access to God and joy in approaching him, making him into an accessible king. This conception is unparalleled in the human realm. A different type of asymmetry is evident in the use of the the word *qešer*, 'domestic rebellion'. Within the Bible as a whole, verbs and nouns from the root *qšr* are not used of rebellions against God, emphasizing that a rebellion against God is not comparable to a mere rebellion against a sovereign, but is more serious, like overthrowing an overlord. Although the Temple is depicted in literary terms that parallel the king's palace, its architecture is distinct from royal architecture. In this case, pragmatic concerns prevented the metaphor from being realized. Finally, it is noteworthy that the metaphor 'God is king' would have allowed two easy solutions to theodicy, by depicting God as a royal (self-serving) judge and showing how God's decisions become bogged down in the royal bureaucracy. However, these options were not taken up by the biblical theologians. The metaphor was used in Israel to illustrate an idealized and superlative God, but not to explain his possible weaknesses.

Chapter 6

BECOMING KING

The Israelite Royal Ritual: The Historiographic Texts

Scholars continue to debate the interpretation of the so-called 'enthronement psalms'[1] (Psalms 47, 93, 96, 97, 98 and 99), which may refer to God's accession as king. According to the methods developed in this study, it is necessary to examine the accession of Israelite kings to the throne before these psalms may be fruitfully interpreted. Not all elements of the accession need be examined in detail; for example, the various methods through which a king rose to power, which would be prominent in a discussion of human kingship, have few parallels in the realm of the divine as described in the Bible, so they will not be studied here.

Reconstructing the institutions surrounding 'becoming king' is very difficult since we have no complete texts which fully describe or proscribe 'coronation rituals'. Most rituals must be reconstructed from the historical narratives. The uncertainty as to whether these narratives accurately reflect the period which they are describing or project back practices contemporaneous to their authors vitiates any attempt to create a diachronic picture of Israelite enthronement rituals. Judaean kingship lasted for close to half a millennium and Northern Israelite kingship lasted for two centuries and incorporated five dynasties[2] plus four kings who did not establish a dynasty; it is *a priori* unlikely that one set of rituals would have persisted throughout this entire period in both geographical centers. Therefore, we cannot speak of *the* coronation ritual. Finally, the Bible leaves us with a very incomplete picture of these rituals, which cannot be completed using other types of sources. This is typically done by using ancient Near Eastern materials, or by locating remnants of the earthly enthronement ritual in Psalms, or by projecting divine enthronement rituals onto the human king. Each of these methods is problematic. Ancient

Near Eastern material may not be used to fill in such gaps because
the Israelite coronation ritual may have differed significantly from
that of its neighbors. The use of Israelite divine 'enthronement'
rituals to fill the gaps is especially problematic because these rituals
are often themselves reconstructed; even if they could be properly
reconstructed, there might be a disparity between the human and
divine spheres.[3] The problems arising from reconstructing the royal
enthronement rituals imbedded in the psalms will be examined
below (pp. 135-39). With all of these caveats in mind, I will now
describe the rituals which were part of the royal coronation.

Most historiographic texts do not describe the enthronement
rituals; instead they say only וימלך X בנו תחתיו, 'and X, his son,
reigned instead of him' (e.g. 1 Kgs 11:43) or note the succession in
the synchronic formula . . . מלך Z . . . ליX בשנת, 'In year X of (King)
Y, Z reigned' (Bin-Nun, 1968). Other non-formulaic accession notes
which contain the name of the king and the verb מלכ, 'to reign', but
give no details of the enthronement ritual, are found scattered
throughout Samuel and Kings (e.g. 2 Sam. 2:8-9; 2 Kgs 13:13; 21:24).
Only in unusual circumstances are details of the coronation given.
The accession of the kings of the short-lived united monarchy (Saul,
David, Absalom, Adonijah and Solomon) is significant enough for
detailed narration. The accession of Jehu (2 Kings 9) was preserved
in detail because of Jehu's role in exterminating the 'accursed' house
of Ahab. This narrative is preserved in a prophetic source within
Kings, and not in Kings' usually laconic narrative. Joash's coronation
(2 Kings 11) is highlighted because it illustrates how the 'illegitimate'
Queen Athaliyah is deposed. Jehoahaz' accession is narrated in some
detail (2 Kgs 23:30) because of the unusual circumstances of his
accession after Josiah's death and because he was not the oldest heir
(2 Kgs 23:31, 36). The special role of foreign kings in the
enthronement of Jehoiakim and Zedekiah encouraged the inclusion
of certain details of their coronation. In none of these cases is there
reason to believe that the details of the coronation are described in a
tendentious manner, although they might be anachronistic, conform-
ing to the period of the author rather than the period being described.
Furthermore, for literary or ideological reasons, each account might
emphasize certain details at the expense of others.

Reconstructing the rites surrounding the accession of Saul is
complicated by the multiple sources reflecting on that important
event. Scholars usually distinguish between three sources: the early
folk-story of the lost asses to which a layer concerning Saul's

anointing by Samuel has been added (e.g. Mettinger, 1976:72-78); the story of Saul being chosen by lot, which is seen as Northern and from the period of David or Solomon (Mettinger, 87); an account of accession after military victory (where Samuel is absent) which is considered the oldest and most reliable description of Saul's accession (Mettinger, 83-87; but see Edelman, 1984) and spliced onto the previous accounts by an inaccurate editorial comment (McCarter, 1980:205, 207) ונחדש שם המלוכה, 'let us renew the monarchy there' (1 Sam. 11:14). The early layer of the first account (9:20, 22-24)[4] consists primarily of a banquet at which Saul is honored by having a special seat and a special sacrificial portion. In this section Samuel says to Saul (9:20): ולמי כל־חמדת ישראל הלוא לך ולכל בית אביך, 'And for whom is all of Israel yearning, if not for you and your ancestral house?' The function of this utterance is difficult to evaluate—is it a performative utterance,[5] which makes him king (like the contemporary utterance 'I hereby declare you man and wife'), or is this a type of foreshadowing of Saul's future kingship, with no actual designation of kingship (Mettinger, 1976:98)? The absence of חמדה, 'yearning' elsewhere in sources of this type makes this issue particularly difficult to resolve. The later revision of this story, especially as found in the LXX to 10:1 (S.R. Driver, 1960:78, McCarter, 1980:171 and Mettinger, 171) leaves no doubt that Saul was actually crowned; the LXX implies that Samuel said: 'Has not the LORD anointed you as a divine designee over his nation, Israel, and you will rule over the nation of the LORD and you will deliver it from its enemies'. According to this source, the coronation consisted of a (performative) utterance and anointing.[6] The coronation described in 10:19-25 is much more complex: the king stood amidst the nation (v. 23), the prophet proclaimed him as king (v. 24a), the people shouted (v. 24bα וירעו) and said יחי המלך, 'long live the king' (v. 24bβ), and a royal charter of sorts was read to the people and then recorded (v. 25a). The final description in 11:14-15 contains different elements: at Gilgal the people וימלכו שם את־שאול, which may be translated as either 'they declared Saul king there' or 'they declared there, "Saul is king"'[7] (v. 15aα), they offered sacrifices (v. 15aβ) and were joyous (v. 15b). Each text reflects parts of the royal ritual as practiced in different periods and perhaps different places; it is impossible, however, to place them in a definite locale or time.

David's coronation is recounted in various reports which are incorporated into a section of Samuel usually called the 'History of David's Rise' (HDR; see Mettinger, 1976:33-47). The 'first coronation' is privately performed by Samuel and ritually consists of only anointing by oil (16:13). There is a general consensus that this account is based on that of the prophetic anointing of Saul in 10:17-27, and thus considerably postdates the period that it describes. A depiction of David's coronation dating from an earlier period which focuses on the same ritual event of anointing is in 2 Sam. 2:4. A final depiction of David's coronation is in 2 Sam. 5:1-3. These verses are problematic; verses 1a ויבאו כל־שבטי ישראל אל־דוד חברונה, 'All the tribes of Israel came to David at Hebron' and 3a ויבואו כל־זקני ישראל אל־המלך חברונה, 'All the elders of Israel came to the king at Hebron' may be doublets, and most scholars separate vv. 1-2 and v. 3 as separate accounts; some claim that vv. 1-2 are deuteronomistic (see McCarter, 1980:131-133; contrast Mettinger, 1976:44-45). If these verses indeed represent separate sources, the ritual in vv. 1-2 consists of a declaration of filiation (v. 1b), suitability based on military experience (v. 2a) and divine designation (v. 2b). The ritual in v. 3 comprises a ברית, 'covenant, pact' and anointing. Since vv. 1-2 and 3 do not reflect separate bodies of vocabulary and vv. 1b-2 and v. 3aβ do not contain any doublets or contradictions, it is worth considering the possibility that vv. 1a and 3aα are double readings (see Talmon 1960), and vv. 1-3 present a unified ritual.

The second half of 2 Sam. 15:10 כשמעכם את־קול השפר ואמרתם מלך אבשלום בחברון, 'When you hear the blast of the horn announce, "Absalom has become king in Hebron"' presents two problems. First, is 'the blast of the horn' part of the coronation ritual, or was it a cry to (civil) war, as in Jer. 51:27? Second, how should ואמרתם מלך אבשלום בחברון, 'announce, "Absalom has become king in Hebron"' be understood? At least three possibilities present themselves: (1) it could be a performative utterance, through which Absalom's kingship is validated; (2) it could be an utterance which encourages others to reflect on the event and to decide whether they accept Absalom's kingship[8]; (3) אמר, usually translated 'announce' or 'say' should be taken in the sense of 'to realize' (Baumgartner, 1967:64 #4), in which case the verb indicates that when you hear the blast of the horn, you should know that the rebellion has begun. Since all of these positions are equally possible, one cannot determine if 2 Sam. 15:10 definitely describes a coronation ritual, so it should not be included as a certain text describing a royal ritual.

Adonijah's pretension to the throne is recounted three times (1 Kgs 1:9, 19, 25; cf. Alter, 1981:100). All three accounts describe a royal banquet, while the third description notes a royal acclamation

יחי המלך אדניהו, 'long live king Adonijah'. The threefold repetition of Adonijah's 'illegitimate' coronation is paralleled by a similar repetition of Solomon's legitimate succession, first as a command from David (1 Kgs 1:32-37), then as a narrated ritual (vv. 38-40) and finally as an event heard in the camp of the enemy (vv. 41-48). The elements of all three tellings are essentially the same: a group of people (vv. 33aα, 38aα, 44a) take Solomon on David's she-mule (vv. 33aβ, 38aβ, 44b) down to the Gihon (33b, 38b, 45aβ) where he is anointed by Zadok and Nathan (vv. 34a, 45aα). The idiom משח למלך, 'to anoint as king', indicates that the anointing was the performative action, making him king. The subsequent reaction of the people is the blowing of the שופר, 'ram's horn' (vv. 34bα, 39bα), which is represented in v. 45 as a general outcry (ותהם הקריה, 'the city went into an uproar', but cf. v. 41) and the acclamation יחי המלך שלמה, 'long live the king, Solomon' (vv. 34bβ, 39bβ). The third telling instead narrates general joy (v. 45aβ), which is found later and in greater detail in v. 40a (MT) of the second telling, והעם מחללים בחללים ושמחים שמחה גדולה, 'the people were playing on flutes and making merry'. The ceremony is completed when the new king sits on the throne (vv. 35a, 46) and is blessed with the wish that he will be even greater than his predecessor (vv. 37, 47a).

2 Kings 9 contains the only lengthy account of the coronation of a Northern king. Certain unique elements in this coronation narrative similarly suggest that it is not Judaean in origin. In his recent study of the prophetic story, Rofé (1982:73-76) posits that the kernel of Jehu's liquidation of the house of Ahab, including most of 2 Kgs 9:1-13, incorporates a contemporaneous account, which has become secondarily associated with Elisha. The text probably provides us with accurate information of a Northern coronation. It includes anointing by a prophet (vv. 3aα, 6), and recitation of the formula כה אמר יהוה משחתיך למלך (אל-עם יהוה)[9] אל-ישראל, 'Thus says the LORD, "I anoint you as king (over the nation of the LORD,) over Israel"' (vv. 3aβ, 6b, 12b). This is followed by three actions: placing peoples' clothes under the king (v. 13a), blowing the שופר, 'ram's horn' (v. 13bα) and proclaiming מלך יהוא, 'Jehu has become/is king' (v. 13bβ). It is unclear which of these are performatives and which are simply reactions of joy; namely, did Jehu become king when he was anointed, or when the anointing formula was recited or when his kingship was publicly recognized on the part of the people through the actions described in v. 13? The text provides no clues that would allow this problem to be resolved.

The detail lavished upon the description of Joash's coronation in 2 Kings 11 reflects the author's joy as Athaliyah, the female pretender to the throne, is deposed. The ceremony in vv. 10-11 where the king is surrounded by armed guards in the Temple probably reflects the special circumstances surrounding Joash' installation by Jehoiada, the high priest, rather than a typical part of the coronation ritual. The ritual proper begins in v. 12: the נזר, 'crown' and עדות, 'testimony' (but probably read צעדות, 'royal bracelet'; see above, pp. 78-79), symbols of kingship, are placed on Joash. This is followed by וימליכו אתו (either, 'he was enthroned' or, 'the phrase מלך יהוא, Jehu has become/is king was proclaimed'); he was then anointed, and the people clapped and said יחי המלך, 'long live the king' (v. 12). While standing on the royal platform, the people[10] rejoiced and blew חצצרות, 'trumpets' and possibly sang (v. 14 LXX). A three-way ברית, 'covenant, (com)pact' is made between God, the people and the king (v. 17).[11] Finally, the king was escorted to the palace, where he sat on a royal throne (v. 19) amidst jubilation (v. 20aα).

A very brief description of the coronation of Jehoahaz is found in 2 Kgs 23:30. The ritual is characterized by anointing by עם־הארץ, 'the people of the land', and the statement וימליכו אתו, 'they made him king' or "they said 'Jehoahaz is king'". The assumption of a new name (a 'throne-name') upon ascending to the throne is explicitly found only in 2 Kgs 23:34 and 24:17, where a foreign overlord renames the Israelite king whom he has just installed. The renaming is strange because the new names do not reflect any special relationship that the new king was supposed to have in relation of the overlord.[12] This suggests that the assumption of a throne name may have been part of the coronation ritual. This is argued most forcefully by Honeyman (1948), who notes the double names יהואחז־שלום, Jehoahaz-Shallum and ידידיה־שלמה, Jedidiah-Solomon (see Wyatt, 1985). This implies that taking a throne name might have been part of the (Judaean?) ritual from its earliest stages.

This material is summarized in the following chart. It notes the possible components of the coronation ritual, the Hebrew terms associated with them, and their dispersion. The chart allows a complete picture of all the rituals associated with coronation to emerge and indicates which sources mention specific rituals.

Elements of Biblical Coronations

Biblical Texts	1 Samuel					2 Samuel			1 Kgs		2 Kings				
	9:20-23	10:1-9	10:24-25	11:15	16:13	2:4	5:1-3	15:10	1:9-25	1:33-45	9:3-13	11:11-20	23:30	23:34	24:17
declare past dealings							*								
prophetic declaration or acclamation	*	*	*									*			
special meal	*							*							
crown (and armband)										*					
mule										*					
anoint		*			*	*	*			*	*	*	*		
kiss		*													
cause to reign				*								*	*	*	*
change name														*	*
sign		*													
peace offerings				*											
clothes on floor												*			
noise			*					*		*	*	*			
X has become king מלך X								*				*			
(long) live the king יחי המלך			*						*	*		*			
compact			*				*					*			
platform												*			
joy				*						*		*			
sit on throne										*		*			
officer blesses										*					
old king blesses										*					
in front of the group	*		*	*	*	*	*		*	*		*			

The chart is self-explanatory. The horizontal columns indicate how common a particular element is and with which kings it was associated. It is necessary to emphasize again that no text intended to depict a complete description of the royal ritual, and there might have been substantial differences in the royal ritual as practiced under different kings due to various factors (e.g. chronological, geographical, whether the successor succeeded through primogeniture or was a usurper). Therefore, these descriptions may not been conflated into a 'complete' description of the royal ritual.

We must focus on the statement made by the people about the king to understand the enthronement pslams. Two such phrases are found: (Y ב) X מֶלֶךְ, 'X has become/is king (at Y)' and (X) יחי המלך, 'long live king (X)'. Although other scholars have insisted that these formulae must not be dealt with in tandem (Mettinger, 1976:131-137 and Lipiński, 1965), I treat these two formulae together because: (1) they are both words spoken by the public; (2) they structurally appear at approximately the same place in the ritual; (3) they never appear together. Their exact function or purpose, however, is not clear. X מלך, 'X is/has become king' is used twice (of Absalom and Jehu), each time by a usurper (Lipiński, 1965:374 and Mettinger, 1976:132). This formula indicates that X has just become king, so that the kingship of the previous monarch should be considered over. This contextual observation may be borne out by the syntax of X מלך, 'X is/has become king' since מלך, 'to be/become king' appears as a verb, stressing an action (and not as a noun). יחי המלך literally 'may the king live', is formally a 3ms *Qal* jussive of חיה, 'to live', + המלך, 'the king', but it is often rendered idiomatically as 'long live the king'. In 2 Sam. 16:16, Hushai, implying that he has defected to Absalom's camp, says to 'King' Absalom יחי המלך יחי המלך, 'long live the king, long live the king'. This suggests that the phrase indicates the subject's acceptance of the sovereignty of a new king. This wish of a long life implies a wish for a long reign. Several scholars, however, have claimed that this is an insufficient explanation of the formula's function. De Boer (1955) for example, claims that יחי, usually rendered 'may he live' should be understood as an indicative, and its use should be connected to the oath formula חי המלך, 'by the life of the king'. According to this theory, the formula is a recognition of the king's power over life and death and connects the royal power to the divine. Mettinger (1976:134) notes the general vagueness of de Boer's proof and calls attention to the El Amarna Akkadian phrase *libluṭ šarru*, 'long live the king', which is used as an oath in letters originating from Canaan. He concludes that the biblical phrase in question (יחי המלך) expresses the people's willingness to enter into a compact with the king (pp. 135-37). These types of suggestions are certainly plausible, though it is difficult to prove that the biblical phrase harked back either to a divine oath or to a compact formula, either in terms of its historical development or in its associations within ancient Israel. It is therefore preferable to understand יחי as a jussive ('may he live'), expressing the subject's acceptance of the king. If this is correct, X מלך, 'X is/has become king' and יחי המלך, 'long live the king' would have similar functions; this explains why they are never found together in descriptions of coronations.

Scholars have debated at length the exact function of these phrases. This debate may not be resolvable. Ideally, one would need to observe a *complete* ancient enthronement and ask an informed bystander such questions as, 'is he king yet?' and, 'what exactly has made him king at this point?' Furthermore, a ritual cannot always be analyzed so that each element serves only one function. If I have correctly interpreted both יחי המלך, 'long live the king' and X מלך, 'X is/has become king' as expressions of loyalty by the subjects, these expressions *could* be characterized as enthronement formulae and/or acts of homage.

Modern Western analogies lead us to expect that the coronation was a quiet, dignified event; biblical evidence, suggests the contrary, that it was a quite noisy affair. This noise is only recorded when the formulae X מלך, 'X is/has become king' or יחי המלך, 'long live the king' are invoked, and could be made before or after the recitation of the formula. A שופר, 'ram's horn' is sounded before the recitation of the X מלך ('X is/has become king') formula. יחי המלך, 'long live the king' may be preceded by a שופר, 'ram's horn' (1 Kgs 1:34, 39), clapping hands (2 Kgs 11:12) or וירעו (1 Sam. 10:24), which indicates either general noise-making (Humbert, 1946:16-21) or playing a noisy instrument such as a שופר, 'ram's horn' or חצצרה, 'trumpet' (e.g. Lev. 25:9; Num. 10:7). The recitation of this formula may also be *followed* by מחללים, 'playing on flutes' (1 Kgs 1:40), חצצרות, 'trumpets' (2 Kgs 11:14) and possibly שרים, 'singers' (2 Kgs 11:14 LXX). This may be so loud that ותבקע הארץ בקולם (1 Kgs 1:40), 'the earth was split open by their uproar' or ותהם הקריה, 'the city went into an uproar' (1 Kgs 1:45). This noisemaking was a collective ritual,[13] which is mentioned in sources of coronations reflecting different time-periods (1 Sam. 10:24; 2 Kgs 11:12, 14). The noise was probably a reflection of the subjects' joy during the coronation (1 Kgs 1:40, 45; 2 Kgs 11:14, 20).

Anointing is firmly anchored in the complex of royal coronation rites. There have been many attempts to explain the ritual's origin and function (e.g. Kutsch, 1963, Mettinger, 1976:185-232 and Pardee, 1977). Pardee's explanation of anointing as 'a desire of purification as part of a *rite of passage*' (1977:18) is most attractive; it is simple and explains most instances of anointing in the Bible and surrounding cultures. It is not necessary to further discuss anointing since it has no parallel in the realm of the divine enthronement. It is only worth noting its prominence, and that in some complexes or coronation rituals the anointing is the main or only ritual (1 Sam. 16:13; 2 Sam. 2:4; 2 Kgs 23:30), suggesting that it was (one of) the main performative rite(s) of the coronation. This is supported by the use of משיח, 'anointed one' as a royal appellation.

The coronation includes a compact.[14] It is twice called a ברית, 'covenant, (com)pact' (2 Sam. 5:3 of David and 2 Kgs 11:17 of Joash), and once expressed through the term משפט המלכה, 'the manner of kingship' (1 Sam. 10:25 of Saul; cf. Mettinger, 1976:87-88). In the cases of Saul and Joash, this compact follows the main rituals, while with David it immediately precedes the anointing. The order described in David's coronation seems more logical, especially if we understand ויכרת להם המלך דוד ברית, 'and David made a pact with them' (2 Sam. 5:3) as David obligating himself to the people, and then being granted the kingship (Mettinger, 1976:139). The existence of the reverse order suggests that the recitation of the compact became a fossilized element within the ceremony, placed at a point where the people could no longer say 'we refuse', leaving the ceremony before it was formalized, as was once done according to the tradition in 1 Kgs 12:1-16. There are many uncertainties about this compact. There are no references to it in the coronation of most kings, including all the Northern kings (contra Fohrer, 1959:15-17). This suggests that a compact was not always made at the coronation or that it existed as an institution only in Judah.[15] It is impossible to reconstruct the content of this compact. This problem is connected to the polysemic nature of the word ברית, 'covenant, (com)pact'. Weinfeld (1975:124-125) points out that the insistence of Kutsch (1963) that ברית must be rendered *Verpflichtung*, 'obligation' may be correct etymologically, but in actual usage, the term covers mutual agreements as well. This makes us unsure whether the ברית, 'compact' contained only the king's responsibilities or also incorporated those of the people.[16] Although the sources indicate that a compact was *an* element of the coronation ritual, it is impossible to discern its contents or its geographical and chronological extent, although this has been attempted (Widengren, 1957 which is criticized in Rosenthal, 1958; Halpern, 1981:16-49).

Certain other aspects of the coronation which might play a role in God's 'enthronement' need to be highlighted. The coronation usually had an audience, sometimes a small group of important officers (1 Sam. 9:22; 1 Kgs 1:38, 44; 2 Kgs 11:11). According to 2 Sam. 5:2, a declaration of the acts that make the king worthy of kingship were recited. This is not more widely attested to since most kings ascended the throne through primogeniture, but this custom might have been followed when primogeniture was not practiced, e.g. with the descendents of Josiah or during the political upheavals in the

Northern kingdom. The gathered assemblage might have celebrated the coronation with a festive meal (Schmidt, 1970; cf. 1 Sam. 9:23; 1 Kgs 1:25; cf. 1 Sam. 11:15). Finally, 1 Kgs 1:35-36 and 2 Kgs 11:19 suggest that sitting on the throne was one of the concluding rites of the coronation ritual.

The Israelite Royal Ritual: Non-Historiographic Texts

Various aspects of the coronation ritual have been reconstructed using non-historiographic texts, especially from Psalms. This can only be done once we determine how many 'royal Psalms' are contained in the Psalter. This issue was already raised by the 'father' of form-criticism, Hermann Gunkel, whose changing positions indicate the difficulty of determining how various psalms might be connected to the enthronement ritual. In his well-known *RGG* article ([1930] 1967:24) he claims that Psalms 2, 21, 72 and 110 belong to the enthronement ritual *or* the autumn festival, while in the posthumous *Einleitung* (Gunkel-Begrich, 1933:145), he notes that only 2 and 110 belong to the 'Feste der Thronbesteigung' while 21 and 72 commemorate the anniversary of the enthronement (see similarly Westermann, 1980:106). I will briefly examine Psalms 2, 21, 72 and 110 along with some other psalms (1, 89) to determine whether Psalms may aid our reconstruction of the coronation ritual.

Brownlee (1971) claims that Psalms 1 and 2 were combined into one psalm late in the history of Judah for use in the coronation ritual. Psalm 2 has often been connected to the coronation (see below); Brownlee's stronger claim is that the two psalms should be understood as one unit (at least at the early editorial level; pp. 322-325), where 'Ps 1 may be a wisdom poem for the instruction of would-be courtiers, who expect to minister in the royal court of Israel' (p. 327). Brownlee's understanding of 1-2 as one unit follows ancient traditions, and may be supported by some evidence of vocabulary and structure, but the topics, styles and poetic structures of the two are so dissimilar that it is difficult to argue that they formed a liturgical unit (see Willis, 1979). Therefore, it is necessary to reject Brownlee's assertion that Psalms 1 and 2 together formed a 'coronation liturgy'.

The situation with Psalm 2 is very different. Ps. 2:7b-9, in which the Davidic king is speaking, represent an important addition to what we have reconstructed from the historical sources—a divine oracle of

the king's adoption by God (v. 7b) and a promise of victory in battle
(vv. 8-9). The word היום, 'today' (v. 7b) inescapably leads to the
conclusion that this ritual transpired on the day when the king's
status changed from commoner to king, namely at the coronation.
The notion that this verse reflects an annual anniversary of the
coronation (e.g. Widengren, 1957; Kraus, 1966:179-88) is very
doubtful since there is no certain evidence among the historiographical
texts or in Psalms that such an anniversary was celebrated. It is not
surprising that part of the 'traditional' divine promise to David
(2 Sam. 7:14, אני אהיה־לו לאב והוא יהיה־לי לבן, 'I will be a father to
him, and he shall be a son to me'; cf. Ps. 89:27-28), indeed the part of
the promise phrased in the theologically most daring fashion, would
be repeated at the coronation.[17] Although the language of Ps. 2:8-9, a
promise for military victory is not found in the Davidic promise,
these verses clearly reflect the king's fears at accession, especially
since the transition between kings was often accompanied with
revolts by vassals. A divine assurance concerning military power is
indeed reflected in 2 Sam. 7:9 and 11 and in 1 Kgs 3:7b[18] and 11aβ, a
divine oracle placed immediately after Solomon's accession. In fact,
the terminological similarity between 1 Kgs 3:7b and Psalm 2:8 (cf.
the use שאל and נתן, 'to ask' and 'to give') might suggest that at some
point 1 Kgs 3:7 belonged to a coronation narrative. Thus, Psalm 2
suggests that part of the coronation ritual was a proclamation by
God's representative, perhaps a 'cultic prophet'[19], of the king's
adoption by God (Rosenthal, 1958:5, Cooke, 1961 and Paul, 1978)
and of the king's military power. This proclamation could be called a
חק, which covers the sense of an 'ordinance' and often implies
immutability (see Jones, 1965).

    Scholars have debated whether Ps. 2:7b-9 alone or if Psalm 2 in its
entirety reflects the practices of an enthronement ritual. This
question is extremely difficult to answer because the psalm presents
some major textual cruxes, frequently presents changes in speakers
and must be treated in relation to a complex set of elements usually
called the 'Zion Tradition' (see Roberts, 1973 and 1982). Three
general options for the exegesis of the entire psalm are frequently
posited: (1) This is a historical psalm, depicting actual events that
transpired at a particular king's accession. (2) The battle is real and is
taking place after the king's accession. The accession is being recalled
retrospectively. (3) This is a general enthronement psalm and the
rebellion depicted in vv.1-3 is a ritual re-enactment of a central motif
of the Zion Tradition (e.g. Kraus, 1966:224, esp. n. 100 and Gottlieb,

1980:72-76). Only if we accept the third possibility need we assume that the entire psalm reflects accession imagery; however, there is nothing in this psalm that forces us to accept this reading. The second possibility must be seriously considered, namely, that a battle long after the accession is being recounted and v. 7 is a verbatim quote (note היום, 'today') by the king of the divine promise of encouragement given long ago. Thus, the only definite piece of evidence for the royal accession ritual that may be garnered from Psalm 2 is the ritual adoption of the king and the promise of the defeat of enemies. It is unclear why these elements are not clearly reflected in any of the historiographical texts surveyed earlier; perhaps the editors of these texts were not interested in the activities of the type of cult-prophet whose activities are probably reflected in Psalm 2.

Psalms 21 and 72 are best treated together since Gunkel had earlier considered them as possibly belonging to the enthronement ritual, but later considered them as commemorating the anniversary of royal accession. The exact genre of each psalm is difficult to determine, but each contains a petition to God to grant to the king typical royal desires, such as long life and victory (Psalm 21) or justice and might (Psalm 72). Such thoughts would be appropriate to many occasions, including the accession, but there is nothing in these psalms to indicate that the accession must be their setting. Gunkel's later position should also be rejected since there is no hard evidence that a royal anniversary was celebrated. We know little of the role played by the royal singers—perhaps these two psalms are the remnants of the corpus of royal songs typically sung before the king.

J.-B. Dumortier (1972) has suggested that the first half of Psalm 89 is 'Un Rituel d'intronisation'. The article, however, never argues in detail that the psalm need be a ritual. The author infers its ritual status from vv. 16-19, which he considers a liturgical fragment, reflecting the autumnal coronation of the king (pp. 182-85, 192). However, these verses do not share the form of a ritual. In contrast to Psalm 118 which has vocabulary which is clearly ritual in nature (cf. vv. 2-4 and 24), nothing in Psalm 89 indicates that it is transpiring during the ritual of coronation; therefore it should not be considered in this context.

Psalm 110 is often considered to be an enthronement psalm. Anderson (1983, II:767) entitles it 'The Enthronement of the King'. It is one of the most difficult psalms; v. 3 is nearly unintelligible in its present form (see Cooke, 1961:218-24), it is often difficult to determine to whom a particular verse is referring (see Gilbert and Pisano, 1980), and several unusual expressions adorn the psalm.[20] The psalm's interpretation becomes even more difficult to evaluate when considering its prominent place in traditional exegesis, especially within Christian circles (Fitzmyer, 1963 and Hay, 1973).

A complete exegesis of Psalm 110 is impossible here; instead a general interpretation of the psalm, with an emphasis on the question of its *Sitz-im-Leben*, will be attempted. The psalm's concern is military victory; each verse except for v. 4 contains battle allusions. Its theme is that the king can only be victorious with divine help. This is said explicitly (vv. 1, 2a) and is accomplished literarily by blending references to divine help with those of royal power. Furthermore, God and the king literarily switch places: in v. 1 the king is at God's right while in v. 5 God is at the king's right. The predominance of military references in the psalm suggests that the dawn of a battle is its most likely *Sitz-im-Leben* (Dahood, 1970).

Nothing in Psalm 110 decisively indicates a coronation setting for the psalm as a whole or for any of its parts. This contrasts with Ps. 2:7, which says אני היום ילדתיך, 'I have fathered you today'. No word equivalent to היום, 'today' is found in Psalm 110. Many scholars see enthronement imagery in v. 1, ישׁב, 'be seated, enthroned', but given the psalm's general imagery, v. 1 should be understood as: sit here and relax while I, God, do the hard work for you and trample your enemies.[21] No enthronement is mentioned; rather the image of a throne and footstool is invoked to express easy victory. Verse 2 follows up this image by mentioning divine help and royal victory. Verse 3 is too difficult to interpret with any certainty—it seems to be a bridge between vv. 2 and 4 by referring to military (עמך נדבת, 'your army comes forth willingly')[22] and sacral (קרשׁ, 'holiness') matters. The end of v. 3, לך טל ילדתיך is very difficult. Even if MT, 'your youth' is changed according to some of the versions to 'I begat you', we need not understand this verse as transpiring on the day of enthronement. In theme it might parallel Ps. 2:7b, but it lacks the decisive word היום, 'today'. Verse 4 is an oracle of confidence to the king, which assures him of God's care by noting the royal function as priest. The exact sense of the end of v. 4, על־דברתי מלכי־צדק remains unclear. If מלכי־צדק refers to the Melchizedek known from Gen. 14:18-19, too little is known about that individual to judge what a priesthood like Melchizedek's meant in ancient Israel. Alternately, מלכי־צדק may be understood as 'O righteous king.' The *yod* of מלכי־צדק (following the medieval Jewish tradition[23] and some moderns) represents an old construct ending (cf. Gesenius, 1974 §90 l), as in דברתי of the same verse. Verses 5-7 return to the motif of 1-2, divine aid helping the king in battle. Indeed, it is unclear where in these verses the portrayal shifts from the divine warrior to the human royal warrior. Verse 7, however, clearly refers to the human king who is expected to be victorious, and is portrayed as a victor drinking during battle (Gilbert and Pisano, 1980:355), winning the battle as an exalted[24] king. There is no compelling reason to connect this battle to the Zion motif and then to the coronation; therefore, this psalm should be understood as a royal psalm of encouragement to the king before battle. This suggested *Sitz im Leben* represents a break with an important tradition within biblical scholarship that used Psalm 110 as a major text in reconstructing the ancient Israelite coronation ritual. This position, represented in different forms by Dürr (1929), Widengren (1955:44-49), Mowinckel (1956:63-64) and Kraus (1966:222-24) must be rejected.

This survey has shown that the only material to be added to the chart on page 131 is the recitation of a portion of the Davidic promise and an assurance of military victory. The absence of an explicit reference to these elements in the historiographic books is an important warning, suggesting that the coronation ritual may not be reconstructed using historiographical texts alone; however, the complexity involved in Psalm exegesis does not allow that picture of coronation to be modified in any substantial fashion.

The Enthronement of God in the Psalms: An Introduction

One of the most difficult problems of Psalms' scholarship is evaluating the extent to which the rituals surrounding the enthronement of kings were projected on to God, and whether these projections function on the literary or on the cultic plane (see Sarna's summary in Buttenweiser, 1969:xxiv-xxvii). The dispute over this question is reflected in the opposite opinions of the two early form critics of Psalms. Gunkel ([1930] 1967:36-37) stated:

> One such transformation [=loss of the original 'pure' form] is seen for example, in the songs celebrating Yahweh's enthronement, in which the characteristic expression is 'Yahweh has become king' (an example is Psalm 97). Such psalms praise Yahweh's dominion and are thus imitations of the Royal Psalms which were customarily sung at the enthronement of the earthly king but then, under

prophetic influence, were transformed into songs heralding the
coming dominion of Yahweh.

Thus, Gunkel claims that the enthronement motifs in Psalms
referring to God reflect a literary development rather than cultic
reality.[25] Mowinckel in his *Psalmstudien II: Das Thronbesteigungsfest
Jahwës und der Ursprung der Eschatologie* ([1930] 1961) devoted over
two hundred pages to disproving Gunkel's position.[26] Mowinckel
again strenuously defended this position thirty years later in his
Offersang og Sangoffer, which was revised and translated as *The
Psalms in Israel's Worship* ([1961] 1979). There he states:

> What the poets have seen in their imagination, and describe or
> allude to, is an event and an act which was linked with an
> enthronement, Yahweh's ascent to the throne (I, 107).
>
> Everything contained in the enthronement psalms, then, gives
> the strongest impression of belonging to the actual present (I,
> 111).
>
> In the cultic festival, past, present and future are wedded
> together into one (I, 113).
>
> At the 'enthronement festival'—as we may primarily call it—
> ancient Israel witnessed Yahweh's arrival as king, when he literally
> founded his kingdom (I, 113).

This synthesis of Mowinckel still commands great support. One
more recent advocate of this position is Gottlieb (1980:63), who
examines the current state of Psalm study within the Myth and
Ritual School:

> A number of psalms belong within the context of the New Year
> Festival. The events which feature in these psalms. . . were events
> in the cultic drama of the New Year Festival. Thus when we read in
> a number of psalms (e.g. 47; 93; 95-100) of Yahweh's enthronement,
> there is reference to a performance which was actually enacted in
> the temple. The enthronement of Yahweh was not primarily either
> an event of the primeval era which the worshippers tried to
> recapture, or something that was expected at the end of days.
> Yahweh's enthronement was primarily an event that was exper-
> ienced 'now' in the cultic drama of the New Year Festival.

The subsequent history of the positions articulated by Gunkel and
Mowinckel is very complex, and no consensus has been reached
within contemporary scholarship on who is correct. In a 140 page
survey of the problem, Lipiński concluded (1962:272; cf. Welten,
1982), 'Comme on le voit, le problème du *Sitz im Leben* précis des

psaumes de la royauté de Yahwé n'a pas encore trouvé de solution qui satisfasse vraiment les exégètes'. In a more recent examination of Psalm 47, one of the 'enthronement psalms', Beuken (1981:38) noted, 'the present situation is one of stalemate' because (1) the psalm contains cultic terminology which does not clearly point to one occasion; (2) the relationship between cult and history remains unclear; and (3) the use of the Hebrew tenses has not been adequately explored. These observations could be extended to the 'enthronement psalms' in general.

The largely negative assessments of Lipiński and Beuken are too pessimistic. An examination of these so called 'enthronement psalms' which seek out in detail their relation to the sub-vehicle, the activities surrounding the Israelite king when he ascended the throne, sheds new light on this problem. However, since the interpretation of these psalms is so bound up with the grammatical issues underlying the interpretation of יהוה מלך, 'the LORD has become/is king', this phrase must be explored first.

The Phrase Yahweh Mālāk

A major, if not the major building block of Mowinckel's cultic theory is his insistence on translating יהוה מלך as 'Jahwë is König geworden' (1961:3) or 'Yahweh has become king' (1979, I:107). He defends that translation with three arguments (1979, II:222): (1) the verbal form *mālak* as opposed to the substantive *melek* implies an activity, not a state; (2) although Hebrew verbs may be either ingressive or durative, 'From the point of view of Hebrew psychology and way of thinking the "ingressive" or perhaps rather the active sense is always superior. . . '; (3) the parallel to אבשלם מלך [sic], 'Absalom has become king,' שלמה מלך, 'Solomon has become king' and *mardukma šarru*, 'Marduk has become king' in *Enūma Eliš* IV (cf. ANET p. 66) indicate that the king 'has now "become king" and therefore hereafter reigns'. Each argument is flawed: (1) *mālāk* indeed may be differentiated from *melek* and is correctly classified as a verb, but it is a stative verb (Ulrichson, 1977:364); (2) generalizations concerning Hebrew psychology are difficult to defend (cf. Barr, 1961), and this particular generalization is not adequately backed up with evidence by Mowinckel; (3) the parallels are incorrect: MT reads מלך שלמה, while אבשלום מלך is not found in the Bible and *mardukma šarru* is syntactically a proper noun + an emphatic particle (+ implicit copula) + a noun in the nominative. It differs from the biblical examples which are a proper noun + verb. Furthermore, the function of this phrase in *Enūma Eliš* is not certain, and Mowinckel's assertion that it is 'a type of investiture formula'[27] is unproven. These flaws in the classical formulation of the cultic interpretation do not mean that Mowinckel's position is wrong; rather they suggest that a new investigation of the phrase is in order.

Two grammatical issues have generally been raised in connection with the phrase *yhwh mālāk* (Pss. 93:1; 96:10; 97:1; 99:1): (1) the significance of the verbal form *mālāk* as opposed to the noun *melek* and (2) the significance of the word order of predicate + verb. Finally, it might be significant that the phrase is always written *yhwh mālāk*, as if it were pausal, despite the fact that its attendant accentuation marks are not considered major disjunctive accents. Many of these issues have been addressed in previous studies; what follows begins with a critical evaluation of earlier suggestions.

Michel (1956) completely examines the verbal root *mlk* in its various syntactical uses. His underlying principle is: 'Wo gleiche Satzstellung und gleiche גבר, מהר, חיה ist anzunehmen, dass auch der Sinn des Verbs gleich ist'. Using this principle, יהוה מלך is translated as 'Mit Jahwe verhält es sich so, dass er Königsherrschaft ausübt' or 'Jahwe ist einer, der Königsherrschaft ausübt'. However, Michel's underlying principle is incorrect, and has been sharply criticized by Ulrichson (1977:366), undercutting Michel's analysis. The problem of Michel's model may be illustrated with the following English examples: 'ate' in 'he sat down and ate the appetizer' might be ingressive (namely, indicating that an action is just beginning), while 'ate' in 'he ate potatoes' might be durative (namely, indicating a continuing action), even though 'ate' appears in both sentences in the syntactically equivalent: 'He' + 'eat,' past + direct object. Thus context, and not syntax alone, helps determine the sense of a syntagma (Ulrichson, 1977:366, 368). Ulrichson plausibly suggests that *mālāk* belongs to a class of verbs such as חיה מהר, גבר which have two different Aktionsarten,[28] one durative, another ingressive (p. 362), and in different contexts the perfect might be translated as 'ist König' or 'wurde König' (pp. 365-66). This analysis by Ulrichson is sensitive to current linguistic research and is balanced; it implies that the use of the perfect (rather than the noun) in the phrase *yhwh mālāk* may not be used to decide between the translation 'The LORD has (now) become king' and 'The LORD is king'.[29]

The significance of the word order of *yhwh mālāk* as S(ubject)-P(redicate) has been hotly debated. Koehler (1953) suggested that the unusual order of *yhwh mālāk* implies an emphasis on the subject, that Yahweh and not another god is king, and it should be translated as (p. 188) 'Es ist Jahwä, der König (geworden) ist'. Ridderbos (1954) countered by citing Gesenius §142a: 'In the great majority of instances, however, the position of the subject at the beginning of a verbal-clause... [is used] to describe a state'. Each of these positions is flawed; neither brings together a sufficient number of like cases to develop a general syntactic rule. The correctness of Gesenius §142a is apparent only; almost all of the examples cited there are within a longer narrative and the order S-P is used either to indicate the pluperfect[30] or as the initial clause of the story.[31] The semantic significance of the S-P order has been questioned in the more recent studies of Michel (1956) and Ulrichson (1977). The clue for understanding the syntax of *yhwh mālāk* comes from the study of emphasis in Biblical Hebrew by Muraoka (1985). In discussing the less frequent syntactic order Snom [=Subject, nominative]-V (as opposed to V-Snom), where V is not a converted finite verb, he notes that this order often occurs when the subject is God as a result of 'a kind of religious psychology in which God occupies the dominant place determined the arrangement of words giving S the initial position'. Muraoka's explanation which depends on understanding the Israelite 'religious psychology' may not be correct, but this must be distinguished from his statistical observation that when Snom=God, Snom-V is the usual order. Thus, the noun-first position of *yhwh* in *yhwh mālāk* is a general *stylistic* feature of Biblical Hebrew, and is of no exegetical significance. Although Muraoka's corpus is largely narrative and legal material, a cursory examination indicates the validity of the observation for Psalms as well.[32] Therefore, the subject-predicate order of *yhwh mālāk* need not imply special emphasis on יהוה.

The pausal form of *mālāk* in *yhwh mālāk* has not generally been noted in studies of this phrase; indeed many scholars transliterate this word as *mālak*. The significance of this pausal form is difficult to evaluate because no one has systematically studied when non-major disjunctives cause pausal changes. General comments such as Gesenius §29 i 'Apart from these principle pauses, there are often pausal changes with the lesser disjunctives...' are remarkably unhelpful. The suggestion of Revell (1981:188) that, 'The pausal forms, must, therefore, have been fixed at some time prior to the fixing of the accentuation in its present form' is compelling. This might suggest that the phrase *yhwh mālāk* functioned as a (complete) cultic cry in ancient Israel and was therefore pausal, and MT's vocalization is a fossilized reflection of this use.

The grammatical study of *yhwh mālāk* yields largely negative results: the psalmists' use of the perfect cannot distinguish between the translations 'the LORD is king' and 'the LORD has become king', nor does the syntax suggest that this verse is describing either a general state or a new fact. The pausal form *mālāk* might suggest that *yhwh mālāk*, whatever its original meaning, might have served as a self-sufficient cultic exclamation. Morphological and syntactic considerations alone do not clarify the nuance or function of *yhwh mālāk*, so the existence of Mowinckel's *Thronbesteigungsfest* must be decided using other methods.

Lipiński (1965) devotes over fifty pages to determining the genre of the phrase *yhwh mālāk*, surveying previous opinions that it is a formula of investiture, acclamation, homage and proclamation, concluding that it is a declaration of fidelity (pp. 336-91). Lipiński's survey is comprehensive and useful, but it suffers from two flaws. He examines the function of *yhwh mālāk* by comparing it to syntactically and semantically similar phrases in ancient Near Eastern literature whose function is contextually clear. He tacitly assumes that the same type or form of utterance in different ancient Near Eastern cultures must have the same function. This is false; similar expressions used by different cultures may have different functions because of the inner dynamic of each culture's ritual system. Even if it could be shown that Israel borrowed *yhwh mālāk* from a neighboring civilization, it is uncertain that its use in psalms which probably considerably postdate this borrowing preserves the original usage. Lipiński's second flaw is his strict categorization into five *mutually exclusive* categories. It is certainly possible that an utterance such as מלך אבשלום בחברון, 'Absalom is/has become king in Hebron' or יהוה מלך, 'the LORD is/has become king' could incorporate several of these elements—it could be part of the enthronement ritual, and in that sense a proclamation of investiture, while at the same time acknowledging or proclaiming the king's sovereignty. In that sense it is also a proclamation, a profession of fidelity and perhaps even an acclamation or an act of homage (see Coppens, 1977-78:10). It is best therefore to turn to the so-called 'enthronement psalms' themselves, to see the extent to which context might clarify the proper understanding of the phrase *yhwh mālāk*.

The Enthronement Psalms

The following section is arranged in concentric circles. First, the psalms containing the phrase *yhwh mālāk* will be examined to see whether their contexts can decide between the translations 'the LORD is king' and 'the LORD becomes king'. I will then examine texts with phrases similar to *yhwh mālāk*. Finally, I will attempt to see which of the other rituals of becoming king are projected onto God.

Psalms 93, 96, 97 and 99 contain the phrase *yhwh mālāk*.[33] These psalms can be broken into two groups: 96, 97 and 99 all contain calls to praise God or predictions that he will be praised, while Psalm 93 lacks this element and is a general description of God's strength (see Westermann, 1981:145-51).[34] A 'complete exegesis'[35] of these four psalms is beyond the scope of this study; instead I will tie them into this metaphor study by briefly exploring each psalm's theme and discussing how its description of God might be picking up on the images of the Israelite (earthly) enthronement ceremony.

Psalm 93, the shortest of the 'enthronement psalms', is particularly difficult to exegete. Firmness is clearly the *leitmotiv* of Psalm 93: God has created a 'firm' world (v. 1 תכון תבל בל־תמוט), his throne is 'stable' (v. 2 נכון) and his ordinances are 'firm' (v. 5 נאמנו). This physical firmness is echoed by God's temporal fullness—he is מאז מעולם, 'Of old, from eternity' (v. 2) and he will be לארך ימים, 'for all times' (v. 5). The spatially central image of the psalm is in vv. 3-4, which must hark back to the myth of God conquering the rebelling sea, a myth which can be reconstructed from fragmentary references throughout the Bible (Cassuto, 1972:81 and Lipiński, 1965:123-35, esp. 125, n. 8.). The rabbinic tradition found in the Babylonian Talmud, *Rosh Ha-Shanah* 31a, that this psalm was recited liturgically on Friday, the day active creation was completed by God, coupled with the Psalm's similar superscription in the LXX, further connects this psalm to creation. The use of 'staircase parallelism' in v. 3, perhaps harking back to Canaanite poetic tradition, and the supposed Canaanite vocabulary of the psalm[36] support the suspicion that in this psalm, God has taken over certain aspects of Canaanite[37] deities. Perhaps, following a hypothesis of Cross (1973:174-94) that Yahweh has assimilated several characteristics of Baal, this psalm may be based on a poem in which Baal, as vanquisher of Yamm, becomes king (CTA 4.4.41-44). If the background of the psalm is God's defeat of enemies, it is natural to interpret verse 1aα, יהוה מלך

as 'God *has become* king', in which the perfect reflects the psalmist placing himself at the end of the 'mythological period', when God had finally asserted himself over his enemies, becoming king.

However, the psalm presents a paradox: although it opens with a statement that God becomes king as a result of this victory, the image of v. 2 ('Your throne stands firm from then, from eternity...') implies that he has always been king. This verse seems to undercut the myth which is about to be obliquely introduced—it is saying that despite the little power struggle or interregnum, God has always been king. The verse revises God's *becoming* king gradually—its first temporal word is מאז, 'from then', which to the reader would initially mean the time of God's defeat of the enemies; the referent of מאז, 'from then' is revised by the following parallel מעולם, 'always', implying a God who always 'was' and never 'became' king. A similar rhetorical use of מעולם, 'from eternity', redefining מאז, 'from then', is found in Prov. 8:22b and 23a.

Perhaps this conflict may be resolved on the textual level, by assuming that v. 2 is secondary, and was inserted to piously argue that God's kingship was never really threatened, undercutting the ancient Canaanite myth. Two factors might support the secondary nature of verse 2: (1) In terms of subject matter, v. 3 reads much better after v. 1; (2) In MT vv. 1, 2, 4, 5, are all composed of tricola while only v. 2 is a bicolon. However, these criteria are not wholly objective, so it is not certain that v. 2 is a later addition.

Certain additional elements of the enthronement ritual are reflected in this psalm: God's throne is mentioned (v. 2) after the formula *yhwh mālāk*, probably reflecting the king's ascent to the throne which was the culmination of the royal ritual, the scene is quite noisy (vv. 3-4), and laws, which formed a part of the royal ceremony, are mentioned (v. 5).[38] Especially if verse 2 is secondary, these elements combined with the likely mythological background of the psalm favor rendering (v. 1) יהוה מלך as 'the LORD has become king'. Perhaps a unified reading of this psalm, combining (the possibly secondary) v. 2 ('... from then, from eternity...') with the imagery of the rest of the psalm is meant to imply that despite God's defeat of enemies in 'mythological times' through which he became king, he really always was the firm and strong king.

Psalms 96, 97 and 99, the remaining three psalms with the formula *yhwh mālāk*, belong together because they share a common general structure of calls (in the imperative or jussive) to worship God or to rejoice before him, and they give justifications for these actions.

From the perspective of this study, the central problem of these psalms is that this call in never addressed specifically to Israel, but is always addressed to the nations.[39] In what sense, in which contexts and in what time-period could the nations be asked to praise the God of Israel?

The notion that non-Israelite nations should praise God is not unique to this group of 'enthronement psalms', but the psalms which purport such a notion are not all of the same mold. A cursory examination of Psalm 117, the shortest psalm in the Psalter, is a useful starting point for examining this concept. The theology of Psalm 117 is unusual: non-Israelite nations are called upon to praise God (v. 1) because he has bestowed his חסד, 'steadfast love' upon Israel, and is always אמת, 'faithful' in the sense of fulfilling an agreement (v. 2). Linguistic factors suggest that this psalm must be post-exilic (Hurvitz, 1972:169-70). Therefore, it is reasonable to connect Psalm 117 to the theology represented by Deutero-Isaiah, specifically the notion developed in Isaiah 45:20ff., that the nations should acknowledge God because he has correctly predicted the salvation of Israel (see Haran, 1963).

Buttenweiser (1969:358-61) correctly sensed the tenor of Psalm 117 and dated it to the early post-exilic period. It clearly reflects the return to Zion; the term חסד, 'steadfast love' refers to God's redemptive acts of remembering his covenant with Israel (Isa. 54:8,10), and אמת, 'faithfulness' refers to the fulfillment of God's earlier prophecies of restoration, a major theme of Deutero-Isaiah. In the exilic period, a time shaken by the overthrow of the great Babylonian empire, a period in which Babylonian and Israelite priests could counter each others' claim that their god brought Cyrus (Tadmor, 1964), I can imagine a poet infused with ideas known from Deutero-Isaiah who would dare to claim that the liberation of Israel constitutes the proof for the claim that Israel's God should be recognized by all.

I intentionally avoid the term 'universalism' in this discussion. The term is used in many different ways; Ringgrenn (1966) seems to be aware of the problem, and distinguishes between the types of universalism presumed by Amos (p. 265), Second Isaiah (p. 292) and Jonah (pp. 305-306). Many scholars continue to use 'universalism' in a vague undefined sense, and insist that it typifies post-exilic texts only (e.g. Clements, 1982:40 on Isaiah 2). Kaufmann (1972a:228-29) sees both the universal and nationalistic tendencies as original to the beginning of Israelite religion, and claims that Isaiah 2 is the composition of Isaiah son of Amoz. Kaufmann (1972b: II 461) claims emphatically: 'The desire to break out of the national realm permeated the depths of Israelite religion even in the ancient period'. He further notes that pre-prophetic universalism may be found in certain psalms (1972b:II, 723). Thus, 'universalism' may not be used to date biblical material.

The theology of Psalms 96, 97 and 99 is different from Psalm 117; it lacks the equivalent of the nationalistic 117:2 כי גבר עלינו חסדו, 'for great is his steadfast love toward us'. In Psalm 96, God should be praised for his greatness, his acts as creator and his royal qualities. In Psalm 97 the nations should rejoice and pay obeisance before God who appears in a theophany and is the all-powerful God of justice. Ps. 99:1-5[40] insists on praise because of God's just nature. None of these psalms exhibit signs of post-exilic Hebrew diction (Hurvitz, 1972 and Qimron, 1978). It is difficult to believe that they could all date from the period of Deutero-Isaiah (or even later according to Lipiński, 1965:268 and Jeremias, 1987) and exhibit no signs of Late Biblical Hebrew, especially in areas of syntax. Furthermore, with one exception, all the psalms that according to linguistic criteria (Hurvitz, 1972) are clearly post-exilic are found in the fifth book of the Psalter (107-150). That book also contains the two psalms whose contents force us to assume that they are exilic or post-exilic (126, 137). This would suggest a gradual editing of the Psalter, in which books 1-4 were largely completed by the exile. Therefore, Psalms 96, 97 and 99, which are in the fourth book of the Psalter, are probably pre-exilic. Contrary to the contention of Buttenweiser (1969:317-40) and others (e.g. Feuillet, 1951, Westermann, 1981:146-47), they do not show the influence of Deutero-Isaiah.[41] Rather, these psalms and Deutero-Isaiah are 'from the same tradition' (Mettinger, 1986-87:157). Contrary to most scholars, the 'universalism' exhibited in these psalms need not be post-exilic. How then should these pre-exilic calls to the nations to follow Yahweh be understood? Is there a possible cultic reality which stands behind them? In other words, would these compositions have been recited to a foreign audience as part of the Temple ritual?

It is very difficult to reconstruct a clear picture of the role the spoken word played in pre-exilic Israel, since very few rituals are described with accompanying words (e.g. Lev. 16:1 and Deut. 26:3-10, 13-15). Post-biblical evidence suggesting that the new year festival is directly connected with God's kingship and certain 'enthronement psalms' (e.g. Mowinckel, 1961:82 and 1979:122-23) is separated from the biblical period by many centuries and may not be automatically retrojected backwards (Rosenthal, 1958:2). The Mesopotamian evidence frequently adduced to support the centrality of the recitation of religious works dealing with the enthronement of gods at the new year festival (Mowinckel, 1961:32; 1979:135) has been strongly questioned (Tadmor, 1976 and Welten, 1982). Thus, there is no clear evidence that psalms such as 96, 97 and 99 had a central, cultic role in pre-exilic Israel.

It is important to evaluate whether biblical evidence suggests that in the pre-exilic period a cultic festival connected to the enthronement of God would call for foreign participation in the ritual. In discussing laws pertaining to the use of blemished animals for sacrifices, Lev. 22:25a notes: ומיד בן־נכר לא תקריבו את־לחם אלהיכם מכל־אלה, 'nor shall you accept such animals from a foreigner for food offering as food for your God', indicating that in certain circumstances a non-Israelite could bring a sacrifice. The dating of this passage depends on the date assigned to P and H.[42] A section in Solomon's prayer in 1 Kgs 8:41-43 also implies that foreigners could worship at the Temple, but this section is an exilic addition (Levenson, 1981) and may not be used to reconstruct earlier practices. In 2 Kings 8, the story of Naaman's cure from leprosy, the opposite tendency is visible—the foreigner worships God on 'Israelite soil' imported to a foreign land. In any case, it is reasonable to assume that this story was originally of Northern Israelite provenience (Rofé, 1982:108-10), so it has no bearing on the participation of foreigners in the Jerusalem Temple cult. The evidence for foreign participation in the Temple cult is thus very limited, especially when compared to the wide variety of sources noting this practice in the Second Temple period (Safrai, 1972:979).[43] If this practice were prevalent in biblical times, we would expect to find it explicitly referred to more often, since it would support the biases and interests of many pre-exilic sources by glorifying God, Jerusalem and the Temple. The lack of a contingent of non-Israelites at the Temple presents a serious problem for our understanding of the pre-exilic Psalms 96, 97 and 99 as 'enthronement psalms' reflecting a ceremony in which non-Israelites are enjoined to worship at the Temple. Israelite enthronement psalms, if they existed, would be expected to emphasize more directly God's sovereignty over Israel (see Ps. 117:2), and would have called on all of Israel to praise God as their king.

How then might these calls for rejoicing in Psalms 96, 97 and 99 be understood? Gunkel interpreted them as 'songs heralding the coming dominion of Yahweh', as 'prophetic, eschatological poetry' (1967:37; cf. Gunkel-Begrich, 1933:94-116). This position has been elaborated upon by Feuillet (1951). This characterization is wrong, since the events portrayed in these poems are not depicted using the typical terms for the eschatological future (ביום ההוא, 'in that day' or באחרית הימים, 'in the days to come'). Furthermore, it is difficult to evaluate the use of prefix (*Yaqtul*) forms of the verbs in Psalms 96, 97 and 99; it is unclear if they should be parsed as imperfects, implying an incomplete or future action, or as jussives. For example, should (96:11) ישמחו השמים be translated 'the heavens will rejoice' (favoring Gunkel) or 'may the heavens rejoice'?[44] Given the absence of explicit eschatological terminology, I would suggest that context favors that these verbal forms should be parsed as jussives.

I understand these psalms as a (wishful) *projection* into the present of a period in which God is sovereign, and his sovereignty is recognized by all, allowing Israel to live in peace and prosperity. The composer(s) of these psalms were faced by attitudes similar to those encountered by the author of the Gideon passage in Judg. 6:13, ויש יהוה עמנו, 'Is the LORD really with us?' In Judges a narrative was composed to prove that God was imminent, יש יהוה עמנו, 'God is with us'. These psalms accomplish the same goal of reshaping reality by claiming that the popular perception of God's inactivity is incorrect— יהוה מלך, 'the LORD is/has become king'. A similar position has been advocated by Weiss (1987, 192), who says in reference to Psalm 47: 'The psalmist, in his spiritual vision sees the fulfillment of his longing for the day in which "The LORD alone shall be exalted" (Isa. 2:11, 17)'.

Projection of a desire of divine imminence as historical reality was well-known in ancient Israel, and was a major factor involved in the creative rewriting of historiography in the biblical period. An extreme example of this was when the events of 701, the reduction of the Judaean state by Sennacherib were written to emphasize the great salvation of Jerusalem and the miraculous defeat of the Assyrian army (see esp. 2 Kgs 19:35). A 'historian' has turned a humiliation at the hands of the Assyrians to a humiliation of the Assyrians by God. Such a text serves as powerful internal propoganda. Garbini (1988) has powerfully argued that ideology and theology typically shaped history-writing in ancient Israel, with historical writings often acting as a type of nationalistic encouragement. Thus, some thinkers within ancient Israel used theology to shape 'history'. Psalms 96, 97 and 99 function similarly: the psalmist(s) insists that יהוה מלך, 'the LORD is/has become king', although historical reality would seem to the contrary. The psalmist(s) of these three psalms has been influenced by the 'Zion traditions' especially as known to us in the pre-exilic Isa. 2:2-4 and Mic. 4:1-3 (see Wildberger, 1972:88-90 and Hillers, 1984:53) which stress the acknowledgement of God as *judge of all nations*, but this eschatological vision has been projected into the present. This is the matrix in which these psalms should be understood.

The interpretation of the phrase *yhwh mālāk* in each psalm depends on the extent to which the psalmist is seen as identifying with the non-Israelites, who are only now seeing God's sovereignty. It might also be appropriate to see if kingship imagery in the psalm is specifically enthronement related (see the chart above, on p. 131), which would suggest 'the LORD has become king', or is predominantly general, which would suggest 'the LORD is king'.

Psalm 96 shares the elements of joy (vv. 11a, 12) and noise (v. 11b, possibly vv. 1-2) with coronations, and might include the element of the recitation of God's past deeds (vv. 5b, 10aβ). These elements are noted as superlatives: the entire land sings to God every day, the entire world, heaven and earth, rejoices (v. 11a), and the usual תרועה, 'noise' is replaced by ירעם הים ומלאו, 'let the sea and all within it thunder' (v. 11b). These possible references to enthronement are balanced by descriptions of God's enduring actions as king, e.g. greatness (v. 4; see above, pp. 71-72), creator (vv. 5b, 10aβ; see above, pp. 116-18), הוד והדר כבוד, words for divine strength (vv. 6-9; see above, pp. 66, 57), bowing (v. 9b; see above, p. 98), fear of him (v. 9b; see above, p. 98) and judge (vv. 10b, 13; see above, pp. 113-16). Psalm 97 is similar to 96, but contains fewer possible references to coronation rituals. Rejoicing, again at a superlative level, is present (v. 1)[45] as is a depiction of God's past great activities (vv. 4-6), but these possible reflections of enthronement are overshadowed by God's general royal attributes, e.g. justice (vv. 2b, 6a, 8b; see above, pp. 113-16), sitting on a throne (v. 2b; see above, pp. 82-85), fear before him (vv. 4-5; see above, p. 98), אדון כל־הארץ, 'master of the whole world' (v. 5b; see above, p. 41), *kbwd* (v. 6b; see above, p. 57), being bowed down to (v. 7b; see above, p. 98) and being supreme (v. 9; see above, p. 72). Psalm 99:1-5 is almost totally lacking in enthronement imagery; only God sitting enthroned (v. 1b)[46] and the recollection of God's past great deeds (v. 4) might recall enthronement. Elements of God's continuing kingship predominate, such as fear (v. 1; see above, p. 98), greatness (vv. 2, 3; see above, pp. 71-72), justice (v. 4; see above, pp. 113-16) and being bowed down to (v. 5; see above, p. 98). To summarize: Psalms 96, 97 and 99 show decreasing amounts of imagery which might be considered as specifically enthronement related, while all three have substantial general kingship motifs. In Psalm 99 it would be difficult to understand יהוה מלך as 'God has become king' since the imagery of being, rather than becoming king predominates so significantly. In Psalms 96 and 97 we have two options: (1) *mālak* may be rendered 'is king' if the references to joy and noise, which reflect enthronement ('becoming king') are allowed to recede into the background; (2) *mālak* may be rendered as 'has become king', and the psalm incorporates images of God from all spheres of kingship, including static images of his enduring qualities as king alongside those of his becoming king. The second option is more likely, although 'becoming king' is less prominent in Psalm 96 and 97 than in Psalm 93.

Gerald Wilson (1984:340-344) has shown that psalms belonging to the same genre are often grouped together. This further supports the contention that Psalms 93-99, with the exception of 94 which form-critically is a lament of the individual (Westermann, 1981:257), should be grouped together, perhaps as 'enthronement psalms' (Mowinckel, 1979:I 106). I will briefly analyze Psalms 95 and 98 to see how they might bear on the issue of God's enthronement. I will begin with Psalm 98 since it is more similar to Psalms 96, 97 and 99 in terms of vocabulary and structure.

Psalm 98 begins with imperatives that closely resemble Psalm 96 and ends almost identically to it. These similarities are probably evoked by a 'common cultic situation' (Anderson, 1983:II 690; cf. Culley, 1967), but need not imply common authorship (contra Jefferson, 1952). Like Psalm 96, it notes God's kingship approximately two-thirds of the way through the psalm rather than at its outset. Like the *yhwh mālak* psalms, it is the nations who are called on to praise God. Enthronement rituals might be reflected in the recollection of God's past deeds (vv. 1-3), which lead up to a total (v. 4 כל־הארץ, 'the whole earth'; v. 7 הים ומלאו תבל וישבי בה, 'the sea and all that is in it, the world and its inhabitants') noisy acclamation of God as king and universal joy (vv. 4, 8b). Many of the phrases could reflect human coronation rituals (v. 4 הריעו, 'raise a shout', v. 6 חצצרות, שופר, הריעו, 'trumpets, horn, raise shout'; v. 8 ימחאו־כף, 'clap hands'). However, we again encounter the problem that these phrases might reflect general exclamations of joy at God being (rather than becoming) king, i.e. his being a victorious war-leader

(vv. 1b-3) and just (v. 9). Much will depend on the unresolvable problem of translating *bā'* in v. 9. If it is taken as a perfect in the sense of 'has (just) come', (and ישפט is a jussive, 'may he judge',) the enthronement imagery would be foregrounded, but if it is taken as an active participle, 'coming,' (and ישפט is an imperfect, 'he will judge',) the coronation imagery would be weakened. Therefore, it is difficult to know the extent to which this psalm specifically reflects 'enthronement' rather than being king.

Psalm 95 is exceptional because the opening call to praise God is not addressed to foreign nations and the body of the psalm is clearly addressed to the Israelites (vv. 6-7; contrast 96:9 and 97:7). It would be especially significant if it contained references to enthroning God, since it might then indicate that the *Israelites* enthroned him in an actual ritual rather than merely projecting into the present the hope for his kingship. However, the only possible reference to enthronement rituals in this psalm is to noisemaking (vv. 1-2). The note that God is king reads (v. 3) כי אל גדול יהוה ומלך גדול על־כל־אלהים, 'For the LORD is a great God, the great king of all divine beings'. It lacks the phrase *yhwh mālāk* and is very general, and does not reflect God having just become king. General kingship imagery is reflected in the images of God as creator (vv. 4-5; see above, pp. 116-18) and bowing down before God (v. 6; see above, p. 98). Psalm 95 celebrates God's kingship and not his enthronement.

To summarize: this analysis of Psalms 93, 95-99 has suggested that individual psalms might be called 'enthronement psalms' with various degrees of assurance. That label is most appropriate to 93, where God is enthroned after defeating enemies who might have been vying for his throne, and possibly to 96 and 98, which contain several motifs borrowed from the human enthronement ritual. However, even in these psalms there is ambiguity as to whether the psalmist is envisaging God as becoming king, or as king, depending on whether the perspective is from the nations, who are *only now* seeing the great extent of God's sovereignty, or from the Israelites, who *always* knew that God is sovereign. In either case, the fact that the call is addressed to non-Israelites suggests that these were not cultic psalms in which God was ritually (re-)enthroned. Contrary to Mowinckel's claim, Psalms 93-99 do not belong together because they form the backbone of an annual ritual; rather they share common vocabulary, motifs and styles and were edited together for that reason.[47] Since they picture God as king, and might, to varying degrees, portray his becoming king, I follow Anderson (1983:33-35) who gives this group of psalms the ambiguous title 'Psalms Celebrating the Kingship of Yahweh'.

Psalms 81 and 47 have often been considered 'enthronement psalms'. Psalm 81 is especially important for the reconstruction of the putative enthronement festival because many scholars (e.g. Mowinckel, 1979:I 124; Kraus, 1961:563-65; Anderson, 1983:586-87) claim that verse 4 (תקעו בחדש שופר בכסה ליום חגנו, 'Blow the horn on the new moon, on the *ksh* for our feast day') explicitly refers to the new year. This follows the rabbinic interpretation of this psalm (Seeligmann, 1980/81:25). However, v. 4 is quite unclear—*ksh* in that spelling is hapax, and although it might be connected to the *ks'* of Prov. 7:20, that context does little to clarify its meaning. Specifically, it is uncertain whether *ksh/'* refers to the full moon (e.g. Kirkpatrick, 1902:489; Snaith, 1947:99-100; Kraus, 1961:563; Baumgartner, 1974:463-464; Anderson, 1983:586-87), in which case 81:4 refers to two different festivals, or whether it refers to the new moon, i.e. when the moon is covered (so ibn Ezra ad loc., cf. Levy, 1876-89:361 s.v. כסא, כסה,) in which case one festival is described. Although according to later Jewish tradition, the month began with the new crescent (see Mishnah *Rosh Ha-Shanah*, esp. chapters 1-2), there is no indication that this was the case in the biblical period. Perhaps as in ancient Egypt (Parker, 1950:9-23), the new month began at conjunction, when the moon was 'covered'. Thus, 'new moon' is a legitimate and even likely translation for *ksh*. Furthermore, it is unclear if בחדש refers to an annual festival or should be rendered 'every new moon' (see Gesenius, 1974 §208 g), in which case the blowing of the horn is connected to the monthly new moon festival, which is clearly important in pre-exilic Israel, although we have little information about how it was celebrated.[48] Verse 2 might be modeled after the enthronement (joy and הריעו, 'raise a shout'), but it should be noted that the musical instruments listed in v. 3 are never among those used in the royal ritual. Given the ambiguities of v. 4, the paucity of possible parallels to human enthronement, and the fact that after v. 4 there are no thematic or verbal connections to rituals surrounding the enthronement of human kings, this psalm should not be considered an enthronement psalm.

Psalm 47 shares much in common with 96-99—it opens with an imperative addressed to non-Israelites commanding them to acknowledge God, it contains possible references to elements of the human enthronement ritual, and states in v. 9: מלך אלהים על-גוים, 'God reigns over the nations' which is similar to *yhwh mālāk*. It contains more possible references to elements of the enthronement ritual than any other psalm. These are: noise (esp. vv. 2, 6), joy (v. 2b), at least one reference to sitting on the throne (v. 9b; possibly v. 6, עלה, 'ascend') and it even mentions the witnesses of the enthronement (v. 10). The *mlk* formula (v. 9 מלך אלהים על-גוים, 'God reigns over the nations') syntactically parallels the human X מלך, 'X reigns' formula, suggesting that the psalmist might be consciously patterning God's enthronement after human enthronement. The unusually large amount of enthronement imagery in this psalm has been previously noted by Gelston (1966:511) and Weiss (1987:187-88)' and Kraus (1966:204-205) claims that only in this psalm may we speak of 'Thronbesteigungsakt'. Given the placement of Psalm 47 in the Elohistic Psalter, and not with the cluster of Pss. 93-99, it is not surprising to see that it differs substantially from the other 'enthronement psalms'. God's accession to the throne in Psalm 47 is totally superlative: all nations make noise (v. 2), God is a universal king (vv. 3, 8, 9) and the important officers of many nations gather to attend the coronation (v. 10). Certain general royal qualities such as being a war-leader (vv. 4-5), supreme (vv. 3, 10b; see above, p. 72) and a מגן, 'shield' (v. 10b; see above, p. 46) are attributed to God, but images associated with becoming king predominate in number and structure over those of God being king. This suggests that the phrase *mālak 'ĕlōhîm 'al gôyîm* should be rendered 'God has (now) shown himself as king over the nations' (see Seeligmann, 1980/ 81:33). However, there are no indications of any cultic underpinnings for this exclamation; like Psalms 96, 97 and 99, it reflects a projection or wish, not a cultic celebration.

Two prophetic texts use phraseology similar to *yhwh mālāk* to represent God acting in his role as king. Isa. 52:7, speaking of God's role as the restorer of Israel to Zion, tells of a messenger speaking to Zion, *mālak 'ĕlōhāyik*. The pericope refers to joy (vv. 8, 9) and noise (v. 8aα), and seems to recall terminology of God defeating his mythological enemies,[49] after which he became king. In this context of God redeeming Israel from its exile and rebuilding Jerusalem, the sense of *mālak 'ĕlōhāyik* is God acting as king by showing his power in redeeming Israel. It might be rendered 'God has really or finally become your king' (Stuhlmueller, 1970:34 and Klein, 1978:131), i.e. the metaphor no longer represents a projection but is a reality. Zeph. 3:15 is beset with textual difficulties. However, whether we read with MT מֶלֶך ישראל, 'the king of Israel' or we follow the Lucianic family of LXX mss., and read the verb 'reigns' and delete Israel,[50] the vocabulary and image are very close to Isaiah 52. Israel should rejoice (v. 14aα) and make noise הריעו (v. 14aβ) because God has arrived as righteous king. The verbs in Isaiah and Zephaniah are in the perfect; in Zephaniah they are prophetic perfects, referring to ביום ההוא, 'in that day' (v. 16),[51] while in Second Isaiah, the perfect is used to narrate completed (past) events. Therefore, although these two prophetic pericopes share vocabulary and stylistic elements with the psalm passages previously analyzed, the stance of the psalm and the prophetic material is different. The perfect in the psalms indicates a future action projected into the present; in Zephaniah it indicates a definite future action and in Second Isaiah a completed past/present action. Despite this important difference, the sense of *mlk* (perfect) is similar—God is no longer otiose, he is again acting like a king. To the extent that this new royal action is similar to the power that a human king gains upon accession, terminology of accession (יהוה מלך, 'the LORD is/has become king' and its variants) and the populace's reaction to the accession (joy, noise) are at home in these texts.

If I am correct in assuming that the confluence of יהוה מלך, 'the LORD is/has become king' and the images associated with it that also appear in human coronation (e.g. joy, noise) reflect the *recognition* (rather than the cultic *realization*) of God's kingship, it is possible that at times elements of the enthronement ritual without reference to the יהוה מלך formula may be used for the same purpose. This is probably the case when shouting and rejoicing are associated with the manifestation of God's power, as in Isa. 12:6 צהלי ורני יושבת ציון כי־גדול בקרבך קרוש ישראל, 'Oh, shout for joy, you who dwell in Zion, for great in your midst is the holy one of Israel', Isa. 44:23 רנו שמים כי־עשה יהוה הריעו תחתיות ארץ פצחו הרים רנה יער וכל־עץ בו, 'Shout, O heavens, for the LORD has acted; shout aloud, O depths of the earth, shout for joy, O mountains, O forests with all your trees', Zech. 2:14 רני ושמחי בת־ציון כי הנני־בא, 'Shout for joy, fair Zion, for I am coming' and Ps. 100:1 הריעו ליהוה כל הארץ, 'raise a shout for the LORD, all the earth'. The content, tone and general royal imagery of these contexts allows the rejoicing or noisemaking to be seen as part of a new recognition of God's sovereignty, and in that sense, his (re-)enthronement. However, since shouting and rejoicing are not confined to enthronement rituals in the Bible, it is difficult to state unequivocally that the image of God as newly enthroned stands behind these passages.

Conclusions

This section has explored the extent to which the rituals surrounding the enthronement of the human king were projected on to God and what these projections might imply. The following tentative conclusions may be offered. The phrases יהוה מלך, 'the LORD is/has become king' and מלך אלהים, 'God is/has become king' and their variants reflect the enthronement formula X מלך, 'X is/has become king' which is used in certain human coronations. Only in Psalm 93 does the phrase appear in a context which clearly parallels its human counterpart—there God ascends the throne as a newly enthroned king after a victory against adversaries. However, at least in its final form, this psalm suggests a counter-image, of God as king from eternity and until perpetuity. When the phrase 'God is/has become king' is used in other psalms (96, 97, 98, 99), there is no trace of an image of God ascending the throne after a mythological victory. These psalms all portray foreigners acknowledging God, which probably cannot reflect a cultic reality. This suggests that the phrase יהוה מלך, 'God is/has become king' is a projection of the desire of God's sovereignty as a reality, placed in mouth the of foreigners who are viewed as accepting God's yoke. In that sense, from the foreigner's perspective, God is becoming king. Various elements of the human enthronement ritual, such as joy and noise and in one case a list of those witnessing the coronation (Ps. 47:10), are therefore incorporated into these psalms alongside general divine royal qualities. These enthronement subrituals are often expressed in superlative terms, reflecting the great extent of God's kingship; everyone accepts his sovereignty and the joy at his accession extends to nature itself. This is consistent with what we have seen in the other chapters.

According to this interpretation, no specific cultic festival stands behind the call יהוה מלך, 'the LORD is/has become king' as it appears in Psalms. Mowinckel's thesis is based upon a faulty set of interpretations of this phrase. He connects this phrase to a New Year Festival on the basis of an uncertain exegesis of the ambiguous Ps. 81:4. His attempt to connect nearly one-third of the Psalter to one particular *Sitz im Leben*, an attempt effected in a different way by Kraus (1951), who creates a 'königliches Zionfest', is interesting but not compelling. Neither Mowinckel nor his followers can bring sufficient proof from non-Psalm texts for a *Thronebesteigungsfest Jahwe*, nor has anyone explained why the psalms that are central to this festival would particularly emphasize the acceptance of God's sovereignty by the nations rather than by Israel. Until these problems are adequately addressed, Mowinckel's hypothesis is best rejected.

Within the framework of a study of the metaphor 'God is king', it is important to see which aspects of the human enthronement ritual are carried over to God. Certain aspects could not be transferred, e.g. God could not say to himself בני אתה, 'you are my son' nor could the old king bless him. Certain rituals such as the placing of the crown and riding on a mule were probably excluded because of the aniconic nature of Israelite religion (see above, pp. 73 and 78). Oil is never mentioned in the divine enthronement texts. Perhaps anointing was such a central portion of the performative ritual of kingship, that if it were transferred, people would have actually believed that God went through a *rite de passage*, only now (re-)becoming king. The 'Psalms Celebrating the Kingship of Yahweh' function on the literary and not the literal plane; had an oil ritual been involved, the distinction between literary and literal might have been broken, and the Israelites might have thought that God is not eternal king, but becomes king.

CONCLUSIONS

The Hebrew Bible insists that God is the 'incomparable one' (Labuschagne, 1966). If this claim were taken seriously on the level of language in ancient Israel, the vocabulary used of God in the Bible would be unique to him. There is some movement in that direction; for example, the second word of the Bible, *bārā'*, usually translated 'created', is only used of God in the Bible, thus suggesting that his action as ברא שמים וארץ, 'creator of heavens and earth', differs from any type of human creative activity.[1] It is precisely the lack of use of *bārā'* with human referents, namely its *un*metaphorical nature, that makes its translation so difficult. If the entire vocabulary used of God were distinct to him, he would be 'incomparable', but also not grounded in human experiences, and therefore, not understandable. For this reason, biblical rhetoric uses language typically belonging to the human sphere and applies it to God. These uses may be considered metaphorical because the biblical God does not generally possess these human attributes in their usual form. For example, the Israelite king is crowned and is part of a dynasty; God as king lacks these qualities. Metaphor becomes a major tool, if not the major tool, used to describe God in Israel. The metaphor gains its usefulness by applying ideas and terms familiar from everyday use to depict God (see Sawyer, 1972:53-54). Furthermore, since by its very nature a metaphor 'A is B' does not imply that A and B are the same in all respects,[2] the use of metaphorical language of God does not conflict with the notion of his incomparability.

Some metaphors are infrequent and are used only in very specific situations, while others are used often and are fundamental to the language of a society. The metaphor 'God is king' is in this second category. Its use is largely coterminous with the biblical period,[3] and it is invoked both explicitly, through the use of the root *mlk*, 'to be king' and implicitly, by projecting entailments of human kingship (e.g. enthroned, resident of a palace) on to God. In fact, it is the predominant relational metaphor used of God in the Bible, appearing much more frequently than metaphors such as 'God is a lover/ husband' (e.g. Jeremiah 3, Ezekiel 16 and Hosea 2) or 'God is a father' (Deut. 32:6; Isa. 63:16; Jer. 3:19).

The kingship of God has been the subject of many studies by biblical scholars. However, no study has taken as its starting point the metaphorical status of 'God is king', and has used the methods for 'unpacking' metaphors to understand the theologoumenon of the kingship of God. Instead, biblical scholars have expended much energy, paper and ink on determining when the conception of God's kingship entered into Israel (e.g. Eissfeldt, 1962b and Buber, 1967), how God's kingship is related to the kingship of gods in other ancient Near Eastern cultures (e.g. Schmidt, 1961 and Smith, 1982) and whether the image implied the cultic actualization of God's kingship (e.g. Mowinckel, 1961). These issues are all important for recon-structing the history of Israelite religion, but they are no substitute for *understanding* what 'God is king' meant to the ancient Israelite community. It is this understanding that I have tried to reconstruct.

This was done by uncovering the 'associated commonplaces' between 'God' and 'king' in the biblical period. It must be stressed that no metaphor can be completely explicated or 'unpacked'; it is impossible to enumerate completely the terminology and images shared by the vehicle and tenor. Furthermore, the nature of the biblical texts often makes it difficult to completely describe the vehicle, human kingship, impinging on our understanding of the metaphor. Also, it is sometimes unclear if certain qualities attributed to God are perceived specifically as entailments of his kingship. Nevertheless, by outlining many associated commonplaces between God as king and human kings, as well as noting the images and terms that are not shared by God and the human king (namely exploring the metaphor's 'extent',) it is possible to develop an understanding of what it meant to call God 'king' in ancient Israel.

The metaphor 'God is king' was extremely productive in ancient Israel as evidenced by the large number of associated commonplaces between God as king and the Israelite king. They share the royal appellations מלך, 'king', רעה, 'shepherd', אדון, 'master', שפט, 'judge', ג(י)ר, 'lamp', מגן, 'shield' and probably משל, 'ruler'. God may be addressed as המלך יהוה, 'the king, Yahweh' in the same way that

David, for example, is called המלך דוד, 'the king, David'. אדני יהוה, 'my master, Yahweh' parallels the royal use of אדני המלך, 'my master, the king'. Immortality is connected to both of them. They are both depicted as wise, wealthy and strong. God, like the human king sits on a throne and sets his feet on a footstool. Some of the same terminology is used to refer to the royal and divine palace; God's palace (the Temple) is called בית יהוה, 'the house of the LORD' parallel to בית המלך, 'the house of the king', and the term היכל, 'palace', used to refer to the Temple (or its parts), is borrowed from the human royal sphere. The heavenly and royal courts are structured similarly: court members stand around the king; the king may consult a courtier or may ask him to volunteer for a royal mission; courtiers may act as middlemen, providing access to the king. They bow to him, sing his praises and are depicted as wise. The members of the courts share some of the same names, including עבד, 'servant', בן, 'son', שר, 'officer', מלאך, 'messenger' and משרת, 'attendant', and they issue proclamations using the same כה אמר, 'thus says' formula. God's roles as judge and builder are sometimes contextually depicted as entailments of his kingship; indeed, as royal builder, the construction of a palace (namely the Temple) and a royal city (Jerusalem) is projected on to him. According to some traditions, access to the divine palace (Temple) is limited, and the worshipper, filled with fear would visit the king there, paralleling the human royal domain. Upon arrival, the worshipper bowed down to God, a gesture probably borrowed from the royal court. שמרי משמרת, 'doers of guard duty', and שמרי הסף, 'guards of the threshhold', referring to Temple guards, are borrowed secular royal terms. Tithes are paid to both God and king, and certain types of Temple gifts may be patterned after royal gifts. God also shares certain aspects of the enthronement rituals with the Israelite king, including the formula מלך X, 'X is/has become king', the ascent of the king onto the throne, the noise and joy of the coronation and its witnessing by important officials. The large number of associated commonplaces which have been uncovered suggests that any scholarly attempt to understand God's kingship which is limited to an examination of the root מלכ, 'to reign', is fundamentally incorrect; 'God is king' was a productive metaphor throughout the biblical period and its entailments must be enumerated and examined to understand what the kingship of God meant in ancient Israel.

The metaphor's strength or predominance is visible in other ways as well. When it became taboo to pronounce the tetragrammaton

יהוה, then אדני, 'my master', a term entrenched in the royal sphere, was used as its surrogate. The associated commonplaces of the metaphor kept up with the changing world of human kingship: when in the post-exilic period משרתים, 'attendants' and royal spies joined the human court, these officials were incorporated into the divine court; this illustrates the vibrant, 'live' nature of the metaphor. Also, the application of the metaphor in areas where it is not strictly appropriate, such as 'God built the Temple', which contradicts historical reality, or in contexts where it seems counter-intuitive, such as 'God is handsome', illustrates the metaphor's pervasiveness in ancient Israel.

The metaphor does not directly map Israelite royal qualities on to God; it often attempts to stress the incomparability of God as divine king by adding superlatives to his royal qualities. Evidence of God's superiority was seen at work in every chapter of this study—instead of being merely מלך, 'king', he is מלך הגוים, 'king of the nations', מלך (ל)עולם (ועד), 'eternal king', מלך כל־הארץ, 'king over the whole earth', מלך רב, 'great king', מלך שמיא, 'king of the heavens', מלך גדול, 'great king', and מלך גדול על כל אלהים, 'great king over all the divine beings'. As מלך, 'king', he never loses a battle. As שפט, 'judge', God's justice is absolute. God has lived forever and will outlive the astral bodies. God uses his supreme wisdom for supra-human projects such as building the world. His royal resources are unlimited and instead of holding mere wealth in his אוצרות, 'treasure houses', they store ever-powerful meteorological phenomena. His *kbwd* qualitatively far surpasses royal *kbwd*. God possesses incomparable strength; he alone is ישגיב בכחו, 'beyond reach in his power'. This superlative strength may be expressed by stringing together terms from the semantic field of strength, forming a long divine titulary; this practice is notably absent with human kings in Israel, especially when we consider the prevalence of royal titularies in the ancient Near East, particularly in Mesopotamia (Seux, 1967). In a word, unlike his royal Israelite counterpart, God is גדול, 'great'. His throne stands for absolute justice and is of exceptional material and size, in one case encompassing the entire heaven. God's royal garb is of extraordinary size. His palace is no mere בית, 'house', but is a בית זבל, 'an exalted house'. According to one tradition, the courtiers of God are very numerous, reflecting his great prestige. Unlike his human counterparts, the king of heaven is fully able to control his officials. As superior judge, God stands while judging. The contrasting images of the world rejoicing or quaking at God's judgement both reflect this overwhelming judicial power. As royal builder he has perfectly constructed the world and its inhabitants and does not tire at the conclusion of his building. When enthronement imagery is projected on to him it reflects superlatives—the joy at his reigning is on a universal scale and is extremely noisy. Thus, most entailments of human kingship that are projected on to God convey God's superlative nature, combining the metaphor 'God is king' with the theological notion 'God is incomparable'.

God's superiority as king over human kings is also emphasized by juxtaposing the abilities of God as king to those of the human king. It is God who as מגן, 'shield' strengthens the human מגן, 'shield'. God the king's eternal nature is expressed in the indicative while the human king's immortality is expressed in the jussive. The great king Darius acknowledges God's preeminence. It is God who dispenses חכמה, 'wisdom', a prerequisite to reigning well. God dispenses עז, 'might', to human kings. His מטה עז, 'mighty scepter', is powerful in contrast to the weak royal מטה עז, 'mighty scepter'; his יד חזקה, 'strong arm' can deliver Israel while Pharaoh's יד חזקה, 'strong arm', ironically represents the human king's weakness. God may grant kings הוד והדר, 'strength'. He is powerful enough to kill מלכים אדירים, 'powerful kings'. Ezekiel 34 depicts in detail God's superiority as shepherd-king over the Israelite shepherd-king. Proverbs 16:11 attributes absolute judicial ability to God, countering the claim of human royal judicial abilities in the previous verse. The Israelite king may ask God for a share of divine משפט, 'justice'. A depiction of such an uneven kingship, where the human kings' royalty depends on God and is not at all on par with God's royalty, stresses God's superlative kingship.

The special morphological patterning of אֲדֹנָי, 'my master' and ניר, 'lamp' and the syntactic differentiation of יהוה אדנינו, 'the LORD our master' from e.g. אדנינו דוד, 'our master, David' suggest that God's royal nature differs from that of the Israelite king. This patterning combines with the frequent contextual emphases of God's superlative nature as king and the statements that God as king gives human kings their royal power to push the metaphor to the edge, suggesting that as king, God is more than king.

The superlative nature of God's kingship is also emphasized by the lack of projection on to God of expressions from the human sphere which imply royal weakness. For example, God is never called נשיא, 'exalted one' or ראש, 'head', since the usage (and not etymology) of these terms suggest diminished royal power. No קשר, 'internal rebellion' is ever perpetrated against God because this might suggest that he was a petty king. Instead, apostasy terminology is borrowed from rebellions against an overlord. God's courtiers have no independent power, emphasizing God's absolute power. The ability of the human bureaucracy to circumvent royal orders is never projected on to God's attendants. Finally, perhaps the absence of oil rituals with God which would parallel the (performative) annointing of the king stresses that God always was, and never becomes, king.

Although God is often depicted as king, God sometimes possesses royal attributes in a unique fashion that threatens the bounds of the metaphor. As רעה, 'shepherd' he uses his שבט, 'staff' beneficently rather than for punishment.[4] He may use עז, 'might' for the anti-militaristic purpose of granting peace and loving משפט, 'justice'. Similarly, he uses his כה, 'strength' to forgive. His זרוע, 'arm' may be gentle, and his right hand, normally a symbol of power, may stand for righteousness. When as royal judge he acquits his subjects, he shows the former accused unusual tenderness. According to certain traditions, all had free access to God the king and people approach him with joy, rather than with the fear which typified the royal visit. These examples illustrate how the expected entailments of the metaphor may be reversed to show how God could not be bound by the metaphor.

In other cases, certain considerations prevented the metaphor from being fully operative. Royal appellations such as נגיד, 'divine designee', משיח, 'anointed one', and בחיר יהוה, 'the chosen of the LORD', which suggest the king's role in relationship to God could not be applied to God. Certain components of the enthronement ritual such as recitation of בני אתה, 'you are my son', and blessing by the old king would be inappropriate to him. In the case of the royal palace (= Temple), the architectural application of the metaphor would have led to functional problems, so it was avoided. Elsewhere, a full application of the metaphor would have conflicted with the iconic prohibition. This explains why God is generally not called beautiful, or depicted as wearing a crown, the royal bracelet, or specific royal clothing; these might have encouraged the plastic representation of him. One exception to this may predate the iconic prohibition, while in the rabbinic period, when there was little danger of Judaism becoming iconic, God was depicted with various royal trappings. Thus, various types of external factors could influence the 'extent' of the metaphor.

Sometimes the metaphor was overactive, divesting royal qualities from the Israelite king and giving them solely to God. Certain words which were once certainly used of human kings became at some time 'disinfected', that is used only of God. This is particularly evident in the area of strength. In contrast to God, no Israelite king is ever called the substantive חזק, 'strong'. Also, human kings are rarely עז, 'mighty' and only God is עזוז, 'mighty'. By the post-exilic period, God had appropriated the root גבר, 'to be strong' from the king. The *qaṭṭîl* form adjectives אדיר, אמיץ, אביר and כביר, all words for 'strong', are used of God and not of human king, as are the strength related words זמר II, 'warrior', and various words for 'fortress', 'rock' and 'refuge' (מפלט, משגב, מצודה, מנוס, מחסה and צור). The large number of theophoric names incorporating an element from the 'strength' field illustrates the centrality of God's strength. Even more striking is God's appropriation of גדול, 'great' at the expense of the Israelite king, leaving Israel with a (paradoxically) un-majestic king. This semantic development is especially noteworthy because it sharply contrasts with the narrative texts that frequently depict kings as great. This suggests that the lack of words for גדול, 'great' with Israelite kings is an intentional feature of the language of the biblical authors, who are trying to emphasize God's royal superiority. The process of divine appropriation of royal terminology is also especially clear in the word היכל, 'palace', which the comparative Semitic evidence indicates belonged originally to the royal palace, but was used in Israel of the Temple. In these cases, God became the king at the expense of the human king.

Although I have referred in general terms to 'the' metaphor 'God is king', it is not a single, unified metaphor. Individual uses of the metaphor in different contexts and in different time-periods recall different specific entailments of God's kingship. Some of the changes are determined by shifts in the structure of the vehicle, human kingship, throughout time. For example, in the post-exilic period, when משרתים, 'royal attendants' and royal spies joined the royal bureaucracy, the divine court changed correspondingly to incorporate these roles. Different ways the metaphor was unpacked may also have been determined by different perceptions that various groups in ancient Israel had about God. For example, according to some conceptions (especially in P), access to the Temple (=palace) was strictly controlled by שמרי הסף, 'guards of the threshhold', who are שמרי משמרת, 'doers of guard duty'. This directly parallels the human royal sphere. Connected to this is the conception that one approaches

God fearfully and cautiously. However, the diametrically opposite viewpoint is adumbrated by other theologians (especially in D), who claim that all have free access to the divine king in his palace, and he should be approached with joy. The submetaphor 'God as king sits on a throne' is also unpacked in different ways throughout the Bible. Thus, one group may accept certain entailments of God's kingship while another may strongly reject them.

Not every entailment is recalled every time the metaphor is used. For example, Isa. 6:1-5 stresses the divine king's power, and depicts his royal court, garb and throne; Isa. 41:21 stresses his role as judge; Jer. 10:7 notes his wisdom; Ps. 5:3 stresses his position as the powerful head of society who can fulfill any request; Psalm 47 is very rich in images taken from the human enthronement ritual. The metaphor functioned as a storehouse of entailments, any number of which may be recalled by an ancient Israelite as appropriate to particular contexts.

The primary result of this study is the description of what calling God a king meant in ancient Israel. Applying the methods of metaphor study to 'God is king' also suggested that two theories which are predominant in biblical scholarship should be modified. The heavenly court is usually treated as a group of demoted pagan deities. This study suggested that they must also be understood within the metaphor 'God is king', as a reflection of the human royal court. This was accomplished by adducing a substantial number of parallels between the human royal and heavenly courts, including correspondences of names, functions and formulae. This could serve as a case example illustrating that any history of Israelite religious institutions must not be confined to understanding where various practices originated or how they are paralleled in the ancient Near East, but must also consider how a particular institution functioned within the ancient Israelite socio-religious system. Some new light was also shed on the so-called 'enthronement psalms', whose interpretation is central to the reconstruction of the ancient Israelite cult. The study of 'God is king' highlighted the literary rather than literal aspects of God's kingship, suggesting that entailments of the metaphor such as 'God becomes king' need not be actualized in the cult. God becoming king could have been a literary image in the same way that God building the Temple was a literary conceit. More specifically, a reexamination of the phrase יהוה מלך, 'the LORD is king' or 'the LORD has become king' suggested that neither syntax nor morphology favored either the durative or the ingressive meaning for *mālāk*, so specific contexts need to be examined to determine if יהוה מלך should be translated 'Yahweh is king' or 'Yahweh has become king'. A close examination of the contexts in which the phrase appears uncovered a significant anomaly—it is generally used in contexts where the non-Israelite nations are supposed to acknowledge God's kingship. Given the pre-exilic date of these psalms and the fact that foreigners did not generally participate in Temple rituals in the pre-exilic period, these psalms should be understood as a projection of Israelite (human) enthronement imagery on to God with one crucial twist—instead of *celebrating* God the king as *newly enthroned*, the nations are projected as *newly (recognizing and) celebrating* the achievements of God (who has *always* been *enthroned*). In its final form, even Psalm 93, which at one point seems to depict God as becoming king, has the countervailing image of God as eternal king. Thus, a study of how the metaphor functions suggests that the 'enthronement psalms' are not the libretto of an annual 'enthronement festival'.

This study is not a complete exploration of the metaphor 'God is king'. No metaphor can be totally 'unpacked'; according to some theorists, strong metaphors use infinite associated commonplaces to convey their meaning. I have concentrated on God's role as sovereign; it would be important to know to what extent God as king is patterned after an overlord rather than after the native Israelite king. An exploration of certain additional details of the metaphor's function in ancient Israel would be fruitful: it would be interesting to note in exactly what genres (e.g. psalms of thanksgiving, hymns, prophecies of consolation) and time-periods the kingship metaphor is used most, to what extent specific biblical authors develop and revitalize the metaphor, and how they used it in conjunction with other metaphors to aid in the depiction of God. Also, many comparative avenues have been probed, but have not been explored systematically. It would be worth investigating how the metaphor differed from Israel in Mesopotamia, where kings were frequently militarily powerful and there was no iconic prohibition, and in Egypt, where in some respects the king was regarded as divine. It would be worthwhile seeing how the metaphor developed in post-biblical times. The metaphor was used by the Jewish rabbinic and the early Christian communities as they became differentiated; how did the use of 'the same metaphor' differ between these communities, and to what extent did the metaphor gain new entailments as the communities came into contact with different forms of monarchy? Finally, I hope that this study has shown how the modern study of metaphor can help us understand what the Israelite meant by calling God 'king', and others will refine this method and use it to understand additional aspects of the biblical depiction of God.

NOTES

Notes to Introduction

1. On this tripartite division, see Kutscher, 1982:12. An attempt to provide a more nuanced method of dating is suggested by Rooker, 1988, but this method is in its infancy.

2. Whenever possible, translations follow *TANAKH: A New Translation of The Holy Scriptures According to the Traditional Hebrew Text* (Philadelphia, PA: Jewish Publication Society, 1985). I thank the publisher for its permission to use this translation.

3. There are certain lingering questions about the song's unity, but v. 18 is a fitting and original conclusion to this poem, as shown by Muilenberg, 1966:250.

4. Other possibly pre-monarchical texts where God may be explicitly depicted as king are Num. 23:21 and Deut. 33:5.

5. See Smith, 1982. Additional Mesopotamian examples are collected by von Soden, 1981:1190 s.v. *šarru(m)* B 'als Gottestitel'; for the Ugaritic evidence, see Schmidt, 1961.

6. Contrast, for example, Johnson, 1967, Gottlieb, 1980 and Halpern, 1981:61. I agree with North, 1932:38: 'We must conclude that however exalted above his brethren the king might be, his place was on the human rather than on the divine side of reality'. Cooke, 1961 substantiates North, while Mowinckel, 1959 offers an intermediate position.

7. Compare a simplistic attempt to define the common Hebrew word אמר, 'to say', on the basis of its cognates (see Barr, 1974:4-7).

8. Compare Talmon, 1977.

Notes to Chapter 1

1. On this tripartite division, see Kutscher, 1982:12. An attempt to metaphor. The metaphor 'God is king' is a simple type of metaphor, consisting of two nouns and the copula; accordingly, much of the discussion pertaining to the more complex types of metaphors need not be examined. For a historical survey on metaphor, see Johnson, 1981:3-47.

2. For a more detailed critique of Searle, see Levin, 1979:125-27.

3. For examples, see the discussion of חיכל and גרול (pp. 91, 70-72).

4. The clearest discussion of this theory is in Soskice, 1985:31-51.

5. Though the terms 'vehicle' and 'tenor' have been criticized for suggesting too static a view of metaphor (e.g. Black, 1962:47, n. 23), they are

God is King

appropriate to the metaphor 'God is king'. They do, however, become problematic in some bidirectional metaphors (Levin, 1979:129).

6. For this term, see Smith, 1971.

7. The ongoing debate whether 1 Kings 1–2 is anti-Solomonic or pro-Solomonic is particularly instructive in this regard; cf. Langlamet, 1976 and the comments of Ackroyd, 1981:394, 'The reader of the text and of the commentaries may, not surprisingly, find himself somewhat bewildered by the alternatives offered. . . '.

8. Texts will be considered post-exilic if they show clear signs of Late Biblical Hebrew (e.g. Psalm 119), are attributed by their authors to that period (e.g. Zechariah) or contain clear references to that period (e.g. Isaiah 40ff.). Other criteria traditionally used to determine lateness are too subjective to be of much use, as shown by Ackroyd, 1953.

9. A detailed refutation of the position that the kings are usually the 'I' is found in Brettler, 1986:23-27.

10. Contrast, for example, Haran, 1978.

11. Schmidt, 1983 is an exception, devoting a section to 'The Kingdom of God' (144-52), in which he restates the views earlier developed in his dissertation (published 1961).

12. In fairness, it must be noted that some more recent studies have more reasonable attitudes about biblical anthropomorphisms. Particularly useful is Dion, 1981, who entitles his concluding section 'Le langage anthropomorphique, indispensable à la religion d'Israël'.

Notes to Chapter 2

1. For example, 'the head of the tribes of Israel' is found only in 1 Sam. 15:17, and seems to be a coined by Samuel for this particular occasion, so it is not classified as a 'royal appellation'.

2. These are: Num. 23:21; Deut. 33:5 (likely); 1 Sam. 12:12; Isa. 6:5; 19:4; 33:17,22; 41:21; 43:15; 44:6; Jer. 8:19; 10:7,10; 46:18; 48:15; 51:57; Mic. 2:13; Zeph. 1:5; 3:15; Zech. 14:9,16,17; Mal. 1:14; Pss. 5:3; 10:16; 20:10; 24:7,8,9,10 (2x); 29:10; 44:5; 47:3,7,8; 48:3; 68:13,25; 74:12; 84:4; 89:19; 95:3; 98:6; 145:1; 149:2; Dan. 4:34. There is a scholarly consensus that מלך, 'king' in most of these verses refers to God. The following are exceptions: Deut. 33:5 is a difficult verse, especially since it is probably a poetic fragment, and presents serious textual problems. (See Cross-Freedman, 1975:111, n. 20.) The context, the theophany on Sinai, suggests that God is the subject (Miller, 1973:82-83). The syntax of ויהי בישרון מלך, 'then he became king in Jeshurun' is difficult; we would expect ויהי מלך על ישרון, 'then he became king over Jeshurun'. The closest parallel is Mic. 5:1, להיות מושל בישראל, 'to rule Israel', but the syntax of that verse is different because there היה is the object of יצא. Perhaps the syntax in Deuteronomy is explained by a desire to parallel בהתאסף ראשי עם, 'when the heads of the people assembled'.

Alternately, בישרון, 'in Jeshurun' may be a graphic error for בשרר, 'while ruling' (cf. Judg. 9:22). Some older exegetes (e.g. Dillmann, 1898:297) suggested that מלך, 'king' in Isa. 33:17, a notoriously difficult verse, refers to God. The following factors favor this interpretation: 1. The image of v. 17, of seeing the king, parallels phrases with the idiom ראה פני יהוה, 'to see the face of the LORD' (Exod. 23:15; 34:23; Deut. 16:16; 31:11; Isa. 1:12; Ps. 42:3; on these passages see Geiger, 1928:337-339). 2. V. 18 is similar to Ps. 48:13, and in that psalm, 'king' probably refers to God (v. 3). 3. Verses 18-21 refer to the invincibility of Jerusalem, which is under *divine* protection (v. 21). 4. V. 22 reads יהוה מלכנו, 'the LORD is our king'. If vv. 17 and 22 are part of the same unit, then 'king' in v. 17 probably also refers to God. The references to God as king in Jer. 46:18; 48:15 and 51:57 are missing in the LXX, whose reading should be preferred according to Janzen (1973:79 and 216 n.22). However, the expression נאם־המלך יהוה צבאות שמו 'declares the king, whose name is LORD of Hosts' is unique to these three verses; if it is secondary to all three, it is unclear why or from where it was added. Therefore, with Tov (1972), I prefer to see the MT and the Hebrew *Vorlage* of the LXX of Jeremiah as two different *ancient* recensions of Jeremiah, so I include these verses in this discussion. Mic. 2:13a is very obscure, but the parallelism in B of מלכם לפניהם, 'the king before them' and יהוה בראשם, 'the LORD at their head,' and the general anti-royal ideology of Micah suggest that מלך, 'king' refers to God. Most scholars revocalize Zeph. 1:5 בְּמַלְכָּם, 'by their king' to 'Milcom', following the Lucianic family of the LXX. However, context favors the MT. Verses 4-5a clearly refer to pagan worship, while v. 5bα and 6 refer to Yahwistic worship, so the MT of 5bβ is best retained, rather than reintroducing the motif of pagan worship. Ps. 68:13, like much of Psalm 68, is notoriously difficult. In general, the position of Miller (1973:103) that it contains a 'series of (divine) war songs or pieces of war poetry' is reasonable, in which case מלכי 'the king(s) of' in this obscure verse probably refers to God. Some older exegetes assume that מלכנו, 'our king' in Ps. 89:19 refers to the Davidic king (Briggs, 1976, II:258), but the isolation of the emphatic *lamed* makes this exegesis unlikely. Verse 19 concludes God's attributes; David's attributes begin only in v. 20b.

3. Note Deutero-Isaiah's general preference for the term Jacob over Israel; proportionally, Second Isaiah uses יעקב, 'Jacob' relative to ישראל, 'Israel' more than any other major prophet, and when he uses both together, Jacob is frequently the favored A word (e.g. 41:14; 44:1; 49:6; cf. esp. 48:1).

4. This expression may be a calque of *šar kiššāti* (Seux, 1967:308-312) or *šar kibrat arba'im* (Seux, 305-308). Certainly some Israelite officials were aware of Assyrian royal practices and propaganda (cf. 2 Kgs 18-19 and the loanwords שלמנים and אשכר), but it is unclear how extensive this group was and if they had influence on prophetic and psalmic language.

5. Cf. the Aramaic of Ezra 5:11 and Jean-Hoftijzer, 1965:270, רב A3,

BDB 913, רב 2, Sefire I B 7 and Gordon, 1965, III:482 #2297. Another case of a qualitative רב is תהום רבה (3x), which might also be a calque in Hebrew.

6. For a survey on *nāgîd* see Ishida, 1977; his conclusions, however, are not adequately sensitive to certain text-critical problems.

7. Jer. 20:1, the sole exception, is a late pre-exilic text where the word has already developed its general post-exilic sense of official. The evidence often cited (e.g. in Bright, 1981:190, based on Albright, 1961:16) from Sefire I 10 that נגד in the sense of official existed in the pre-exilic period remains uncertain, especially since the reading נגרי and not נגדי is posited there by some scholars (Donner-Röllig, 1979, II:268). In any case, an Aramaic attestation of נגד as 'official' would not prove that the Hebrew נגיד had the same meaning at the same time.

8. These two points need not be, but usually are held simultaneously; for a summary see Mettinger, 1976:151-58 and Lipiński, 1974:497 n. 2.

9. They were largely anticipated by Thornton, 1963:8.

10. For a similar treatment, see Tsevat, 1980d:93 and Halpern, 1981:1-12.

11. 1 Chr. 29:22 וימשחו ליהוה לנגיד, 'they anointed the LORD as a *nāgîd*' is clearly an error by haplography for וימשחוהו, 'they anointed him' (Rudolph, 1955:194; RaDaK glosses this verse, 'its meaning is they anointed him').

12. This interpretation of משיחי, found in Dahood, 1970 III:33 was anticipated by Rashi and RaDaK.

13. The suggestion of Driver, 1960:351 to read בגבען בהר יהוה (so LXX) is possible, but not compelling.

14. David is portrayed as a shepherd (1 Sam. 16:11) who zealously guards his flock (1 Sam. 17:34-35). The connection between shepherding and becoming king is explicit in the rabbinic midrash in which David was an extraordinarily sensitive shepherd, leading God to conclude 'since he knows how to shepherd, he should shepherd my sheep, Israel'. (Cf. Buber, 1967:357 to Ps. 78:71 and Exodus Rabbah 2:2.) Similar traditions are extant about Moses (Ginzberg, 1968 II:300-302 and V:414 n.109) who is never called a king, but nevertheless has many royal qualities, especially in the military and the judicial spheres (see Whitelam, 1979:214). With the possible exception of the difficult Isaiah 63:11, Moses is never called a shepherd in the Bible, even though he is depicted as leading sheep (cf. Exod. 3:1, Num. 27:16-17). In rabbinic literature, Moses is often called a shepherd (cf. Ginzberg V ibid., Targum and Rashi to Qoh. 12:11, and תנחומא וילך א). The tradition in 1 Samuel 9 that Saul was anointed while searching for his father's asses may be a transformation of this shepherd topos aimed at portraying Saul in a negative light.

15. I am not including Gen. 48:15, where רעה, as a participle ('who shepherds me'), is not an appellation, but is acting verbally, taking a direct object.

16. BHS' emendation יִנְחֵנִי, 'they will lead me' (cf. Dahood, 1978, I:147) has no versional support, and does not assume that this biblical poet had the power to creatively modify his metaphor, to show how God surpasses the human shepherd. As noted in the previous chapter, a single metaphor may be used differently in different contexts, thus, in Isa. 10:5, God's crook is used to represent his anger.

17. The veracity of these texts has often been questioned. For a summary and a general defense of the accuracy, see Williamson, 1977:71-82.

18. The translation of נשיא in the LXX of v. 25 as ἄρχων is of no text-critical value; see Levenson, 1976:64-65.

19. Num. 10:4; 36:1; Num. 25:15 (cf. v.18). For details, see Bartlett, 1969.

20. For similar arguments in a different context, see Barr, 1968:151-55.

21. Kraus (1961, I:331) suggests an original אלהים > יהוה > יהוה. See the collection of emendations and interpretations in Mulder, 1972:33-80 and Whitley, 1986:280-82.

22. For similar haplographies, see Delitzsch, 1920:5-11.

23. Note the general use of מר for kings in Aramaic, e.g. in the Assur ostracon line 6; for a comprehensive list, see Jean-Hoftijzer, 1965, s.v. מר (pp. 166-67).

24. The exegesis of the eighth case (Mal. 3:1) is difficult; the contrasting opinions of Rashi ('the God of justice') and ibn Ezra ('the angel/messenger') reflect the verse's ambiguity.

25. Exod. 23:17 and 34:23. Even here, it may be used to emphasize God's power to punish those who do not partake in these festivals; cf. (the much later) Zech. 14:16-17.

26. It is tempting to see this title as a reflex of the Akkadian *šar šarrāni* (perhaps via an intermediate Aramaic מר מריא), especially if the thesis of Weinfeld, 1972 concerning the royal element in Deuteronomy is generally correct.

27. אדונך, 'your master' written with defective spelling always refers to a human master, so it is tempting to see אדניך, 'your master', written plene, and read *'ădŏnayik*, as a special form, resembling the pausal form which is used only of God. However, though *'ădŏnayik*, is used once of God (Isa. 51:22), it is used in Ps. 45:12 of the human king. It is however possible that the tradition behind this vocalization is the same as in the midrash Genesis Rabbah 39:1 (to Gen. 12:1; Theodor-Albeck, 1965:365), which understood the referent as divine.

28. Cf. Pss. 8:2, 10; 135:5; 147:5; some of these are more certain than others.

29. Eissfeldt bases his arguments on these texts: CTA 15.5.20 (1970:25) 2.4.5 and 51.1 (1974:67). The ending -ny in CTA 15 is usually taken as a dual (Ginsberg, 1946:43; Caquot, 1974:546 and n. i). CTA 51.1 *lumy.adtny* is problematic, but it is likely that the scribe of this letter began with the usual

formula in the singular *lumy* (cf. CTA 50.2 and UT 1013.1), and then
remembered that the letter was from two sons, so then correctly wrote *adtny*.
CTA 2.4.5 *larṣ.ypl.ulny wl.'pr.ʾẓnny* is Eissfeldt's strongest case. However,
the immediately preceding context is badly broken, and the suffixes might be
construed as duals (Gibson, 1977:43, n. 4), though Caquot, 1974:135, n. k
doubts this. In any case, the Ugaritic evidence for a *-(n)y* emphatic suffix is
tentative at best.

30. In Ps. 35, יהוה is used in vv. 1, 5, 6, 9, 10 (see further), 22, 24, 27. ארני is
used in 17a and 22b as a vocative, opening a colon; perhaps v. 23 should be
parsed העירה והקיצה למשפטי אלהי / וארני לריבי in which case וארני is also
an invocation of God. V. 10 uses יהוה rather than ארני as a vocative since it is
quoting Exod. 15:11. In Ps. 51 God is always called אלהים (3, 12, 16, 19),
except for v. 17 when God's name begins the verse.

31. So according to the count of the Massorah at Gen. 18:3.

32. For example, see BHS or Ginsburg, 1926 to Ps. 130. The major
versions do not usually distinguish between יהוה and ארני, so they are of no
assistance in this issue.

33. This is probably the case for six of the seven uses of ארני in Genesis in
the Sodom pericope. The מסורה קטנה is careful to note '134' at Gen. 18:3
and 27, but there is a discussion in RaDaK and Minhat Shai to Gen. 18:3 on
whether ארני there is holy or profane. (Cf. *Soferim* 4:10 [Higger,
1937:143].)

34. Ullmann, 1967:73; on the linguistic status of personal names in the
Bible, see Gibson, 1981:126-39.

35. Over three-quarters of the uses of the phrase are in Ezekiel.

36. In Second Isaiah, aside from the use of ארני אלהים, 'my master, God'
in 40:10, where it clearly conveys God's strength, it is used in 50:4, 7, 9, a
servant passage, and in 61:1-11, a passage related to the servant songs
(North, 1948:137-38). This might suggest a separate authorship for the
servant songs.

37. See its use in the Mesha inscription line 18 (a foreigner would have
written the name as he heard it), in several inscriptions from Kuntillet ʿAjrud
(Meshel, 1978) and throughout the pre-exilic period in many of the Lachish
and Arad letters (Pardee, 1982:235).

38. Note how 'judge' parallels 'official' in the same way that elsewhere (e.g.
Isa. 49:7, Hos. 7:3) 'king' parallels 'official'.

39. Gen. 18:25; Judg. 11:27; Isa. 33:22; Jer. 11:20; Pss. 7:12; 9:5; 50:6;
58:12; 75:8; 94:2; Job 23:7 (MT). I exclude cases where the participle is used
verbally (e.g. 1 Sam. 3:13 and Ezek. 34:17), and thus is not an appellation.

40. Cf. Prov. 13:9 (where ישמח means 'to shine', cf. Greenfield, 1959: 141-
51, esp. 147), 20:20 (note in Ezra 'his lamp' means his soul, as in [Exod.
21:17] 'he shall surely die') and 27, 24:20 and Job 21:17.

41. E.g. Job 10:21-22. Mesopotamian conceptions substantially influenced
the picture of the underworld as a dark place; there too it is lacking in light
(*nūru*! cf. CAD N II 350a).

42. See further the next section on 'breath of our life' and 2 Sam. 18:3, where the troops said to King David, 'But you are worth ten-thousand of us'.

43. The text of 2 Sam. 22:29 is to be preferred over the parallel Ps. 18:29, according to which *nyr* is not an appellation.

44. For רוח as an 'animating spirit' see e.g. Ps. 14:4 and Wolff, 1974a:32-39, 234.

45. The use of צל, 'shade' in the sense of 'protection' (see Baumgartner, 1983:960 צל 2. Schutz) in the same verse supports this interpretation of רוח אפינו, 'our life-spirit' in Lam. 4:20.

46. BDB, s.v. רוח p. 296, gives a meaning 'ancient angel of the presence and later Shechinah'. However, in none of the verses cited is רוח, 'spirit,' a divine name, as it is in post-biblical literature, though it is possible that רוח 'spirit' developed its meaning of shechinah from a close (mis)reading of certain biblical verses such as Ps. 139:7.

47. According to the older exegetes (e.g. Briggs, 1907:258), מגנינו, 'our shield' in Ps. 89:19 refers to the king. However, if we accept the existence of the emphatic *lamed* in Hebrew (cf. Baumgartner, 1974:485-86), that verse is best understood as the conclusion of the psalm's hymn, not as the opening of the oracle. Dahood (1965:16-18) posits that מגן means 'a suzerain'. The usual critiques of Dahood's methodology apply here too—he imports meanings to Hebrew only known from other Northwest Semitic languages, vastly increasing the complexity of the Hebrew lexicon and giving novel interpretations to texts which present no lexical, morphological or syntactic problems.

48. Gen. 15:1; Deut. 33:29; 2 Sam. 22:3, 31; Pss. 3:4; 18:3, 31; 28:7; 33:20; 59:12; 84:12; 89:19; 115:9, 10, 11; 119:14; 144:2; Prov. 30:5. Ps 7:11 may be added if we emend the text with Baumgartner (1974:517) and others.

49. The arguments of Baldwin, 1964 to include Isa. 4:2 are unconvincing; the verse is purely agricultural and is an image of restoration to counter such images as Isa. 1:7, and has nothing to do with the monarchy.

50. An alternate solution is to interpret צמח צדק(ה) as 'legitimate heir' (Sweetman, 1965 and others), but the evidence is largely based on a third century Pheonician inscription (Donner-Röllig, 1979: 43:1). There is no evidence in Biblical Hebrew that indicates that צדק can mean 'legitimate'. Evidence based on the posited meaning 'legitimate wife' for *aṭt ṣdqh* in KRT (CTA 14) line 12 (cf. Gordon, 1965, III:72-73) is inconclusive, since the context preceding this line is broken. Furthermore, the evidence that Zedekiah was seen as an illegitimate king is not compelling; for details see Brettler, 1986:78, n. 102.

51. E.g. Pss. 22:29; 59:14; 89:10; 1 Chr. 29:12; 2 Chr. 20:6.

52. Dan. 8 is probably an exception, but this very late text which uses very unusual images in describing the heavenly scene is atypical of the Bible.

Notes to Chapter 3

1. Though the form יחיה is morphologically an imperfect, this form is used as a jussive in biblical literature (Bergsträsser, 1962:II:30b), especially in Ezra-Nehemiah (see Japhet, 1968:335 on the converted לה) and in Rabbinic Hebrew (Segal, 1980:155).

2. The classical position of Alt, 1967b concerning the distinctions between southern dynastic and northern charismatic kingship has been controverted by Buccellati, 1967:195-208.

3. Verses in which מלכ, 'to reign' is explicit: Exod. 15:18; Jer. 10:10; Mic. 4:7; Pss. 10:16; 29:10; 145:13; 146:10; Dan. 3:33; 4:31; 6:27; 7:14. Verses where kingship is implied through the throne image (ישׁ, 'to be enthroned' and/or כסא, 'throne'): Pss. 9:8; 45:7 (in the simile); 68:17; 102:13; Lam. 5:19. Ps. 48 (cf. v. 15) is full of kingship imagery.

4. Although נמות, 'we will die' is posited by the earliest textual evidence, e.g. the pesher in 1QpHab and the LXX, this verse is included among the lists of the תקוני ספרים, 'scribal corrections' and the earlier lists of כינה הכתוב, 'euphemisms' (see Lieberman, 1962:28-37). Targum posits the reading לא תמות, 'you never die'.

5. Isaiah chapters 40ff. are particularly rich in allusions to earlier biblical traditions. It has often been noted that Davidic kingship, a typical topos in prophecies of consolation, is absent there. Eissfeldt, 1962a and Conrad, 1985 have shown how Davidic kingship was projected on to Israel as a whole. To the extent that there is continuity between Second and Third Isaiah, Isa. 62:3 may strengthen his thesis. However, Davidic kingship was also appropriated and transformed by projecting some of the Davidic royal qualities on to God. Thus it is no accident that it is specifically in Isaiah 40ff. that the royal image known from Psalm 72 becomes a divine image.

6. The extent of wisdom literature's influence on ancient historiography should not be exaggerated as in Whybray 1968; cf. the critique of Crenshaw, 1969:137-140. McKenzie's position is even more radical; he claims to 'have identified the wise men of Israel with the historians...' (1967:8). This involves a misunderstanding of both wisdom and historiography. One solution is to follow Whybray's later position (1974) and to abandon the term 'wisdom literature' altogether.

7. Cf. Job 12:13; Prov. 20:24; possibly 30:3; Isa. 19:11b-12; 40:14; Jer. 10:7; Ezek. 28:1-6; Ps. 139:1-18.

8. Read ברים as ברים (cf. Jer. 50:36) from the Akkadian *bārû*. So Baumgartner, 1967:146, but cf. idem, p. 105.

9. 3:28 is an additional example if אלהים there signifies God and is not being used as a superlative; cf. Thomas, 1953.

10. However, the king owned some royal property; cf. Whitelam, 1979:74-75, 243 n. 57.

11. The superscription 'to Solomon' should be characterized with other

superscriptions studied in Childs, 1971 as ahistorical and midrashic (so Slomovic, 1979:373-74).

12. Gen. 31:1 (TO נכסיא); Isa. 10:18; 22:24; 61:6; 66:12; Nah. 2:10; Ps. 49:17; cf. Baumgartner, 1974:436 ('Besitz'), Ben Yehuda, 1959:2234 and Weinfeld, 1982:26.

13. Cf. Hebrew חיל and כח; cf. Fohrer, 1968.

14. The royal nature of this passage is recognized by TO and pTJ who translate ואדני האדנים, 'and master of masters' in v. 17 as ומרי מלכין, 'master of kings'.

15. A single likely exception, where *kābôd* of God refers to wealth is in the mouth of foreigners (1 Sam. 6:5). (McCarter, 1980:127 'tribute', comes closest to this suggestion.) On the general meaning of *kābôd* as applied to God, see Mettinger, 1982a:80-115, esp. 106 n. 22.

16. See de Vaux, 1965:70 and Tadmor, 1971:63 n. 33.

17. The context suggests that גבורים should by read as גבור, and the final *mem* is either enclitic (McCarter, 1984:71) or is a dittography, perhaps influenced by the frequent mention of גבורים elsewhere in the lament.

18. This shift and a partial explanation are noted in Kosmala, 1975:370. The *kḥ* of kings as a general quality is only noted in post-exilic texts, e.g. 2 Chr. 13:20; 22:9; Dan. 8:6, 22, 24; 11:6.

19. The one exception is David in 1 Chr. 29:29-30.

20. In Isaiah, the king is probably God; cf. above, p. 173 n. 2. I do not include cases where עז, 'mighty' is used (adjectivally) to describe an action performed by a king which is unrelated to strength, such as 2 Sam. 6:14.

21. It is unclear if this late text uses *mlkm h'dr* in the same sense as *'dr* in the earlier inscriptions (see Dönner-Rollig, 1979:ii:28) or whether it reflects the Greek μεγαλοδόξος (Gibson, 1982:120). Avishur, 1979:106 correctly draws the parallel between the Phoenician and the Hebrew *mlkm 'drm*, but incorrectly assumes that Phoenician and Hebrew *'dr* should be translated as *gdwl*.

22. It is likely that the meaning of 'glory' (e.g. Halpern, 1981:132-33) for *hdr* (and then *hwd*) derives from the Aramaic *hdr* (cf. above, p. 69). This influence began in the exile (cf. Ezek. 16:14) and continued into post-exilic and rabbinic Hebrew. The translators of the LXX in several contexts interpreted *hwd* in the sense known to them in contemporary usage as δόξα, which has (indirectly) influenced modern translators.

23. Isa. 30:30; Job 39:20 (cf. 40:9-10). This contrasts with the Akkadian *mellammu*, which according to Oppenheim, 1943 had its origin in a mask, and is thus a visual phenomenon. The visual nature of the melammu is confirmed by the Shamash hymn (Lambert, 1975:126) where amidst various royal images, line 11 reads *melammuka ištene'û*.

24. With כח, 'strength', Ps. 29:4, with עז, 'might', Prov. 31:25, of oxen Deut. 33:17, of mercenaries Ezek. 27:10 and with פחד, 'fear', and גאון, 'majesty', Isa. 2:10, 19, 21.

25. Mulder, 1972:5-7 is probably correct that the repetition of *hādār* is due

to dittography, so one *hādār* should be deleted and verse 4 should be read together with the beginning of verse 5.

26. See Warmuth, 1978:338 and bibliography there.

27. In general, arguments from parallelism are dangerous, but elsewhere in this psalm the ideas in each hemistich are generally related, so the same is likely true here. In Psalm 145:11-12, there is a disagreement between MT and some versions whether גבורה is in the singular or plural. This typically happens when גבורה used of God is followed by a personal pronoun. This has little exegetical significance for us, so further cases of this phenomenon will not be noted.

28. The difference implied by using simile rather than metaphor is debated in the literature; see Soskice, 1985:58-61.

29. The royal nature of this formula is indicated by the rendition of the Targumim to אדני האדנים, 'master of masters' earlier in the verse.

30. Commentators often emend כח, 'power' to חסד, 'kindness' so that this case conforms with the others (so Smith, 1974:298; BHS). This emendation is based on the incorrect assumption that the formula has fossilized. However, as shown by Fishbane, 1977:279-81, the formula was not fixed and was often adapted to fit new contexts.

31. It might be noteworthy that Akkadian *ezzu* is used of gods and not of kings (CAD E, 432-34), but other words from the root *ezēzu(m)* do not show similar usage patterns.

32. Here and elsewhere I count parallel references and inner-biblical quotations as one reference.

33. The versions to Deuteronomy 32 are quite instructive; LXX usually translates צור there as θεός, clarifying that its referent is God, and the Peshitta renders it from the root תקף, implying that strength is the major component of the metaphor.

34. Cf. the name מעזיה(ו) at Elephantive (Noth, 1928:157). מעוז in Psalm 31:3 is read as מעון in the parallel Elohistic 71:3. It is impossible to decide which reading is original, especially given the translations in the LXX.

35. מבצר, 'fortified', the most general fortress term, is never applied to God, just as אבן, the most general 'rock' term, is never applied to him.

36. So Gesenius, 1974 §84[b]g, among others. For differing opinions on the morphology of this word, see Sarna, 1979:389-90.

37. See the studies of Avishur, 1977, and 1984:153-88. The term 'synonymous' is misleading; Avishur means either terms that have the same referent or terms from one semantic field; see Gibson, 1981:199-206.

38. The interpretation of בהדרת־קדש, always with the verb השתחוה, is very difficult (Pss. 29:2; 96:9; 1 Chr. 16:29). The *bet* may either indicate a place (so LXX ἐν αὐλῇ), or an attitude of the worshipper. In 2 Chr. 20:21 משררים ליהוה ומהללים להדרת־קדש, the reference of the noun phrase הדרת קדש is God, but this referent may not be imported to בהדרת קדש.

39. On the theophoric elements עם, אח, אב see Noth, 1928:66-77.

40. See the discussions on בעל as a theophoric element in Noth, 1928:119-22, Tigay, 1986:68 and Avigad, 1988:8-9.

41. There is even an intriguing possibility that archeology could indicate that the Israelites did not produce any royal inscriptions; it is especially curious that the Siloam inscription is not structured like a royal inscription and does not even mention the name of the patron king.

42. In 2 Sam. 5:10 (=1 Chr. 11:9) עמו . . . וילך דוד הלוך וגדול ויהוה, גדול is an infinitive absolute coupled with הלוך, and does not indicate that David was גדול in the absolute sense (cf. 2 Chr. 17:12). Also, David's accomplishments are clearly attributed to God—ויהוה עמו. In 2 Sam. 7:21 גדולה is not a general royal attribute, but refers to the following להודיע את־עבדך (so McCarter, 1984:236).

43. The translation 'honor' for יקר found in Rosenthal, 1961:86 and Ginsberg in Rosenthal, 1967 is consistent with Dan 2:6 and with later Jewish Aramaic usage (Jean-Hoftijzer, 1965:110 יקר II), but is too general for the majority of Biblical Aramaic contexts which connect *yqr* specifically with kingship.

44. It is uncertain if this geographical location had this name earlier, and might have been named for the Judaean king, or whether Joel gave it this name in anticipation of the divine judgement, in which case it might not be connected to King Jehoshaphat.

45. Cf. North, 1932:10-11 and Johnson, 1935:75-76, but this notion should not be exaggerated. Let me briefly examine two 'classic' cases where it is usually invoked: 2 Samuel 24 and the sins of Manasseh. In 2 Samuel 24 the plague is brought on by the action of the census, not because it is David who specifically performed it. In the case of Manasseh, it is noteworthy that although many Dtr texts single out his sins as responsible for the national calamity, 2 Kings 21 claims that the entire nation followed his idolatrous ways. Even Chronicles, which is usually held up as the prime attestation of royal responsibility for the national welfare at times stresses the nation's complicity in the royal sin (e.g. 2 Chr. 36:14).

46. I include cases where גדול, 'great' is used of God's כבוד, 'presence' or שם, 'name' since these terms may be used as surrogates for God (see Mettinger, 1982a:38-114), but I do not include cases where God's attributes or actions are called גדולים, 'great' (e.g. Ps. 108:5).

47. Etymologically, עליון, 'most high' probably originated as a divine appellation, as indicated by its Northwest Semitic antecedents (see Wehmeier, 1976: 285-86), but this is not relevant for understanding how עליון, 'most high' was understood within Israelite society.

48. It is difficult to know if the *Polel* uses of רם should be included here, since it is unclear if they mean 'to praise' or 'to make great'.

49. Cf. the biblical personal name שניב/שגוב, probably a hypocoristicon, and אלשגב, known from an 8-7th century Hebrew seal (Heltzer-Ohana, 34).

50. This might have changed to a minor degree in the post-exilic period; cf. Ezra 5:11, 1 Chr. 29:25 and 2 Chr. 1:1. Perhaps Israelite kings in the post-exilic period were so weak that applying to them terms used of God did not involve a true comparison of God to the kings, thus weakening God's power. Alternately, since these texts all refer to Solomon it is possible that only he or perhaps only dead kings could be called 'great'.

51. Possibly the image of the עבד, 'servant' as 'ugly' in Isa. 53:2 (cf. 52:14) is based on the idea that the 'servant' is an anti-king (cf. ולא הדר, 'lacking *hādār*').

52. Mettinger's claim (1978) that Israelite religion became aniconic under the influence of Hosea (p. 24) and that the prohibition of icons is 'to accentuate his [=God's] transcendance' is tantalizing, but not decisively argued. It would, however, explain why the image of God as beautiful is preserved only in the early Isaiah.

53. The eternal nature of God is so often explicitly connected with kingship or the root מלכ, 'to reign', that this divine attribute must certainly be a projection from human kingship. On the other hand, the case with wisdom is less certain.

Notes to Chapter 4

1. This text is difficult; it is unclear if one or two crowns are being made (cf. Rudolph, 1976:128 and esp. Lipiński, 1970:34-35). Myers and Myers, 1987:349-53 argue that two crowns were made, one for the king (6:12-13a) and a second for the high priest (13b), since these two shared leadership roles in the early post-exilic period.

2. The translation of עליו יציץ נזרו is difficult; for a discussion, see Brettler 1986:149 n. 3.

3. For MT עטרת־מלכם some LXX mss. render τὸν στέφανον Μελχομ τοῦ βασιλέως αὐτῶν. This reflects a double reading מלכם מלכם, 'Milcom their king'. Driver (1960:294; cf. McCarter, 1984:311) favors reading מלכם, the god. In any case, the jewel from the crown of a divine statue was incorporated into David's royal crown.

4. See the Assyrian reliefs of Shalmanesser III (The Black Obelisk in ANEP #355) and the relief of Sennacherib at Lachish (ANEP #371).

5. *Ktr* is only used in Esther, though verbs and nouns from the root *ktr* are found elsewhere. *Ktr* later became the standard word for 'crown' in Rabbinic Hebrew. Perhaps its entrenchment in Hebrew was influenced by similar sounding (though non-cognate) words in (old Indo-European) and Greek (Eilers, 1954-56:331).

6. Isa. 62:3 והיית עטרת תפארת ביד־יהוה וצניף/וצנוף מלוכה בכף־אלהיך presents several exegetical problems, which primarily center on the correct interpretation of the rare idiom והיית...ביד. In that context, God is not wearing a crown; the crown is ביד, 'in the hand of' and not בראש, 'on the head of' God (as noted by Luzzatto, 1970:390)—a point not sufficiently

appreciated by most modern scholars (e.g. Westermann, 1969:375).

7. The *aleph* may be prosthetic (cf. Joüon, 1965 §17a; 88La), in which case the אצעדה is related to the (non-royal) צעדה of Isa. 3:20. However, the lack of the article is surprising, and possibly ואצעדה should be emended to והצעדה (Driver, 1960:233; cf. McCarter, 1984:57, 233). For a possible etymology, see Kopf (1958:198).

8. Most scholars emended ערות to צעדות (e.g Montgomery-Gehman, 1976:425), until von Rad 1966b claimed to have found Egyptian parallels to a royal protocol as part of the coronation ritual. Von Rad's suggestion, however, suffers from two problems: the influence of Egyptian institutions on the united monarchy is no longer readily admitted and the syntax ויתן עליו את־הנזר ואת העדות does not favor taking ערות as an abstract noun. Many scholars now favor MT's ערות and discuss its significance at great length (e.g. Widengren, 1957 and Halpern, 1981:16-49).

9. There is no evidence known to me of Hellenistic royalty wearing white. In the Dura-Europas Synagogue, neither of the two kings depicted (David and Ahasueraes) are in white garb (Goodenough 1964:178, 187). Professor Wayne Meeks (oral communication) has confirmed the anomalous nature of the white clothing in Daniel.

10. On the etymological problems and the relationship between שבט and שרבים, see Wagner (1966:116 #317).

11. The common emendation by the Albright-Cross school (e.g. Cross-Freedman, 1975:83 n. 31) of Gen. 49:10 שבט, 'scepter' to שפט, 'ruler' is gratuitous since it is likely that שבט means 'king' through metonymy. This understanding is supported by the Aramaic Targumim TO עביד שלטן (cf. Micah 5:1; pTJ מלכין ושליטין and Neofitti מלכין) and is presupposed by the messianic interpretations of the verse (cf. Prigent, 1959 and Urbach, 1976:606, n. 80).

12. I exclude Jer. 51:19 which is very difficult. Although grammatically God must be the subject of שבט, logically ישראל must be supplied before שבט (so Targum and Rashi). LXX lacks ושבט altogether; Janzen (1973:61) suggests that LXX is correct and MT represents an expansion from 10:16.

13. I do not include Exod. 17:16 *ks* in my discussion since it is anomalous and most scholars emend it to *ns*, 'banner'. (So Baumgartner, 1974:465 and Childs, 1974:311-12; even Driver (1918:161) is inclined toward accepting this emendation.)

14. In this chapter I use the word 'enthroned' in its general sense 'to sit on a throne' and not in its narrow sense of 'ritually sitting on a throne as part of a(n annual) rite'.

15. The last two terms are found only in 1 Chronicles (28:5; 29:23) and refer to the throne which was legitimized by God (Williamson, 1982:136). Japhet (1977:335-40) makes the even stronger claim that the Davidic king was understood as God's representative.

16. Syrian: Ahiram (ANEP #456), Bar Rakab (460) and Yehawmilk (477); Egyptian (415); Mesopotamian (371 [the Lachish reliefs] and many others);

Persian (28, 463); Neo-Hittite (849 [Karatepe]) and Ugaritic (493 [of El]). The iconographic material is now all collected in Metzger 1985, vol. 2.

17. Compare the Lachish relief (ANEP #371) where the inscription describes Sennacherib sitting on his throne while reviewing the booty.

18. Reading ואתה קדוש יושב, 'You are holy, enthroned' (against the accentuation marks) following BHS, NJPS and Kraus (1961:174, 175) among others.

19. The general early dating of Exodus 15 may be defended on linguistic grounds (Robertson, 1972), but the content of v. 17 may argue against this date (see Childs, 1974:246). Furthermore, it is possible that the root *yšb* here should be translated 'to dwell'.

20. Cf. the reference to a *kussât uqnîm* in von Soden, 1981:1426b.

21. Note the image in the verse ותחת רגליו כמעשה לבנת הספיר וכעצם השמים לטהר, 'under his feet was the likeness of a pavement of lapis lazuli, like the very sky for purity'. This however does not exclude the possibility that the verse's image is partly based on a royal palace paved in blue.

22. On 1 Kgs 8:23-53 see Levenson (1981:153-166). Even the conservative Bright (1965:27) assumes that Jer. 3:16-18 is exilic; cf. McKane, 1986:77.

23. Some scholars have suggested that the priestly attire may be based on royal clothing (e.g. Mettinger, 1976:287-88). If they are correct, this may be a deflection of this aspect of royalty from God, where it was religiously inappropriate, to the priests, the divine representatives of God.

Notes to Chapter 5

1. The influence of this semantic development continued into early Jewish Aramaic sources, where *hykl* denotes the Temple (Fitzmyer-Harrington, 1978:316, s.v. *hykl*). In the Aramaic of Hatra *hykl* is both 'temple' and 'palace' (Jean-Hoftijzer 1965, 64. s.v. *hykl*), but this seems to be independent of the Hebrew development, and did not cause the meaning 'palace' to be largely lost from *hykl* in the language.

2. See Aharoni, 1973:6-7, who discusses the possibility that the ark was not separated in a hidden room in certain pre-Solomonic temples.

3. The parallels between the Arad temple and the משכן, 'Tabernacle' (see Aharoni, 1973:4-7) may be significant once we date P as pre-exilic; they might suggest a non-Jerusalemite origin for (parts of) P.

4. Haran, 1978:10-11, 122-131 and passim argues that certain aspects of P are best understood as reflecting utopian ideals.

5. Contrast Haran, 1978:189-194 who contends that the Tabernacle is a conflation of the Shiloh and Jerusalem temples, with Cross, 1981:175, who continues to maintain that it is 'the Tent designed and established by David'.

6. Milgrom, 1970 is confusing at this point. He explicitly draws the royal analogy (p. 47), but then proceeds to explain (and date!) this institution through Hittite parallels.

7. The continuing debate on the root and conjugation of this word (see Emerton, 1977 and Kreuzer, 1985) is irrelevant to the term's use.

8. 1 Kgs 12:19 ויפשעו ישראל בבית דוד עד היום הזה, 'and Israel rebelled against the Davidic house, until this very day' seems to be an exception. However, the attitude reflected in this verse differs from the surrounding material, which generally supports the legitimacy of the Northern kingdom. Thus, this verse is a late addition, which shares its theology with 2 Kgs 17:21 (see Brettler, VT, forthcoming) and with much of Chronicles, that the North rebelled against its overlord, Judah.

9. For specifics, see Brettler, 1986:227, n. 144.

10. In the following discussion, I exclude the interrelationship between God and Moses, which was very atypical; cf. esp. Num. 12:8 and Mann, 1977:144-152.

11. This was pointed out by Jacob Milgrom during a seminar on Numbers at the Hebrew University in fall 1978.

12. Licht, 1978 isolates 15 separate sources.

13. Of a theophany, see Ezek. 1:28; 3:23; 43:3; 44:4; Lev. 9:24; 1 Kgs 18:29 (see Gruber: 133). Gen. 17:3 does not fit this pattern; it is the only time that this action is evoked by an appearance of God to Abraham (contrast e.g. 12:7 and 18:1). מלאכים, 'divine messengers' performing unusual acts may provoke similar actions (Judg. 13:20; Dan. 8:17 and 1 Chron. 21:16; see Gruber:133). In three cases when the existence of the Israelites was threatened, extreme supplication is expressed through ויפלו על־פניהם, 'they fell on their faces' (Num. 16:22; 17:10; 20:6; see Gruber:134-135).

14. This narrative is before David's coronation by the people, but the text still treats him as king because he was so designated by the prophet Samuel.

15. In this chapter, Absalom, having deposed David, is treated as king.

16. The term עבד, 'servant', is relative in Hebrew; for example, in the Yabneh Yam inscription (KAI I, 36, #200) the royal official who is the recipient of the letter is אדני השר (line 1), 'my master, the officer' and the complainent is the עבד, 'servant' (ad nauseum [8x in 14 short lines]).

17. Brin, 1966-67 and Avigad, 1969:9 support Clermont-Ganeau while Rainey, 1968-69, Hestrin and Dayagi-Mendels, 1978:12 and Lemaire, 1979 deny his contention.

18. BDB 1058 includes משרתיו, 'his attendants' in Prov. 29:12 under 'royal officers (late)'. However, in this pre-exilic text (cf. Eissfeldt, 1974a:475), the attendants belong to a משל, 'ruler', and not to a מלך, 'king', and therefore these are not '*royal* officers'.

19. The עם, 'people,' who are מהללים, 'praising' are the שרי המאות, 'chiefs of hundreds', as indicated by v. 9 in conjunction with v. 10 העם ואיש שלחו בידו, 'the people, each man with his weapon'.

20. 21 of 28; if we count parallel texts as one, 14 of 21.

21. All translations from Modern Hebrew are my own.

22. אלהים in such contexts is ambiguous, referring either to deities or to

members of the heavenly council. Deut. 32:8 LXX and Qumran make it clear that the reference is to the council.

23. Cf. some of the versions to 2 Kgs 11:14 which imply *śārîm* for MT *śārîm*.

24. For the texts, see Borger, 1979, I:75; for a translation see ANET, p. 288. If this conjecture is correct, exiling the singers was also a way of depriving the Judaean king of his authority.

25. This theme was originally clearer before the psalm was incorporated into the Elohistic Psalter, creating confusion between the two uses of אלהים, as 'God' and as 'the divine beings' (Tsevat, 1969-70:126 and others).

26. Mr. William Schniedewind, a graduate student at Brandeis University, has suggested that Joseph's and Daniel's roles as dream interpreters might reflect an Israelite reality, in which case Gabriel's role does have an earthly, royal counterpart.

27. A bureaucracy, with the attendant loss of control by a central authority, would have been especially appropriate to the historical setting of the Book of Daniel, but this is not played out.

28. In some texts, it is unclear if צבא השמים refers to the heavenly council or to astral worship. On the identity and provenience of the latter, see Cogan, 1974:84-87.

29. Note the translations of מלאכי, 'Malachai' in the LXX as ἀγγέλου αὐτοῦ and in some Targum traditions as מלאכי דיתקרי שמה עזרא ספרא (Sperber, 1962:500).

30. It is unclear to me why this use of מלאך, 'messenger' should only be post-exilic; perhaps certain polemics against מלאכים in the pre-exilic literature (see Rofé, 112-19) prevented its being used earlier for prophets. For a different explanation, see Ross, 1962:106.

31. The clearest evaluation of the problem using this evidence is Emerton, 1982:3-9, who notes that these inscriptions *allow* for the possibility of translating יהוה צבאות as 'Yahweh of Seba'ôt,' but do not force us to adopt this translation.

32. For a comprehensive discussion of the judicial system of ancient Israel which includes a critique of Wilson and Whitelam, see Niehr, 1987.

33. The only exception is Deuteronomy, and its royal connections have been posited by Weinfeld (1972, esp. 163-64 and 1985:95-98), but see the critique of Rofé (1974).

34. Weinfeld's attempt (1972:153-155) to see many of these as narrow terms equivalent to Mesopotamian *mîšarum* acts does not fit the majority of these texts' contexts. Weinfeld, 1985:26-44 elaborates on his earlier claims. His main argument is that certain terms associated with *mîšarum* have interdialectical equivalents that are used with the terms משפט וצדקה, 'justice and equity,' so these Hebrew terms must refer to the same institution as the *mîšarum*. This type of argument is flawed since similar words may be used in different types of contexts in different languages; furthermore, the parallel terms that Weinfeld notes are certainly too general to prove his point.

35. The verb דן, 'to judge' is used in the juridical field of non-royal people only in Gen. 49:16 and Jer. 5:28. (In Jer. 30:13 MT is too corrupt to be interpreted clearly and in Qoh. 6:10 דן does not have a narrow judicial use.) In my discussion of דן, I make a clear distinction between the verb דן and the noun דין. Barr (1961:100-106) has discussed the 'root fallacy'. His treatment suggests that we need to distinguish between the usages of verbs, nouns and adjectives from the same root. Rabin (1962:23) has made a similar point in his discussion of biblical semantics.

36. For a detailed discussion of the texts attributing justice to God, see Krašovec, 1988.

37. Brunner, 1958 suggests that this image was borrowed from the depiction of the ideogram of *ma'at* on the Egyptian royal platform. Falk, 1960 rejects this position, claiming that the metaphor developed independently within ancient Israel.

38. The phenomenon of juxtaposed diametric sayings has been briefly noted by Murphy, 1981:63. Examples which may be added to his include Prov. 15:15-16; 18:10-11; 28:25-26. Hildebrandt (1988) studies paired verses in Proverbs, but emphasizes their 'cohesion', rather than a possibly polemical interrelationship.

39. For a study and typology of such texts, see Crenshaw, 1970.

40. Although יסד and חזק are used of kings only in post-exilic texts, this is probably coincidental since both terms are used in pre-exilic texts of non-royalty.

41. Kapelrud, 1980 (esp. 10) claims: 'There is no doubt that creation as an idea, event and necessity was of no importance in ancient Ugarit', but this is questionable.

42. Doubling is a stylistic feature of this psalmist. God's *kbwd* is mentioned in v. 3 and vv. 7-8, the call to praise him is found in vv. 1-2 and again in vv. 7-8, and his fairness is recalled in v. 10 and v. 13.

43. The Aramaic verse 11 is clearly a gloss (so Bright, 1965:77, 79 and McKane, 1986:225; contrast Holladay, 1986:324-325) which separates vv. 10 and 12. Vv.10 and 12-13 share common imagery and probably belonged together at some stage of the transmission of the text. The different tradition reflected in 4QJer[a] (Janzen, 1973:175) probably reflects a secondary or 'vulgar' tradition.

44. This interpretation of the plural cohortative נעשה, 'let us make' is at least as old as Genesis Rabbah (Theodor-Albeck, 1965:60) and pTJ. For a review of the exegesis of the 1 plu verb, see Westermann 1984:144-45.

45. On the dating of these verses see above, p. 14. On the problem of the referent of 'temple' see Friedman, 1981; but note the philological objections of Haran and Weinfeld, ibid. 29-30.

46. This usage is particularly common in Second Isaiah: as Weinfeld, 1968:121 notes, 'Second Isaiah is the first prophet who used the notion of creation as a prime proof for the unity, supremacy and greatness of the God of Israel'. Although this prophet does not explicitly connect God's abilities as

a creator to his kingship, these chapters all have God's royalty as their underpinning, as shown by Mettinger, 1986-87.

47. It is pointless to speculate on the exact nuance of ברא precisely because no human analogy for this action exists. For an analysis of some theories of its reference, see Westermann, 1984:98-99.

48. It is unclear if this text refers to domestic or foreign visitors, especially when it is compared to the parallel in 2 Chr. 9:23.

49. The exact sense of לשלשת ימים, 'on the third day' is difficult; Driver's contention (1915:170) that it is a sarcastic play on the 3-year tithe institution of Deuteronomy is very interesting, especially given the current popularity of theories that posit a Northern origin for Deuteronomy.

50. This can be added to the evidence mustered in Japhet, 1968 to prove that Chronicles and Ezra-Nehemiah are of different authorship.

51. There has been a radical revision by biblical scholars in understanding human sacrifices in Israel. The older view, which assumed that human sacrifice was practiced in ancient Israel, has been called into question; see Childs, 1974:195, Hillers, 1984:79 and Greenberg, 1983b:269-70.

52. Note the language of 1 Sam. 1:11. Although Samuel is not called a nazirite in MT, he is clearly depicted as one; this is made explicit in 4QSam[a] to 1:22 (Cross, 1953:18, but see his n. 5) and Ben-Sira 46:13.

Notes to Chapter 6

1. For this designation and the problems involved in defining their extent, see Lipiński, 1962:134-37, Watts, 1965 and Gray, 1979:9.

2. By 'dynasty' I mean at least a father and son who reigned consecutively.

3. These problems are not sufficiently considered in Halpern's reconstruction of the royal ritual (1981:125-48). He also conflates texts and freely uses Enuma Elish to fill in details.

4. This is not the full extent of the source; in this section I only note the verses within an account which refer to the royal ritual.

5. See Austin, 1975. Although he modifies his position and would deal with such performatives under the 'illocutionary forces of an utterance' and specifically as 'exertatives' (pp. 151, 155-57), I retain the imprecise term 'performative utterance' since it is less cumbersome and more transparent linguistically.

6. The LXX might not be original, however. The text of LXX is very trite, and might have been assembled by a translator on the basis of 1 Sam. 9:16, 17 and 2 Kgs 9:6, because he felt that something was missing in the text. This process probably occurred in the *nūn* verse of Psalm 145 (Sanders, 1965:38 on 11QPs[a] XVII, 2-3).

7. Following Hillers, 1967 that the verbs in *Piel* and *Hiphil* which classical Hebrew grammars consider 'declarative' are actually 'delocutive',

i.e. indicating that a locution is being stated.

8. An example might clarify the difference between (1) and (2). (1) would be equivalent to a principal formally saying to a potential teacher after an interview 'you will teach here' while (2) is similar to the principal saying to the secretary of that school 'X is now a teacher here', which indicates that it is now the secretary's responsibility to help X.

9. The phrase in parentheses is in vv. 6 and 12 but not v. 3.

10. The term used is עם־הארץ, literally 'people of the land', which may be a technical term for a group of the population that was particularly associated with the monarchy; see Talmon, 1967, Oded, 1977:456-58, Mettinger, 1976:124-30 and Gunneweg, 1983.

11. ובין המלך ובין העם, 'between the king and the people' is missing in 2 Ch. 23:16, but this is the type of material which the Chronicler might omit from his source (Japhet, 1977:98-99).

12. Contrast for example *šarru lu dārî*, '(Mr.) The King (=Sennacherib) is Indeed Everlasting', whom Sennacherib places on the throne of Ashkelon in the account of his third campaign (Borger, 1979:I 73, col. II line 65 [62]). The new king was given this name as a constant reminder of his vassaldom.

13. So Humbert, 1946:11-14 of the תרועה in general. I use 'ritual' as it might be used by a folklorist describing a sports crowd jumping up and screaming after a goal has been scored.

14. My use of this term follows Mettinger, 1976.

15. Its mention in 1 Sam. 10:25 with Saul might reflect Judaean practice.

16. The arguments of Mettinger, 1976 that the ברית was unilateral are unconvincing; see Brettler, 1986:284, n. 47 and 285, n. 50.

17. The unity and dating of 2 Samuel 7 remain unresolved in contemporary biblical scholarship. I accept the view of Tsevat, 1980b:115, that vv. 13b-16 are a gloss, but most-likely date from near the Solomonic period. This would allow the assumption that Psalm 2 is quoting from an adoption motif within the Davidic promise.

18. צאת ובא, 'going and coming', is generally acknowledged to have military connotations (see Baumgartner, 1974:406 יצא 4d). The short analysis of this unit in Crenshaw, 1981:46 is especially apposite—he notes that although the passage is Dtr, its mention of Gibeah clearly indicates Dtr's use of an earlier source. Furthermore, Crenshaw posits that the wisdom element in the unit might be secondary. This leaves open the possibility that this chapter is a reworked request for military power.

19. For a discussion of this office, see Johnson, 1962, Wilson, 1980, index, s.v. 'cultic prophecy' and Murray, 1982.

20. These include v. 2 רדה בקרב and v. 6 ארץ רבה, ידין בגוים.

21. Cf. symbolic trampling in Josh. 10:24; 2 Sam. 22:39; 1 Kgs 5:17.

22. Cf. Judg. 5:2 בהתנדב עם (cf. v. 9), which is in a clear military context.

23. Abraham ibn Ezra and David Kimhi following Moses ibn Chiquitilia. Targum renders מלך זכי

24. ראש ירים, 'he holds his head high', is equivalent to *ullû rēšu* in Akkadian (CAD, E 126a-b).

25. The second part of Gunkel's thesis (Gunkel-Begrich, 1933:100-16), that these psalms are eschatological, may be considered separately from his assertion that these are not cultic psalms.

26. Some of Mowinckel's claims were anticipated by Volz, 1912, whose study has remained relatively obscure in comparison to Mowinckel. Like Mowinckel, Volz describes 'das Neujahrsfest Jahwes', but psalms do not play a predominant role in his reconstruction of the festival.

27. For this term see Lipiński, 1965:338.

28. See the discussion of this term in Mettinger, 1973:73-79.

29. However, the conclusion of Kapelrud, 1963 that מלך is both durative and ingressive (p. 231, 'Jahwe herrscht jetzt aktiv als König'), which conflates both possibilities, is not compelling.

30. E.g. Gen. 18:17; 20:4; 39:1; 41:10; Judg. 1:16; 1 Sam. 9:15; 14:27.

31. E.g. Gen. 16:1; 24:1; 1 Kgs 1:1.

32. Cases where S= יהוה, אדני or אלהים and it precedes the predicate (though not always in a simple S-P phrase) include: 9:8; 11:5; 13:2; 14:2; 29:10a, 11; 30:4, 8; 33:10; 34:18; 41:3, 4; 51:17; 53:3, 6b; 55:17 (2X), 20; 59:11; 60:8; 67:2; 68:12; 71:11; 85:13; 87:6; 103:19; 108:12; 121:7, 8; 138:8. Cases of P-S *include*: 37:40; 50:3; 64:8; 78:21; 85:2; 126:2,3; 135:14; 140:13; 146:10. A sizable number of these P-S phrases appear in the fifth book of the Psalter.

33. Lipiński, 1965:371 would include 10:16 emended with the LXX, but he offers no decisive reasons to prefer LXX over MT. In his study, Lipiński only includes Psalms 93, 97 and 99, and excludes Psalm 96, since it does not open *yhwh mālāk*, although it uses the phrase in v. 10. However, given the similarities between 96 and 99, it is best included.

34. Jeremias, 1987 separates the psalms into similar categories, but for different reasons. I have not been able to fully integrate his study into this work, but our underlying differences are obvious: I insist on linguistic dating of texts, while he is willing to date material by using typological factors, from early, mythological texts, to late, universalistic texts. I am also much more hesitant to conclude that one biblical text is quoting from another; it is equally possible that both texts share traditional, cultic language.

35. This is a slippery term. It is interesting to compare Lipiński's methods of exegeting psalms using 'Une manière que l'on souhaiterait exhaustive' (1965:91) with those of Meir Weiss (1984), whose book is subtitled '*The Method of Total Interpretation*'. The former largely relies on external ancient Near Eastern material, while the latter insists on a literary (new-critical) methodology which moves in concentric circles from the word to the larger literary units. The former persistently raises the problems of the limits of the comparative method while the latter raises the issue of 'over-reading' and the limits of inter-textuality.

36. See Jefferson, 1952, Lipiński, 1965:164 and Dahood, 1968:344. The method used in these studies, however, needs refinement—it is irrelevant how many words shared with Ugaritic are used in the psalm; instead we must determine how many *unusual* words in a Hebrew composition could only be explained by assuming that they reflect borrowings from Canaanite.

37. This term is very problematic since it covers a broad geographical and chronological area; Tsevat, 1980d:79, n. 9 calls it a 'spongy term'. If Ps. 93:3 does reflect a 'Canaanite' verse form, it is significant that the exact type of expanded colon it uses is unattested to in the Ugaritic corpus (Loewenstamm, 1969:189).

38. The contention of Anderson, 1983:667 that the image of גאות לבש, 'robed in grandeur', might be 'derived from the investiture of the earthly King [sic] at his enthronement' is interesting, but nowhere in Israelite sources is the donning of a royal garment a part of the investiture ritual.

39. In Psalm 96: v. 1 כל־הארץ, 'all the earth', v. 7 משפחות עמים, 'O families of the peoples', v. 9 כל הארץ, 'all the earth' and in vv. 3 and 10 Israel is told to declare certain things בגוים, 'among the nations' so that all nations will praise God. In Psalm 97: v. 1 הארץ, איים, 'the earth, islands' (cf. v. 6 כל־העמים, 'all peoples'). In Psalm 99: v. 1 עמים הארץ, 'peoples, the earth' and the subject of the plurals יודו, 'they praise' (v. 3) and רוממו, 'exalt' (v. 5) must be כל־העמים, 'all peoples' (v. 2).

40. Briggs, 1976: II 309 and 312 claims correctly that vv. 6-9 are a later addition to this psalm. They contain no royal imagery at all and are stylistically and thematically different from vv. 1-5. Verse 5 was the original conclusion of the psalm; in its earlier form the psalm achieved closure through implicit mentions of the ark in v. 1 and v. 5. V. 5 was repeated almost verbatim in v. 9 as a resumptive repetition after the insertion of vv. 6-8.

41. Indeed, Buttenweiser (p. 330) makes a stronger claim, that Deutero-Isaiah is the author of Psalms 93, 96, 97, 98 (cf. e.g. Feuillet 1951, Westermann, 1981:146–47). He does not adequately consider the possibility that these psalms and Deutero-Isaiah used common motifs. This is especially likely in the case of Isa. 52:7 (מלך אלהיך), which is too common a notion to prove literary dependence, and Isa. 51:9 and Psalm 93:1, which both use ancient motifs (see Cassuto, 1972). Buttenweiser's strongest case is איים, 'islands', of Ps. 97:1, which really does typify Second Isaiah, but this word is not unique to him and is found in late pre-exilic literature (Zeph. 2:11 and Jer. 31:10 [cf. Gen. 10:5]). Finally, the possibility that Second Isaiah used cultic tropes from pre-exilic psalms is not adequately considered by Buttenweiser; contrast Westermann, 1969:23-27, who finds substantial literary dependence of Second Isaiah on Psalms.

42. Contrast Haran, 1978:5-9, Zevit, 1982 and Hurvitz, 1983 to Levine, 1982.

43. If Lev. 22:25 is post-exilic (see previous note), it might reflect the

beginning of this custom.

44. Psalms 97 and 99 resolve the imperfect/jussive problem in opposite directions—97:1 תגל, 'let exalt', is formally a jussive, while 99:1 תנגום, 'will quake', is formally an imperfect. This might suggest that the psalms should not all be cast in the same mold and should be interpreted individually rather than as a group. However, there are a substantial number of cases where a morphologicaly jussive form needs to be taken as an imperfect and vice versa (Bergsträsser, 1962:II §101 m); whether this reflects textual problems or grammatical ambiguity is moot.

45. Vv. 8 and 12 also mention rejoicing, but that is at God's justice, not as a reaction to his enthronement.

46. Some scholars, including Lipiński, 1965:277-279, insist that *yōšēb* be emended to *yāšab*, mostly on the basis of parallelism, but this is uncertain. The exceptional poetic structure of the יהוה מלך line in this psalm as compared to the other יהוה מלך psalms is noteworthy; only in 99:1 does יהוה need to be repeated in the deep structure of the verse (יהוה מלך ירגזו עמים [יהוה] ישב כרובים תנוט הארץ ; for this type of analysis, see Greenstein, 1983). This is the first of many differences between psalm 99 and the other יהוה מלך psalms.

47. Psalm 94 shares much common vocabulary with the surrounding psalms. This thematically related group of psalms may extend from 92-100.

48. The strongest argument against assuming that this refers to a monthly event is that חג is usually taken to only refer to the three pilgrimage festivals. However, in Exod. 32:5 and possibly Judg. 21:19 this is not so.

49. Cf. נשאו קול and Ps. 93:3; on זרוע קרשו see Cassuto, 1972: 78 # 33. The possibility of these phrases echoing ancient myths is fostered by the general mythical predilection of Second Isaiah.

50. See Rahlfs, 1935:541. If this is an early reading, I would reconstruct the development of the MT thus: 1. מלך יהוה. 2. abbreviation מלך י (see G.R. Driver, 1960:119-120). 3. abbreviation י misread as ישראל. 4. readings 1 and 3 conflated to מלך ישראל יהוה (=MT).

51. If Zeph. 3:14-15 is pre-exilic (Eissfeldt, 1974a:425) and originally read מלך יהוה בקרבך, the contention that Psalms 93, 94-99 reflect the influence of Second Isaiah would be considerably weakened.

Notes to Conclusion

1. For a discussion of semantic and morphological differentiation used to distinguish divine actions and qualities, see Melammed, 1948.

2. This would be the implication of the substitution view of metaphor (see Soskice, 1985:8-14, 24-26), which has been generally replaced by the tensive view of metaphor.

3. Its earliest use is probably in Exod. 15:18; Dan. 7:9-10 is among its latest biblical uses.

4. However, it is not certain that 'God is shepherd' is always a sub-metaphor of 'God is king'.

BIBLIOGRAPHY

Ackroyd, Peter
  1953   'Criteria for the Maccabean Dating of Old Testament Literature'. *VT*
          3:113-132.
  1968   'The Meaning of Hebrew דור Reconsidered'. *JSS* 13:3-10.
  1981   'The Succession Narrative (so called)'. *Interpretation* 35:383-398.
Aharoni, Yohanan
  [1969] 1971 'The Israelite Sanctuary at Arad'. Pages 28-44 in *New Directions in
               Biblical Archeology*. Ed. D.N. Freedman and Jonas Greenfield.
               Garden City, NY: Doubleday.
  1973   'The Solomonic Temple, the Tabernacle and the Arad Sanctuary'.
          Pages 1-8 in *Orient and Occident: Essays Presented to Cyrus H.
          Gordon. AOAT* 22. Ed. Harry A. Hoffner Jr. Neukirchen-Vluyn:
          Neukirchener Verlag.
  1975   *The Arad Inscriptions.* Jerusalem: Bialik Institute and IES. (Hebrew)
  1978   *The Archeology of Eretz-Yisrael.* Jerusalem: Shikmonah. (Hebrew)
Ahituv, S.
  1973   Review of Mettinger 1971. *IEJ* 23:126-128.
Albright, William Foxwell
  1932   'The Seal of Eliakim and the Latest Preëxilic History of Judah, with
          Some Observations on Ezekiel'. *JBL* 51:79-106.
  1950   'The Judicial Reform of Jehoshaphat'. Pages 61-82 in *Alexander Marx
          Jubilee Volume*. Ed. Saul Lieberman. NY: Jewish Theological
          Seminary.
  1961   *Samuel and the Beginnings of the Prophetic Movement.* Cincinnati,
          Ohio: HUC Press.
Alon, G.
  1949   'בשם'. *Tarbiz* 31:30-39. (Hebrew)
Alt, Albrecht
  [1930] 1967a 'The Formation of the Israelite State in Palestine'. Pages 223-309 in
               Essays on Old Testament History and Religion. Garden City, NY:
               Doubleday.
  [1951] 1967b 'The Monarchy in The Kingdoms of Israel and Judah'. Pages 311-335
               in *Essays on Old Testament History and Religion*. Garden City, NY:
               Doubleday.
Alter, Robert
  1981   *The Art of Biblical Narrative.* NY: Basic Books.

Anderson, A.A.
[1972] 1983   *Psalms*. NCBC. 2 vols. Grand Rapids, MI: Eerdmans.
Austin, J.L
[1962] 1975   *How to Do Things with Words*. Second Edition. Oxford: Oxford University Press.
Avigad, Nahman
1969   'A Group of Hebrew Seals'. *EI* 9:1-9. (Hebrew, English summary 134*)
1986   *Hebrew Bullae from the Time of Jeremiah*. Jerusalem: Israel Exploration Society. (Hebrew)
1988   'Hebrew Seals and Sealings and their Significance for Biblical Research'. *VTSup* 40:7-16.
Avishur, Yitzhak
1977   *The Construct State of Synonyms in Biblical Rhetoric*. Jerusalem: Kiryat Sepher. (Hebrew)
1979   *Pheonician Inscriptions and the Bible*. Jerusalem: E. Rubenstein. (Hebrew)
1984   *Stylistic Studies of Word-Pairs in Biblical and Ancient Semitic Literatures*. AOAT 210. Kevelaer: Butzon & Bercker.
Baldwin, Joyce
1964   'Ṣemah as a Technical Term in the Prophets'. *VT* 14:93-97.
Baltzer, Klaus
1968   'Considerations Regarding the Office and Calling of the Prophet'. *HTR* 61:567-581.
Barr, James
1961   *The Semantics of Biblical Language*. Oxford: Oxford University Press.
1968   *Comparative Philology and the Text of the Old Testament*. Oxford: Oxford University Press.
1974   'Etymology and the Old Testament'. *OTS* 19:1-28.
Bartlett, J.R.
1969   'The Use of the Word ראש as a Title in the Old Testament'. *VT* 19:1-10.
Bauer, Hans and Pontus Leander
[1922] 1965   *Historische Grammatik der Hebräischen Sprache des Alten Testamentes*. Hildesheim: Georg Olms.
Baumgartner, Walter et al.
1967,1974,1983 *Hebräisches und Aramäisches Lexikon zum Alten Testament*. 3 vols. Leiden: E.J. Brill.
Ben-Yehuda, Eliezer
[1910ff.] 1959 *Thesaurus Totius Hebraitatis*. 8 vols. New York: Thomas Yoseloff. (Hebrew)
Berg, Sandra
1979   *The Book of Esther*. SBLDS 44. Missoula, MT: Scholars Press.
Bergsträsser, G.
[1918,1929] 1962 *Hebräische Grammatik*. Hildesheim: Georg Olms.
Berlin, Adele
1985   *The Dynamics of Biblical Parallelism*. Bloomington, IN: Indiana University Press.
Beuken, W.A.M.
1981   'Psalm XLVII: Structure and Drama'. *OTS* 21:38-54.

Bickerman, Elias
    1967   *Four Strange Books of the Bible.* NY: Schocken.
Bin-Nun, Shoshana
    1968   'Formulas from Royal Records of Israel and of Judah'. *VT* 18:414-432.
Biran, Avraham., ed.
    1981   *Temples and High Places in Biblical Times.* Jerusalem: HUC-JIR.
Bjørndalen, Anders Jørgen
    1974   'Zu den Zeitstufen der Zitatformel ... ‏כה אמר‎ im Botenverkehr'. *ZAW* 86:393-403.
Black, Max
    1962   *Models and Metaphors: Studies in Language and Philosophy.* Ithaca, NY: Cornell University Press.
    1979   'More about Metaphor'. Pages 19-43 in *Metaphor and Thought.* See Ortony 1979a.
Blau, Joshua.
    [1972] 1979 *Phonology and Morphology.* Hakibbutz Hameuchad. (Hebrew)
The Book of Ben Sira
    1973   Jerusalem: The Academy of the Hebrew Language and the Shrine of the Book.
Booth, Wayne C.
    1979a   'Metaphor as Rhetoric: The Problem of Evaluation'. Pages 47-70 in *On Metaphor.* See Sacks 1979.
    1979b   'Ten Literal "Theses"'. Pages 173-174 in *On Metaphor.* See Sacks 1979.
Borger, Rykle
    1979   *Babylonische-Assyrischen Lesestücke.* 2nd Edition. AnOr 54. Rome: PBI.
Brenner, Athalya
    1982   *Colour Terms in the Old Testament.* JSOTSup 21. Sheffield: JSOT.
Brettler, Marc Zvi
    1986   *God is King: Understanding an Israelite Metaphor.* Ph.D. Dissertation, Brandeis University.
    Forthcoming 'Ideology, History and Theology in 2 Kings XVII 7-23'. *VT.*
Briggs, Charles Augustus
    [1906, 1907] 1976 *Psalms.* ICC. 2 vols. Edinburgh: T and T Clark.
Bright, John
    1953   *The Kingdom of God: The Biblical Concept and Its Meaning for the Church.* NY: Abingdon.
    1965   *Jeremiah.* AB. Garden City, NY: Doubleday.
    1981   *A History of Israel.* Philadelphia, PA: Westminster.
Brin, Gershon
    1966-67 'On the Title ‏בן המלך‎'. *Leshonenu* 31:5-20, 85-96. (Hebrew)
Brown, Francis, S.R. Driver and C.A. Briggs
    [1907] 1975 *A Hebrew and English Lexicon of the Old Testament.* Oxford: Oxford University Press.
Brownlee, William H.
    1971   'Psalms 1-2 as a Coronation Liturgy'. *Biblica* 52:321-336.
Brunner, Hellmut
    1958   'Gerechtigkeit als Fundament des Thrones'. *VT* 8:426-428.

Buber, Martin
[1956] 1967   *The Kingship of God*. Translated Richard Scheimann. NY: Harper
                and Row.
Buber, Solomon, ed.
[1891] 1977   *Shocher Tob*. Jerusalem. (Hebrew)
Buccellati, Georgio
1967   *Cities and Nations of Ancient Syria*. Studia Semitici 26. Rome:
                Instituto di Studi del Vicino Oriente.
Buttenweiser, Moses
[1938] 1969   *The Psalms Chronologically Treated with a New Translation*. NY:
                Ktav.
Caird, G.B.
1980   *The Language and Imagery of the Bible*. Philadelphia, PA: Westminster.
Camp, Claudia V.
1987   'Woman Wisdom as Root Metaphor: A Theological Consideration'.
                Pages 45-76 in *The Suffering Heart*, JSOT Sup 58. Ed. K. Hoglund et
                al. Sheffield: JSOT Press.
Caquot, Andre et al.
1974   *Textes Ougaritigues: Mythes et Legendes*. Paris: Les Editions du
                Cerf.
Cassuto, U.
1972   'The Israelite Epic'. Pages 62-90 in *Studies on the Bible and the
                Ancient Orient*, vol. I. Jerusalem: Magnes Press. (Hebrew)
Childs, Brevard
1971   'Psalm Titles and Midrashic Exegesis'. *JSS* 16:137-150.
1974   *The Book of Exodus*. OTL. Philadelphia, PA: Westminster.
Clements, R.E.
1973   Review of Mettinger 1971. *JSS* 18:155-156.
[1980] 1982   *Isaiah 1-39*. NCBC. Grand Rapids, MI: Eerdmans.
Cleremont-Ganneu, Charles
1888   *Recueil d'Archéologie orientale*. Vol 1. Paris: Leroux.
Clifford, Richard J.
1972   *The Cosmic Mountain in Canaan and the Old Testament*. HSM 4.
                Cambridge, MA: Harvard University Press.
Clines, David J.A.
1987   'The Parallelism of Greater Precision'. Pages 77-100 in *Directions in
                Biblical Hebrew Poetry*, JSOT Sup 40. Elaine R. Follis. Sheffield,
                Sheffield Academic Press.
Cogan, Morton
1974   *Imperialism and Religion: Assyria, Judah and Israel in the Eighth and
                Seventh Century BCE*. SBLMS 19. Missoula, MT: Scholars Press.
Cohen, L. Jonathan
1979   'The Semantics of Metaphor'. Pages 64-77 in *Metaphor and Thought*.
                See Ortony 1979a.
Cohen, Ted
1979   'Metaphor and the Cultivation of Intimacy'. Pages 1-10 in *On
                Metaphor*. See Sacks 1979.
Conrad, Edgar W.
1985   'The Community as King in Second Isaiah'. Pages 99-111 in
                Understanding the Word: Essays in Honor of Bernhard W. Anderson.
                JSOT Sup 37. Ed. James T. Butler et al. Sheffield: JSOT Press.

Coogan, Michael David
    1978   *Stories From Ancient Canaan*. Philadelphia, PA: Westminster.
Cooke, Gerald
    1961   'The Israelite King as Son of God'. *ZAW* 73:202-225.
Coppens, J.
    1977-78   'La Royauté de Yahvé dans le Psautier'. *Ephemerides Theologicae Louvanienses* 53:300-362; 54:1-59.
Cowley, A.
    [1923] 1967   *Aramaic Papyri of the Fifth Century B.C.* Osnabrück: Otto Zeller.
Crenshaw, James
    1969   'Method in Determining Wisdom Influence upon "Historical" Literature'. *JBL* 88:129-142.
    1970   'Popular Questioning of God in Ancient Israel'. *ZAW* 82:380-395. (Reprinted in Crenshaw, ed., 1976, 289-304.)
    1981   *Old Testament Wisdom: An Introduction*. Atlanta, GA: John Knox.
Crenshaw, James ed.
    1976   *Studies in Ancient Israelite Wisdom*. NY: Ktav.
Croft, Steven J.L.
    1987   *The Identity of the Individual in the Psalms*. JSOT Sup 44. Sheffield: JSOT Press.
Cross, Frank Moore
    1953   'The Council of Yahweh in Second Isaiah'. *JNES* 12:274-277.
    1973   *Canaanite Myth and Hebrew Epic*. Cambridge, MA: Harvard University Press.
    1981   'The Priestly Tabernacle in the Light of Recent Research'. Pages 169-180 in *Temples and High Places in Biblical Times*. See Biran 1981.
Cross, Frank Moore and David Noel Freedman
    1975   *Studies in Ancient Yahwistic Poetry*. SBLDS 21. Missoula, MT: Scholars Press.
Culley, Robert C.
    1967   *Oral Formulaic Language in the Biblical Psalms*. Toronto: University of Toronto.
Dahood, Mitchell
    [1965] 1978,
    1968, 1970   *Psalms*. AB. 3 vols. Garden City, NY: Doubleday.
Dalman Gustaf
    1889   *Der Gottesname Adonaj und Seine Geschichte*. Berlin: H. Reuther's Verlagsbuchhandlung.
Davidson, Donald
    1979   'What Metaphors Mean'. Pages 29-45 in *On Metaphor*. See Sacks 1979.
de Boer, P.A.H.
    1955   'Vive le Roi!' *VT* 5:225-231.
de Man, Paul
    1983   *Blindness and Insight: Essays in the Rhetoric of Contemporary Criticism*. Minneapolis, MN: Univ. of Minnesota.
de Vaux, Roland
    [1958, 1960] 1965 *Ancient Israel*. NY: McGraw Hill.
Delitzsch, Friedrich
    1920   *Die Lese- und Schriebfehler im Alten Testament*. Berlin: Walter de Gruyter.

Diez Macho, Alejandro
  1968-1979 *Neophyti I.* 6 vols. Madrid-Barcelona: Consejo Superior de Investi-
             gaciones Científicas.
Dillmann, August
  1898   *Der Prophet Jesaja.* Leipzig: S. Hirzel.
Dion, Paul-E.
  1981   'Ressemblance et Image de Dieu'. *DBSup* 55:365-403.
Donner, H. and W. Röllig
  1979   *Kanaanäische und Aramäische Inschriften.* 3 vols. Wiesbaden: Otto
             Harrasowitz.
Driver, G.R.
  1960   'Abbreviations in the Massoretic Text'. *Textus* 1:112-131.
Driver, Samuel Rolles
  [1897] 1915 *Joel and Amos.* CBC. Cambridge: Cambridge University Press.
  1918   *Exodus.* CBC. Cambridge: Cambridge University Press.
  [1913] 1960 *Notes on the Hebrew Text and the Topography of the Books of Samuel.*
             Oxford: Oxford University Press.
  [1891] 1972 *An Introduction to the Literature of the Old Testament.* Gloucester,
             MA: Peter Smith.
Dürr, Lorenz
  1929   *Psalm 110 im Lichte der neuern altorientalischen Forschung.* Münster:
             Aschendorffsche Verlagsbuchhandlung.
Dumortier, Jean-Bernard
  1972   'Une Rituel d'Intronisation: Le Ps. LXXXIX 2-38'. *VT* 22:176-196.
Eaton, J.H.
  1976   *Kingship and the Psalms.* SBT II 32. Napierville, IL: Allenson.
Edelman, Diana
  1984   'Saul's Rescue of Jabesh-Gilead (I Sam 11 1-11): Sorting Story from
             History'. *ZAW* 96:195-209.
Eichrodt, Walther
  1961   *Theology of the Old Testament.* Vol. 1. Translated J.A. Baker.
             Philadelphia, PA: Westminster.
Eilers, Wilhelm
  1954-56   'Neue aramäische Urkunden aus Ägypten'. *AfO* 17:322-335.
Eissfeldt, Otto
  1962a   'The Promise of Grace to David in Isaiah 55:1-5'. Pages 196-207 in
             Israel's Prophetic Heritage. Ed. B.W. Anderson and W. Harrelson.
             N.Y: Harper and Row.
  [1928] 1962b 'Jahwe als König'. Pages 172-193 in *Kleine Schriften* I. Tübingen:
             J.C.B. Mohr.
  [1957] 1966 'Silo und Jerusalem'. Pages 417-425 in *Kleine Schriften* III. Tübingen:
             J.C.B. Mohr.
  1970   *Adonis und Adonaj.* Berlin: Akademie Verlag.
  [1965] 1974a *The Old Testament: An Introduction.* New York: Harper and Row.
  [1970] 1974b 'אֱרוּן'. *TDOT* I:59-72.
Elat, Moshe
  1977   *Economic Relations in the Lands of the Bible.* Jerusalem: Bialik
             Institute. (Hebrew)
Ellis, Richard
  1968   *Foundation Deposits in Ancient Mesopotamia.* Yale Near Eastern
             Researches 2. New Haven, CT: Yale University Press.

Emerton, J.A.
1968   'The Syntactic Problem of Psalm XLV.7'. *JSS* 13:58-63.
1977   'The Etymology of hištaḥawāh'. *OTS* 20:41-55.
1982   'New Light on Israelite Religion: The Implications of the Inscriptions
        from Kuntillet 'Ajrud'. *ZAW* 94:2-20.
Falk, Zeev
1960   'Two Symbols of Justice'. *VT* 10:72-74.
Feininger, Bernd
1981   'A Decade of German Psalm-Criticism'. *JSOT* 20:91-103.
Feuillet, A.
1951   'Les Psaumes Eschatologiques du Règne de Yahweh'. *Nouvelle Revue
        Théologique* 73:244-260, 352-363.
Fiorenza, Elisabeth Schüssler
1988   'The Ethics of Interpretation: De-Centering Biblical Scholarship'.
        JBL 107:3-17.
Fishbane, Michael
1977   'Torah and Tradition'. Pages 275-300 in *Tradition and Theology in the
        Old Testament*. Ed. Douglas Knight. Philadelphia, PA: Fortress.
Fitzmyer, Joseph
1963   "Now this Melchizedek...' (Heb 7:1)'. *CBQ* 25:305-321.
1967   *The Aramaic Inscription of Sefire*. Rome: PBI.
1971   *A Genesis Apocryphon of Qumran Cave I*. Second, Revised Edition.
        Rome: PBI.
Fitzmyer, Joseph and Daniel Harrington
1978   *A Manual of Palestinian Aramaic Texts*. Rome: PBI.
Fohrer, Georg
1959   'Der Vertrag zwischen König und Volk in Israel'. *ZAW* 71:1-22.
1968   'Twofold Aspects of Hebrew Words'. Pages 95-103 in *Words and
        Meanings: Essays Presented to David Winton Thomas*. Ed. Peter
        Ackroyd and Barnabas Lindars. Cambridge: Cambridge University
        Press.
[1968] 1972 *History of Israelite Religion*. Nashville, TN: Abingdon.
1976   'Sophia'. Pages 63-83 in *Studies in Ancient Israelite Wisdom*. See
        Crenshaw, ed., 1976.
Frankfort, Henri
[1954] 1977 *The Art and Architecture of the Ancient Orient*. Harmondsworth:
        Penguin.
[1948] 1978 *Kingship and the Gods*. Chicago, IL: University of Chicago Press.
Fraser, Bruce
1979   'The Interpretation of Novel Metaphors'. Pages 172-185 in *Metaphor
        and Thought*. See Ortony 1979a.
Freedman, D.N.
1981   'Temple Without Hands'. Pages 21-30 in *Temples and High Places*. See
        Biran 1981.
Fretheim, Terence
1984   *The Suffering of God: An Old Testament Perspective*. Philadelphia, PA:
        Fortress.
Friedländer, M.
[1873] ND *The Commentary of ibn Ezra on Isaiah*. New York: Feldheim.
Fritz, Volkmar
1976   'Die Deutungen des Königtums Saul in den Überlieferungen von

seiner Entstehung I Sam 9-11'. *ZAW* 88:346-362.

Garbini, Giovanni
 1988   *History and Ideology in Ancient Israel*. NY: Crossroads.

Gardner, Howard and Ellen Winner
 1979   'The Development of Metaphoric Competence: Implications for Humanistic Disciplines'. Pages 121-139 in *On Metaphor*. See Sacks 1979.

Geertz, Clifford
 1973   *The Interpretation of Cultures*. NY: Basic Books.

Geiger, Abraham
 1928   *Urschrift und Übersetzungen der Bibel*. Frankfurt am Main: Madda.

Gelston, A.
 1966   'A Note on יהוה מלך'. *VT* 16:507-512.
 1974   'Kingship in the Book of Hosea'. *OTS* 19:71-85.

Gesenius, Wilhelm
 [1910] 1974 *Gesenius' Hebrew Grammar*. Ed. E. Kautzsch. Trans. A.E. Cowley. Oxford: Oxford University Press.

Gibson, Arthur
 1981   *Biblical Semantic Logic*. Oxford: Basil Blackwell.

Gibson, John C.L
 1971, 1975,
 1982   *Textbook of Syrian Semitic Inscriptions*. 3 vols. Oxford: Oxford University Press.
 1977   *Canaanite Myths and Legends*. Edinburgh: T and T Clark.

Gilbert, Maurice and Stephen Pisano
 1980   'Psalm 110 (109), 5-7'. *Biblica* 61:343-356.

Ginsberg, H.L.
 1946   *The Legend of King Keret*. BASOR Sup, 2-3. New Haven, CT: ASOR.
 1982   *The Israelian Heritage of Judaism*. NY: Jewish Theological Seminary.

Ginsburger, Moses
 1903   *Pseudo-Jonathan*. Berlin: S. Calvary and Co.

Ginzberg, Louis
 1961   *A Commentary on the Palestinian Talmud*. vol. IV. NY: Jewish Theological Seminary of America. (Hebrew).
 [1909-1938] 1968 *The Legends of the Jews*. Seven volumes. Philadelphia, PA: The Jewish Publication Society.

Ginsburg, C.D.
 1926   *The Torah, The Writings*. London: British and Foreign Bible Society.

Görg, Manfried
 1977   'Eine neue Deutung für Kapporaet'. *ZAW* 89:115-119.

Good, Robert
 1985   'The Just War in Ancient Israel'. *JBL* 104:385-400.

Goodenough, Erwin R.
 1964   *Jewish Symbols in the Greco-Roman Period*. Vol. 9. NY: Pantheon.

Gordon, Cyrus H.
 1965   *Ugaritic Textbook*. 3 vols. Rome: PBI.

Gottlieb, Hans
 [1976] 1980 'Myth in the Psalms'. Pages 62-93 in *Myth in the Old Testament*. Ed. Benedict Otzen, Hans Gottlieb and Knud Jeppesen. London: SCM.

Gray, George Buchanan
 [1903] 1976 *Numbers*. ICC. Edinburgh: T and T Clark.

Gray, John
[1964] 1976   *I and II Kings*. OTL. Philadelphia, PA: Westminster.
1979   *The Biblical Doctrine of the Reign of God*. Edinburgh: T and T Clark.

Greenberg, Moshe
1972   'Exodus, Book of'. *EncJud* 6:1050-1067.
1983a   *Biblical Prose Prayer*. Berkeley, CA: University of California Press.
1983b   *Ezekiel 1-20*. AB. Garden City, NY: Doubleday.

Greenfield, Jonas
1959   'Lexicographical Notes II'. *HUCA* 30:141-151.
1985   'Ba'al's Throne and Isa 6:1'. Pages 193-198 in *Mélanges bibliques et orientaux en l'honneur de M. Mathias Delcor*. AOAT 215. Ed. A. Caquot et al. Kevalaer: Verlag Butzon und Bercker.

Greenstein, Edward
1983   'How Does Parallelism Mean?'. Pages 41-70 in *A Sense of Text. A JQR Supplement*. Winona Lake, IN: Eisenbrauns.

Gruber, Mayer I.
1980   *Aspects of Nonverbal Communication in the Ancient Near East*. 2 vols. Studia Pohl, 12. Rome: PBI.

Gunkel, Hermann
[1930] 1967   *The Psalms: A Form-Critical Introduction*. Translated Thomas M. Horner. Philadelphia, PA: Fortress.

Gunkel, Hermann and Begrich, J.
1933   *Einleitung in die Psalmen*. HKAT suppl. Göttingen: Vandenhoeck und Ruprecht.

Gunneweg, A.H.J.
1983   'עם הארץ—A Semantic Revolution'. *ZAW* 95:437-440.

Hall, Donald
1985   'A Fear of Metaphors'. *NY Times Magazine*. July 14, 6-8.

Hallo, William W.
1957   *Early Mesopotamian Royal Titles: A Philological and Historical Analysis*. New Haven, CT: American Oriental Society.
1988   'Texts, Statues and the Cult of the Divine King'. *VT* 40:54-66.

Halpern, Baruch
1981   *The Constitution of the Monarchy in Israel*. HSM 25. Chico, CA: Scholars Press.

Hanson, Paul
1968   'The Song of Heshbon and David's NÎR,' *HTR* 61:297-320.

Haran, Menachem
1963   *Between Former Prophecies and New Prophecies*. Jerusalem: Magnes. (Hebrew)
1971   'The Graded Numerical Sequence and the Phenomenon of "Automatism" in Biblical Poetry'. *SVT* 22:238-267.
1978   *Temples and Temple-Service in Ancient Israel*. Oxford: Oxford University Press.

Hay, David M.
1973   *Glory at the Right Hand*. SBLMS 18. Nashville, TN: Abington.

Healey, John F.
1984   'The Immortality of the King: Ugarit and the Psalms'. *Or* 53:245-254.

Heidel, Alexander
[1942] 1963   *The Babylonian Genesis*. Second Edition. Chicago, IL: University of
              Chicago.
Heider, George C.
1985   *The Cult of Molek: A Reassessment*. JSOT Sup 43. Sheffield: JSOT
              Press.
Heidt, William George
1949   *Angelology of the Old Testament*. Washington, D.C: Catholic University
              of America Press.
Held, Moshe
1968   'The Root ZBL/SBL in Akkadian, Ugaritic and Biblical Hebrew'.
              JAOS 53 (*Essays in Memory of E.A. Speiser*):90-96.
Heltzer, M. and M. Ohana
1978   *The Extra-Biblical Tradition of Hebrew Personal Names*. Haifa:
              University of Haifa. (Hebrew)
Henle, Paul
[1958] 1967   'Metaphor'. Pages 173-195 in *Language, Thought and Culture*. Ed.
              Paul Henle. Ann Arbor, Michigan: University of Michigan Press.
Herdner, Andréer
1963   *Corpus des Tablettes en Cunéiformes Alphabétiques*. MRS 10. Paris:
              Geuthner.
Hestrin, Ruth and Michal Dayagi-Mendels
1978   *First Temple Seals*. Jerusalem: The Israel Museum. (Hebrew)
Higger, Michael
1937   *Tractate Sofrim*. NY: Devai Rabbanan. (Hebrew)
Hildebrandt, Ted
1988   'Proverbial Pairs: Compositional Units in Proverbs 10-29'. *JBL*
              107:207-224.
Hillers, Delbert
1967   'Delocutive Verbs in Biblical Hebrew'. *JBL* 86:320-324.
1984   *Micah*. Hermeneia. Philadelphia: Fortress Press.
Hoffman, Yair
1976-77   'On the Use of Two "Introductory Formulae" in Biblical Language'.
              Tarbiz 46:157-180. (Hebrew)
Holladay, William L.
1986   *Jeremia 1*. Hermeneia. Philadelphia, PA: Fortress.
Honeyman, A.M.
1948   'The Evidence for Regnal Names Among the Hebrews'. *JBL* 67:13-
              25.
Hönig, Hans Wolfram
1957   *Die Bekleidung des Hebräers*. Zurich: Brunner, Bodmer and Co.
Hornung, Erik
[1971]1982   *Conceptions of God in Ancient Egypt: The One and the Many*.
              Translated John Baines. Ithica, NY: Cornell University Press.
Humbert, Paul
1946   *La 'Terou'a': Analyse d'une Rite Biblique*. Neuchâtel: Université de
              Neuchâtel.
Hurvitz, Avi
1972   *The Transition Period in Biblical Hebrew: A Study in Post-Exilic
              Hebrew and its Implications for the Dating of Psalms*. Jerusalem: Bialik
              Institute. (Hebrew)

1974   'The Date of the Prose-Tale of Job Linguistically Reconsidered'. *HTR*
            67:17-34.
1983   'The Language of the Priestly Source and its Historical Setting—The
            Case for an Early Date'. Pages 53-94 in *Proceedings of the Eighth
            World Congress of Jewish Studies, Panel Sessions: Bible Studies and
            Hebrew Language*. Jerusalem: World Union of Jewish Studies.
Ikeda, Yutaka
1982   'Solomon's Trade in Horses and Chariots in its International Setting'.
            Pages 215-238 in Ishida, ed., 1982.
Ishida, Tomoo
1977   נגיד: A Term for the Legitimization of the Kingship'. *Annual of the
            Japanese Biblical Institute* 3:35-51.
Ishida, Tomoo, ed.
1982   *Studies in the Period of David and Solomon and Other Essays*. Winona
            Lake, IN: Eisenbrauns.
Jacobsen, Thorkild
1970   *Toward the Image of Tammuz and Other Essays on Mesopotamian
            History and Culture*. Ed. W.L. Moran. Cambridge, MA: Harvard
            University Press.
1976   *The Treasures of Darkness*. New Haven, CT: Yale University Press.
Janzen, J. Gerald
1973   *Studies in the Text of Jeremiah*. HSM 6. Cambridge, MA: Harvard
            University Press.
Japhet, Sara
1968   'The Supposed Common Authorship of Chronicles and Ezra-
            Nehemia Investigated Anew'. *VT* 18:330-371.
1977   *The Ideology of the Book of Chronicles and its Place in Biblical
            Thought*. Jerusalem: Bialik Institute. (Hebrew)
Jean, Charles F. and Jacob Hoftijzer
1965   *Dictionnaire des Inscriptions Sémitiques de l'Ouest*. Leiden: E.J.
            Brill.
Jefferson, H.G.
1952   'Psalm 93'. *JBL* 71:155-160.
Jenni, Ernst and Claus Westermann
[1971] 1975 *Theologisches Handwörterbuch zum Alten Testament*. 2 vols. Munich:
            Chr. Kaiser.
Jeremias, Jörg
1987   *Das Königtum Gottes in den Psalmen*. FRLANT 141. Göttingen:
            Vandenhoeck & Ruprecht.
Johnson, Aubrey R.
1935   'The Role of the King in the Jerusalem Cultus'. Pages 71-111 in *The
            Labyrinth*. Ed. S.H. Hooke. London: The Society for Promoting
            Christian Knowledge.
1958   Hebrew Conceptions of Kingship. Pages 204-235 in *Myth and Ritual*.
            Ed. S.H. Hooke. London: Oxford University Press.
[1944] 1962 *The Cultic Prophet in Ancient Israel*. Cardiff: University of Wales.
1967   *Sacral Kingship in Ancient Israel*. Cardiff: University of Wales
            Press.
Johnson, Mark, ed.
1981   *Philosophical Perspectives on Metaphor*. Minneapolis, MN: Univ. of
            Minnesota Press.

Jones, G. H.
1965   'The Decree of Yahweh (Ps. II 7)'. *VT* 15:336-344.
Joüon, Paul
[1923] 1965   *Grammaire de l'Hébreu Biblique*. Rome: PBI.
Kaddari, M.Z.
1973   'A Semantic Approach to Biblical Parallelism'. *JSS* 24:167-175.
Kalugila, Leonidas
1980   *The Wise King: Studies in Royal Wisdom as Divine Revelation in the Old Testament and Its Environment*. CBOT 15. Lund: CWK Gleerup.
Kapelrud, Arvid
1963   'Nochmals Yahwä Mäläk'. *VT* 13:229-331.
1980   'Creation in Ras Shamra Texts'. *Studia Theologica* 34:1-11.
Kaufmann, Yehezkel
[1960] 1972a   *The Religion of Israel*. Translated and Abridged Moshe Greenberg. NY: Schocken.
1972b   *The History of Israelite Religion*. 8 vols. in 4. Jerusalem and Tel-Aviv: Bialik and Devir. (Hebrew)
Keel, Othmar
1977   *Jahwe-Visionen und Siegelkunst*. *Stuttgarter Bibelstudien* 84/85. Stuttgart: Verlag Katholisches Bibelwerk.
Kenik, Helen
1976   'Code of Conduct for a King: Psalm 101'. *JBL* 95:391-403.
Kirkpatrick, A.F.
1902   *The Book of Psalms*. Cambridge: Cambridge University Press.
Klein, Ralph
1978   'A Theology for Exiles—The Kingship of Yahweh'. *Dialog* 17:128-134.
Koch, Klaus
[1964] 1969   *The Growth of the Biblical Tradition*. London: Adam and Charles Black.
Koehler, Ludwig
1953   'Syntactica III:IV *Jahwäh mäläk*'. *VT* 3:188-189.
Koehler, Ludwig and Walter Baumgartner
1958   *Lexicon in Veteris Testamenti Libros*. Leiden: Brill.
Kopf, L.
1958   'Arabische Etymologien und Parallelen zum Bibelwörterbuch'. *VT* 8:161-215.
Kosmola, H.
[1971] 1975   'גבר'. *TDOT*, II:367-382.
Krašovec, Jože
1988   *La justice (ṣdq) de dieu dans la bible hébraïque et l'interprétation juive et chrétienne*. Göttingen: Vandenhoeck & Ruprecht.
Kraus, Hans-Joachim
1951   *Die Königherrschaft Gottes im Alten Testament*. Tübingen: J.C.B. Mohr.
1961   *Psalmen*. BKAT XV1 and XV2. 2 vols. Neukirchen: Neukirchener Verlag.
[1962] 1966   *Worship in Israel*. Translated Geoffrey Buswell. Oxford: Blackwell.
Kreuzer, Siegfried
1985   'Zur Bedeutung und Etymologie von Hištaḥah/yštḥwy'. *VT* 35:39-60.

Kugel, James
1981 *The Idea of Biblical Poetry: Parallelism and its History*. New Haven, CT: Yale University Press.
Kuschke, Arnulf and Martin Metzger
1972 'Kumudi und die Ausgrabungen auf Tell Kamid el-Loz'. *VTSup* 22:143-173.
Kutsch, Ernst
1963 *Salbung als Rechtsakt*. BZAW 87. Berlin: Alfred Töpelmann.
Kutscher, Eduard Yechezkel
1959 *The Language and Linguistic Background of the Isaiah Scroll*. Jerusalem: Magnes Press. (Hebrew)
1982 *A History of the Hebrew Language*. Jerusalem: Magnes Press.
Labuschagne, C.J.
1966 *The Incomparability of Yahweh in the Old Testament*. Leiden: Brill.
Lakoff, George and Mark Johnson
1980 *Metaphors We Live By*. Chicago, IL: University of Chicago Press.
Lambdin, Thomas O.
1953 'Egyptian Loanwords in the Old Testament'. *JAOS* 53:145-155.
Lambert, W.G.
[1960] 1975 *Babylonian Wisdom Literature*. Oxford: Oxford University Press.
Langlamet, F.
1976 'Pour ou contre Salomon? La rédaction prosolomonienne de I Rois 1-11'. *RB* 83:321-379, 481-528.
Leiter, Samuel
1973-74 'Worthiness, Acclamation and Appointment: Some Rabbinic Terms'. *PAAJR* 41-42:137-168.
Lemaire, André
1979 'Note sur le titre *bn hmlk* dans l'ancien Israël'. *Semitica* 29: 59-65.
Levenson, Jon D.
1976 *Theology of the Program of Restoration of Ezekiel 40-48*. HSM 10. Missoula, MT: Scholars Press.
1981 'From Temple to Synagogue: 1 Kings 8'. Pages 143-166 in *Traditions in Transformation: Turning Points in Biblical Faith*. Ed. Baruch Halpern and Jon Levenson. Winona Lake, IN: Eisenbrauns.
1985 *Sinai and Zion: An Entry into the Jewish Bible*. Minneapolis, MN: Winston Press.
1987 'The Jerusalem Temple in Devotional and Visionary Experience'. Pages 32-61 in *Jewish Spirituality: From the Bible Through the Middle Ages*. Ed. Arthur Green. NY: Crossroads.
Levin, Samuel
1979 'Standard Approaches to Metaphor and a Proposal for Literary Metaphor'. Pages 124-135 in *Metaphor and Thought*. See Ortony 1979a.
Levine, Baruch
1982 'Toward an Investigation of the Priestly Source: The Linguistic Aspect'. *EI* 16 (Mazar Volume):124-131.
Levy, Jacob
1876-1889 *Neuhebräisches und Chaldäisches Wörterbuch über die Talmudim und Midraschim*. 4 vols. Leipzig: F. A. Brockhaus.
Licht, Jacob
1978 'The Sinai Theophany'. Pages 251-267 in *Studies in the Bible and the*

Ancient Near East Presented to Samuel E. Loewenstamm. Ed.
Yitschak Avishur and Joshua Blau. Jerusalem: Rubinstein's. Vol. I.
(Hebrew; English Summary Vol. II 201-202.)

Lieberman, Saul
1962   *Hellenism in Jewish Palestine*. NY: Jewish Theological Seminary.
Lipiński, Eduard
1962   'Les Psaumes de la Royauté de Yahwé dans l'exégèse Moderne'. Pages
        133-272 in *Le Psautier*. Ed. Robert de Langhe. Louvain: Institut
        Orientaliste.
1965   *La Royauté de Yahwé dans la Poésie et le Culte de l'ancien Israël*.
        Brussels: Paleis de Academiën.
1970   'Recherches sur le livre de Zacharie'. *VT* 20:25-55.
1974   'Nāgid, der Kronprinz'. *VT* 24:497-499.
Liver, Jacob
1967   'The Book of the Acts of Solomon'. *Biblica* 48:75-101.
Loewenstamm, Samuel
1969   'The Expanded Colon in Ugaritic and Biblical Verse'. *JSS* 14:176-
        196.
Long, Burke 0.
1984   *1 Kings with an Introduction to the Historical Literature*. FOTL 11.
        Grand Rapids, MI: Eerdmans.
Loewenberg, Ina
1974   'Identifying Metaphors'. *Foundations of Language* 12:315-338.
Luzzatto, S.D.
[1855-1897]
1970   *Commentary on the Book of Isaiah*. Tel-Aviv: Dvir. (Hebrew)
Lyons, John
1977   *Semantics*. Vol. 1. Cambridge: Cambridge University Press.
MacCormic, Earl R.
1976   *Metaphor and Myth in Science and Religion*. Durham, NC: Duke
        University Press.
Machinist, Peter
1983   'Assyria and Its Image in the First Isaiah'. *JAOS* 103:719-737.
Macholz, Georg Christian
1972   'Zur Geschichte der Justizorganisation in Juda'. *ZAW* 84:314-340.
Malamat, Abraham
1982   'Longevity: Biblical Concepts and Some Ancient Near East Parallels'.
        AfO 19: 215-224.
Mann, Thomas W.
1977   *Divine Presence and Guidance in Israelite Traditions: The Typology of
        Exaltation. Johns Hopkins Near Eastern Studies*. Baltimore, MD:
        Johns Hopkins University Press.
Marmorstein, A.
1927   *The Old Rabbinic Doctrine of God: The Name and Attributes of God*.
        London: Oxford University Press.
Mauser, Ulrich
1970   'Image of God and Incarnation'. *Interpretation* 24:336-356.
McCarter, P. Kyle
1980   *I Samuel*. AB. Garden City, NY.: Doubleday.
1984   *II Samuel*. AB. Garden City, NY: Doubleday.

McFague, Sallie
    1982   *Metaphorical Theology: Models of God in Religious Language.* Philadelphia, PA: Fortress Press.
    1987   *Models of God: Theology for an Ecological, Nuclear Age.* Philadelphia, PA: Fortress.

McKane, William
    [1970] 1977   *Proverbs.* OTL. Philadelphia, PA: Westminster.
    1986   *Jeremiah.* ICC. Edinburgh: T and T Clark.

McKenzie, John L.
    1967   'Reflections on Wisdom'. *JBL* 86:1-9.

Melammed, Ezra Zion
    1948   'Biblical Phrases Unique to God'. *Tarbiz* 19:1-18. (Hebrew)

Mendelsohn, Isaac
    1956   'Samuel's Denunciation of Kingship in Light of Akkadian Documents from Ugarit'. *BASOR* 143:17-22.

Meshel, Zeev
    1978   *Kuntillet 'Ajrud: A Religious Centre from the Time of the Judaean Monarchy on the Border of Sinai.* Jerusalem: Israel Museum. (Hebrew)

Mettinger, Tryggve N.D.
    1971   *Solomonic State Officials.* CBOT 5. Lund: CWK Gleerup.
    1973   'The Hebrew Verb System: A Survey of Recent Research'. *ASTI* 9:64-84.
    1976   *King and Messiah: The Civil Legitimation of the Israelite King.* CBOT 8. Lund: CWK Gleerup.
    1978   'The Veto on Images and the Aniconic God in Ancient Israel'. Pages 15-29 in *Religious Symbols and their Functions.* Ed. H. Biezais. Stockholm: Almqvist and Wiksell.
    1982a   *The Dethronement of Sabaoth: Studies in the Shem and Kabod Theologies.* CBOT 18. Lund: CWK Gleerup.
    1982b   'YHWH SABAOTH—The Heavenly King on the Cherubim Throne'. Pages 109-138 in *Studies in the Period of David and Solomon and Other Essays.* See Ishida 1982.
    1986-87   'In Search of the Hidden Structure: YHWH as King in Isaiah 40-55'. *SEÅ* 51-52:148-157.

Metzger, Martin
    1985   *Königthron und Gottesthron.* AOAT 15. 2 vols. Kevelaer: Verlag Butzon & Bercker.

Michel, Diethelm
    1956   'Studien zu den sogenannten Thronbesteigungspsalmen'. *VT* 6:40-68.

Milgrom, Jacob
    1970   *Studies in Levitical Terminology, I: The Encroacher and the Levite and the Term 'Aboda.* University of CA Near Eastern Studies 14. Berkeley, CA: University of California Press.

Miller, George A.
    1979   'Images and Models, Similes and Metaphors'. Pages 202-250 in *Metaphor and Thought.* See Ortony 1979a.

Miller, Patrick D.
    1973   *The Divine Warrior in Early Israel.* HSM 5. Cambridge, MA: Harvard University Press.

Miller, Patrick D. Jr., Paul Hanson and S. Dean McBride, eds.
1987   *Ancient Israelite Religion: Essays on Honor of Frank Cross.*
          Philadelphia, PA: Fortress.
Montgomery, James and Henry Snyder Gehman
[1951] 1976   *The Books of Kings.* ICC. Edinburgh: T and T Clark.
Morgan, Jerry L.
1979   'Observations on the Pragmatics of Metaphor'. Pages 136-147 in
          Metaphor and Thought. See Sacks 1979.
Mowinckel, Sigmund
[1951] 1956   *He That Cometh.* NY: Abington.
1959   'General Oriental and Specific Israelite Elements in the Israelite
          Conception of the Sacral Kingdom'. Pages 283-293 in *The Sacral
          Kingship.* Leiden: E.J. Brill.
[1930] 1961   *Psalmstudien II: Das Thronbesteigungsfest Jahwës und der Ursprung
          der Eschatologie.* Amsterdam: P. Schippers.
[1961] 1979   *The Psalms in Israel's Worship.* Translated D. R. Ap-Thomas. 2 vols.
          Nashville, TN: Abingdon.
Muilenberg, James
1966   'A Liturgy on the Triumphs of Yahweh'. Pages 233-251 in *Studia
          Biblica et Semitica* (Vriezen Fss.). Wageningen: Veenman & Zonen.
Mulder, J.S.M.
1972   *Studies on Psalm 45.* Oss: Offsetdrukkerij Witsiers.
Mullen, E. Theodore
1980   *The Assembly of the Gods.* HSM 24. Cambridge, MA: Harvard
          University Press.
Muraoka, T.
1985   *Emphatic Words and Structures in Biblical Hebrew.* Jerusalem:
          Magnes Press.
Murphy, Roland
1981   *Wisdom Literature. Job, Proverbs, Ruth, Canticles, Ecclesiastes,
          Esther.* FOTL XIII. Grand Rapids, MI: Eerdmans.
Murray, Robert
1982   'Prophecy and the Cult'. Pages 200-216 in *Israel's Prophetic Tradition:
          Essays in Honor of Peter Ackroyd.* Ed. Richard Coggins et al.
          Cambridge: Cambridge University Press.
Myers, Carol and Eric
1987   *Haggai, Zechariah 1-8.* AB. Garden City, NY: Doubleday.
Neuberg, Frank J.
1950   'An Unrecognized Meaning of Hebrew DÔR'. *JNES*:215-217.
Newsom, Carol
1984   'A Maker of Metaphors—Ezekiel's Oracles Against Tyre'. *Interpretation*
          38:151-164.
1985   *Songs of the Sabbath Sacrifice: A Critical Edition.* HSS 27. Atlanta,
          GA: Scholars Press.
Niehr, Herbert
1986   *Herrschen und Richtern: Die Wurzel špṭ im Alten Orient und im Alten
          Testament.* Würzburg: Echter.
1987   'Grundzüge der Forschung zur Gerichtsorganisation Israels'. BZ
          31:206-227.
North, Christopher
1932   'The Religious Aspects of Hebrew Kingship'. *ZAW* 50:8-38.

1948   *The Suffering Servant in Deutero-Isaiah*. Oxford: Oxford University Press.

Noth, Martin
1928   *Die israelitischen Personennamen in Rahmen der gemeinsemitischen Namengebung*. BWANT III. Stuttgart: W. Kohlhammer.

Oded, Bustenay
1977   'Judah and the Exile'. Pages 435-488 in *Israelite and Judaean History*. OTL. Ed. John H. Hayes and J. Maxwell Miller. Philadelphia, PA.

Olivier, J. P. J.
1979   'The Sceptre of Justice and Ps. 45:7b'. *Journal of Northwest Semitic Languages* 7:45-54.

Oppenheim, A. Leo
1943   'Akkadian pul(u)ḫ(t)u and melammu'. *JAOS* 63: 31-34.
1968   'The Eyes of the Lord'. *JAOS* 88:173-180.

Oppenheim, A. Leo et al.
1958-   *The Assyrian Dictionary of the Oriental Institute of the University of Chicago*. Chicago, IL: The Oriental Institute.

Ortony, Andrew, ed.
1979a.   *Metaphor and Thought*. Cambridge: Cambridge University Press.
1979b   'Metaphor: A Multidimensional Problem'. Pages 1-16 in *Metaphor and Thought*. See Ortony, 1979a.

Ottosson, M.
[1975] 1978   'היכל'. *TDOT* III, 382-388.

Paivio, Allan
1979   'Psychological Processes in the Comprehension of Metaphor'. Pages 150-171 in *Metaphor and Thought*. See Ortony 1979a.

Paley, Samuel M.
1976   *King of the World: Ashur-nasir-pal II of Assyria 883-859 BC*. Brooklyn, NY: Brooklyn Museum.

Pardee, Dennis
1977   'A New Ugaritic Letter'. *BiOr* 34:3-20.

Pardee, Dennis et al.
1982   *Handbook of Ancient Hebrew Letters*. SBL Sources for Biblical Study 15. Chico, CA: Scholars Press.

Parker, Richard
1950   *The Calendars of Ancient Egypt*. Chicago, IL: University of Chicago Press.

Paul, Shalom
1972   'Psalm 72:5—A Traditional Blessing for the Long Life of the King'. *JNES* 31:351-355.
1978   'Adoption Formulae'. *EI* 14 (H. L. Ginsberg Volume):31-36. (Hebrew, English summary 123*)

Pope, Marvin
[1965] 1973   *Job*. AB. Garden City, NY: Doubleday.
1977   *Song of Songs*. AB. Garden City, NY: Doubleday.

Porten, Bezalel
1978   'The Documents in the Book of Ezra and the Mission of Ezra'. *Shnaton* 3:174-196. (Hebrew; English summary XIX-XX)

Porter, Paul A.
1983   *Metaphors and Monsters: A Literary Critical Study of Daniel 7 and 8*. CBOT 20. Lund: CWK Gleerup.

Prigent, Pierre
    1959   'Quelques Testamonia messianiques'. *TZ* 15:419-430.
Pritchard, James, ed.
    1969a   *Ancient Near Eastern Texts Relating to the Old Testament*. 3rd Edition with Supplement. Princeton, NJ: Princeton University Press.
    1969b   *The Ancient Near East in Pictures Relating to the Old Testament*. 2nd Edition with Supplement. Princeton, NJ: Princeton University Press.
Qimron, Elisha
    1978   'On Second-Temple Language in Psalms'. *Beth Mikra* 23/72:139-150. (Hebrew)
Quintens, Werner
    1978   'La vie du roi dans Psaume 21'. *Biblica* 59: 516-541.
Rabin, Chaim
    1962   'Is Biblical Semantics Possible?' *Beth Mikra* 7:17-22. (Hebrew)
Rabinowitz, Isaac, ed.
    1983   *The Book of the Honeycomb's Flow*. Ithaca, NY: Cornell University Press.
Rahlfs, Alfred, ed.
    1935   *Septuaginta*. Stuttgart: Württembergische Bibelanstalt.
Rainey, Anson
    1968-69 'בן המלך *at Ugarit and Among the Hittites*'. *Leshonenu* 33:304-308. (Hebrew)
    1970   'Compulsory Labour Gangs in Ancient Israel'. *IEJ* 20:191-202.
Ramsey, Ian T., ed.
    1971a   *Words about God: The Philosophy of Religion*. NY: Harper and Row.
Ramsey, Ian T.
    [1966] 1971b 'Talking about God'. Pages 202-218 in *Words about God*. See Ramsey 1971a.
Reade, Julian
    1975   'Sources for Sennacherib: The Prisms'. *JCS* 27:189-198.
    1983   *Assyrian Sculpture*. Cambridge, MA: Harvard University Press.
Redford, Donald
    1970   *A Study of the Biblical Story of Joseph*. VTSup 20. Leiden: E.J. Brill.
    1972   'Studies in Relations between Palestine and Egypt during the First Millenium B.C.: The Taxation System of Solomon'. Pages 141-156 in *Studies on the Ancient Palestian World Presented to Prof. F. V. Winnet*. Ed. J.W. Wever and D.B. Redfield. Toronto: University of Toronto Press.
Revell, E. J.
    1981   'Pausal Forms and the Structure of Biblical Poetry'. *VT* 31:186-199.
Richards, I.A.
    1936   *The Philosophy of Rhetoric*. NY: Oxford University Press.
Richter, Wolfgang
    1965   'Zu den "Richtern Israels"'. *ZAW* 77:40-72.
Ricoeur, Paul
    1977   *The Rule of Metaphor: Multidisciplinary Studies of the Creation of*

Meaning in Language. Translated by Robert Czerny et al. Toronto: University of Toronto Press.

Ridderbos, J.
1954   'Jahwäh Malak'. *VT* 4:87-89.

Ringgren, Helmer
[*1963*] 1966   *Israelite Religion.* Translated David Green. Philadelphia, PA: Fortress Press.

Roberts, J.J.M.
1973   'The Davidic Origin of the Zion Tradition'. *JBL* 92:329-344.
1982   'Zion in the Theology of the Davidic-Solomonic Empire'. Pages 93-108 in *Studies in the Period of David and Solomon and Other Essays.* See Ishida, 1982.
1987   'In Defence of the Monarchy: The Contribution of Israelite Kingship to Biblical Theology'. Pages 377-396 in *Ancient Israelite Religion.* See Miller et al., 1987.

Robertson, David A.
1972   *Linguistic Evidence in Dating Early Hebrew Poetry.* SBLDS 3. Missoula, MT: Scholars Press.

Rofé, Alexander
1969   *Israelite Belief in Angels in the Pre-exilic Sources as Evidenced by the Biblical Traditions.* Ph.D. diss., Hebrew University, Jerusalem. (Hebrew with English Summary)
1970   'The Classification of Prophetical Stories'. *JBL* 89:427-440.
1974   'Review of Weinfeld's *Deuteronomy and the Deuteronomic School*'. *Christian News from Israel* 24:204-209.
1982   *The Prophetical Stories.* Jerusalem: Magnes Press. (Hebrew)

Rooker, Mark
1988   *Biblical Hebrew in Transition: The Language of the Book of Ezekiel.* Ph.D. diss., Brandeis University.

Rosenthal, Erwin I.J.
1958   'Some Aspects of the Hebrew Monarchy'. *JJS* 9:1-18.

Rosenthal, Franz
1961   *A Grammar of Biblical Aramaic.* Wiesbaden: Otto Harrasowitz.
1967   *An Aramaic Handbook* I/2. Wiesbaden: Otto Harrasowitz.

Ross, James.
1962   'The Prophet as Yahweh's Messenger'. Pages 98-107 in *Israel's Prophetic Heritage.* Ed. B.W. Anderson and W. Harrelson. NY: Harper and Row.
1967   'Jahweh ṣebā'ôt in Samuel and Psalms'. *VT* 17:76-92.

Rudolph, Wilhelm
1955   *Chronikbücher.* HAT. Tübingen: J.C.B. Mohr.
1968   *Jeremia.* HAT. Tübingen: J.C.B. Mohr.
1976   *Haggai-Sacharja 1-8-Sacharja 9-14-Maleachi. KAT* XII/4. Gütersloh: Gütersloher Verlagshaus Gerd Mohn.

Sacks, Sheldon, ed.
1979   *On Metaphor.* Chicago: University of Chicago.

Safrai, Shmuel
1972   'Second Temple, Ritual'. *EncJud* 15:969-984.

Saggs, H.W.F.
1984   *The Might that was Assyria.* London: Sidgwick and Jackson.

Sanders, J.A.

1965   *The Psalms Scroll of Qumran Cave 11. DJD* IV. Oxford: Oxford
           University Press.
Sarna, Nahum
1973   'Zedekiah's Emancipation of Slaves and the Sabbatical Year'. *Orient
           and Occident: Essays Presented to Cyrus H. Gordon*. Ed. Harry A.
           Hoffner, Jr. Neukirchen-Vluyn: Neukirchener Verlag.
1979   'The Divine Title 'abhîr ya'ăqôbh'. Pages 389-398 in *Essays on the
           Occasion of the 70th Anniversary of Dropsie University*. Philadelphia,
           PA.
Sawyer, John
1972   *Semantics in Biblical Research*. SBT II 24. London: SCM.
Schmidt, Ludwig
1970   *Menschlicher Erfolg und Jahwes Initiative*. WMANT 38. Neukirchen-
           Vluyn: Neukirchener Verlag.
Schmidt, Werner
1961   *Königtum Gottes in Ugarit und Israel*. BZAW 80. Berlin: Töpelmann.
[1968] 1983 *The Faith of the Old Testament*. Translated John Sturdy. Philadelphia,
           PA: Westminster.
Scholem, Gershom
[1960] 1965 *Jewish Gnosticism, Merkabah Mysticism and Talmudic Tradition*. NY:
           Jewish Theological Seminary.
Searle, John
1979   'Metaphor'. Pages 92-113 in *Metaphor and Thought*. See Ortony
           1979a.
Seeligmann, I.L.
1980/81   'Psalm 47'. *Tarbiz* 50: 25-35 (Hebrew).
Segal, M.H.
[1927] 1980 *A Grammar of Mishnaic Hebrew*. Oxford: Oxford University Press.
Seux, M.-J.
1967   *Epithetes Royales Akkadiennes et Sumeriennes*. Paris: Letouzey et
           Ane.
Shaviv, Shemuel
1984   'Nâbî' and Nāgîd in I Samuel IX 1-X 16'. *VT* 34:108-113.
Shinan, Avigdor
1979   'The Sins of Nadab and Abihu in Rabbinic Legend'. *Tarbiz* 48:201-
           214. (Hebrew)
Simon, Uriel
1967   'The Poor Man's Ewe-Lamb: An Example of a Judicial Parable'.
           Biblica 48:207-242.
Skehan, Patrick W.
1954   'A Fragment of the "Song of Moses" (Deut 32) from Qumran'.
           BASOR 136:12-15.
1980   'The Divine Name at Qumran, in the Masada Scroll, and in the
           Septuagint'. *Bulletin of the International Organization for Septuagint
           and Cognate Studies* 13:14-44.
Slomovic, Elieser
1979   'Toward an Understanding of the Formation of the Historical Titles in
           the Book of Psalms'. *ZAW* 91:350-380.
Smith, Gary V.
1982   'The Concept of God/the Gods as King in the Ancient Near East and
           the Bible'. *Trinity Journal* 3:18-38.

Smith, J.M.P.
[1911] 1974   *Micah, Zephaniah and Nahum*. ICC. Edinburgh: T and T Clark.

Smith, Mark
1988   'Divine Form and Size in Ugaritic and Pre-exilic Israelite Religion'. *ZAW* 100: 424-427.

Smith, Morton
1952   'The Common Theology of the Ancient Near East'. *JBL* 71:135-147.
1971   *Palestinian Parties and Politics that Shaped the Old Testament*. NY: Columbia University Press.

Snaith, Norman N.
1947   *The Jewish New Year Festival*. London: Society for Promoting Christian Knowledge.

Soggon, J. Alberto
1982   'Compulsory Labor under David and Solomon'. Pages 259-267 in *Studies in the Period of David and Solomon and Other Essays*. See Ishida 1982.

Soskice, Janet
1985   *Metaphor and Religious Language*. Oxford: Oxford University Press.
1987   'Theological Realism'. Pages 105-119 in *The Rationality of Religious Belief: Essays in Honour of Basil Mitchel*. Ed. William J. Abraham and Steven Holtzer. Oxford: Oxford University Press.
1988   'Myths, Metaphors and Narrative Theology', in *Proceedings of the Seventh European Conference of Philosophy of Religion*. Utrecht.

Speiser, E.A.
1955   'The Durative Hitpa'el: A tan-Form'. *JAOS* 75:119-121.
1963   'Background and Function of the Biblical Nasi'. *CBQ* 25:111-117.
1964   *Genesis*. AB. Garden City, NY: Doubleday.

Spencer, John R.
1984   'The Task of the Levites: šmr and ṣb". *ZAW* 96:267-271.

Sperber, Alexander
1959-1973   *The Bible in Aramaic*. 5 vols. Leiden: E. J. Brill.

Stuhlmueller, Caroll
1970   'Yahweh-King and Deutero-Isaiah'. *Biblical Research* 15:32-45.

Sweetman, James
1965   'Some Observations on the Background of צדיק in Jeremias 23,5a'. *Biblica* 46:29-40.

Tadmor, Hayim
1964   'The Historical Background of the Cyrus Declaration'. Pages 450-473 in *Oz Le-David*. Jerusalem: Kiryat Sepher. (Hebrew)
1971   'The "People" and the Kingship in Israel'. Pages 46-68 in *Jewish Society Throughout the Ages*. Ed. H. H. Ben-Sasson and S. Ettinger. NY: Schocken.
1976   'New-Year in Mesopotamia'. *EM* 7:305-311. (Hebrew)

Tadmor, H. and M. Cogan
1982   'Hezekiah's Fourteenth Year: The King's Illness and the Babylonian Embassy'. *EI* 16 (Harry Orlinsky Volume):198-201. (Hebrew; English summary p. 124*)

Talmon, Shemaryahu
1960   'Double Readings in the Massoretic Text'. *Textus* 1:144-185.
1967   'The Judean 'Am Ha'areṣ in Historical Perspective'. *Fourth World*

Congress of Jewish Studies, Papers. Vol. 1. Jerusalem: World Union of Jewish Studies, 71-76.

1977 'The "Comparative Method" in Biblical Interpretation—Principles and Problems'. *VTSup* 30:320-356.

1978 'On the Emendation of Biblical Texts on the Basis of Ugaritic Parallels'. *EI* 12 (H. L. Ginsburg Volume):117-124. (Hebrew; English Summary 127*)

Teixidor, James
1967 'Review of Fitzmyer, *A Genesis Apocryphon of Qumran Cave I*'. *JAOS* 87:633-636.

Theodor, J. and Ch. Albeck
1965 *Midrash Bereshit Rabbah*. Jerusalem: Wahrmann Books.

Thomas, D. Winton
1953 'A Consideration of Some Unusual Ways of Expressing the Superlative in Hebrew'. *VT* 3:209-224.

Thompson, Michael E.W.
1982 'Isaiah's Ideal King'. *JSOT* 24:79-88.

Thornton, T.C.G.
1963 'Charismatic Kingship in Israel and Judah'. *JTS* 14:1-11.

Tigay, Jeffrey H.
1986 *You Shall Have No Other Gods: Israelite Religion in Light of Hebrew Inscriptions*. HSS 31. Atlanta, GA: Scholars Press.

Tov, Emmanuel
1972 'The Contribution of Text Criticism to the Literary Criticism of Jeremiah'. *Beth Mikra* 50:279-287. (Hebrew)

Tracy, David
1979 'Metaphor and Religion: The Test Case of Christian Texts'. Pages 89-104 in *On Metaphor*. See Sacks 1979.

Trever, John (photographer)
1972 *Scrolls from Qumran Cave I*. Jerusalem: Albright Institute.

Trible, Phyllis
1978 *God and the Rhetoric of Sexuality*. Philadelphia, PA: Fortress.

Tsevat, Matitiahu
1965 'YHWH ṢEBA'OT'. *HUCA* 36:49-58.
1969-1970 'God and the Gods in Assembly'. *HUCA* 40-41:123-137.
1980a *The Meaning of the Book of Job and Other Essays*. New York: Ktav.
[1963, 1965] 1980b 'The Steadfast House'. Pages 101-117 in *The Meaning of the Book of Job and Other Essays*. See Tsevat, 1980a.
[1972/73] 1980c 'The Throne Vision of Isaiah'. Pages 155-176 in *The Meaning of the Book of Job and Other Essays*. See Tsevat, 1980a.
[1966/67] 1980d 'The Biblical Account of the Foundation of the Monarchy in Israel'. Pages 77-99 in *The Meaning of the Book of Job and Other Essays*. See Tsevat, 1980a.

Tur-Sinai, N.H.
1967 *The Book of Job: A New Commentary*. Revised Edition. Jerusalem: Kiryat Sepher.

Ullmann, Stephen.
[1951] 1967 *The Principles of Semantics*. Oxford: Basil Blackwell.

Ulrichsen, Jarl H.
1977 'JHWH MALAK: Einige sprachliche Beobachtungen'. *VT* 27: 361-374.

Urbach, E.E.
1959   'The Rabbinic Law of Idolatry in the Second and Third Centuries in the Light of Archeological and Historical Facts'. *IEJ* 9:149-165, 229-245.
1976   *The Sages*. Third edition. Jerusalem: Magnes Press. (Hebrew)

Ussishkin, D.
1966a   'Building IV in Hamath and the Temple of Solomon and Tel Tayanat'. *IEJ* 16:104-110.
1966b   'King Solomon's Palace and Building 1723 in Megiddo'. *IEJ* 16:174-186.

Vischer, Wilhelm
1949   'Words and Word: The Anthropomorphisms of the Biblical Revelation'. *Interpretation* 3:1-18.

Volz, Paul
1912   *Das Neujahrsfest Jahwes*. Tübingen: J.C.B. Mohr.

von Rad, Gerhard
[1957, 1960]
1962   *Old Testament Theology*. Vol. 1. Translated by D.M.G. Stalker. New York: Harper and Row.
[1958] 1966a *The Problem of the Hexateuch and Other Essays*. NY: McGraw Hill.
[1947] 1966b 'The Royal Ritual in Judah'. Pages 222-231 in *The Problem of the Hexateuch*. See von Rad. 1966a.

von Soden, Wolfram
1965. 1972.
1981   *Akkadisches Handwörterbuch*. 3 vols. Wiesbaden: Otto Hassasowitz.

Wagner, Max
1966   *Die lexikalischen und grammatikalischen Aramäismen im alttestamentlichen Hebräisch*. BZAW 96. Berlin: Töpelmann.

Wambacq, B.N.
1947   *L'épithète Divine Jahvé Seba'ôt*. Desclée: De Brouwer.

Warmuth, G.
[1974] 1978 'הדר'. *TDOT* III:335-341.

Watts, John D.W.
1965   'Yahweh Mālak Psalms'. *TZ* 21:341-348.

Wehmeier, G.
1976   'עלה'. *THAT* II:272-290.

Weinfeld, Moshe
1968   'God the Creator in Genesis 1 and in the Prophecies of Deutero Isaiah'. *Tarbiz* 37:102-132. (Hebrew)
1970   'The Covenant of Grant in the Old Testament and in the Ancient Near East'. *JAOS* 90:184-203.
1972   *Deuteronomy and the Deuteronomic School*. Oxford: Oxford University Press.
1975   'Berit—Covenant vs. Obligation'. *Biblica* 56:120-128.
1981   'Sabbath, Temple and the Enthronement of the LORD—The Problem of the Sitz im Leben of Genesis 1:1-2:2'. Pages 501-512 in *Mélanges bibliques et orientaux en l'honneur de M. Henri Cazelles*. AOAT 212. Ed. A. Caquot and M. Delcor. Kevalaer: Verlag Butzon & Bercker.
1982   'כבוד'. *TWAT* IV:23-40.
1984   'Divine Intervention in War in Ancient Assyria and in the Ancient Near East'. Pages 121-147 in *History, Historiography and Interpretation:*

Studies in Biblical and Cuneiform Literatures. Ed. H. Tadmor and M. Weinfeld. Jerusalem: Magnes.

1985 *Justice and Righteousness in Israel and the Nations*. Jerusalem: Magnes Press. (Hebrew)

Weiss, Meir

1984 *The Bible from Within: The Method of Total Interpretation*. Jerusalem: Magnes.

1987 *Scriptures in their Own Light: Collected Essays*. Jerusalem: Bialik Institute. (Hebrew)

Wellek, Rene and Austin Warren

[1963] 1973 *Theory of Literature*. 3rd ed. Penguin Edition. Harmondsworth: Penguin Books.

Wellhausen, Julius

[1878] 1973 *Prolegomena to the History of Ancient Israel*. Gloucester, MA: Peter Smith.

Welten, Peter

1982 'Königsherrschaft Jahwes und Thronbesteigung'. *VT* 32:299-310.

Westermann, Claus

[1960] 1967 *Basic Forms of Prophetic Speech*. Translated Hugh Clayton White. Philadelphia, PA: Westminster.

[1966] 1969 *Isaiah 40-66*. OTL. Philadelphia, PA: Westminster.

1975 'כבד'. *TWAT III*:794-811.

1976 'עבד'. *THAT* II:182-200.

[1967] 1980 *The Psalms: Structure, Content and Message*. Translated Ralph D. Gehrke. Minneapolis, MN: Augsburg.

[1965] 1981 *Praise and Lament in the Psalms*. Translated Keith Crim and Richard Soulen. Atlanta, GA: John Knox.

[1974] 1984 *Genesis*. Translated John Scullion. Minneapolis, MN: Augsburg.

Whitelam, Keith

1979 *The Just King: Monarchical and Judicial Authority in Ancient Israel*. JSOTSup 12. Sheffield: JSOT Press.

Whitley, C.F.

1986 'Textual and Exegetical Observations on Ps 45, 4-7'. *ZAW* 98:277-282.

Whybray, R.N.

1968 *The Succession Narrative*. SBT II 9. Naperville, IL: Allenson.

1974 *The Intellectual Tradition in the Old Testament*. BZAW 135. Berlin: de Gruyter.

Widengren Geo

1955 *Sakrales Königtum im Alten Testament und im Judentum*. Stuttgart: W. Kohlhammer.

1957 'King and Covenant'. *JSS* 2:1-32.

Wildberger, Hans

1972 *Jesaja 1-12*. BKAT. Neukirchen-Vluyn: Neukirchener Verlag.

Williamson, H.G.M.

1977 *Israel in the Books of Chronicles*. Cambridge: Cambridge University Press.

1982 *1 and 2 Chronicles*. NCBC. Grand Rapids, MI: Eerdmans.

Willis, John T.

1979 'Psalm 1—An Entity'. *ZAW* 91:381-401.

Wilson, Gerald

1984   'Evidence of Editorial Divisions in the Hebrew Psalter'. *VT* 34:337-352.

Wilson, Robert
1980   *Prophecy and Society in Ancient Israel*. Philadelphia, PA: Fortress Press.
1983   'Israel's Judicial System in the Preexilic Period'. *JQR* 74:229-248.

Wolff, Hans Walter
[1973] 1974a *Anthropology of the Old Testament*. Philadelphia, PA: Fortress.
[1965] 1974b *Hosea*. Hermeneia. Philadelphia, PA: Fortress Press.

Wyatt, N.
1985   '"Jedidah" and Cognate Forms as a Title of Royal Legitimation'. *Biblica* 66:112-125.

Yeivin, Shmuel
1971   ' פקיד,פקידות' *EM* VI:540-575. (Hebrew)

Zevit, Ziony
1982   'Converging Lines of Evidence Bearing on the Date of P'. *ZAW* 94: 481-511.

Zimmerli, Walther
1979, 1983 *Ezekiel*. 2 vols. Hermeneia. Philadelphia, PA: Fortress.

INDEXES

INDEX OF BIBLICAL REFERENCES

INDEX OF AUTHORS